Robert B. Ives
Grantham
December 7, 1979
2305

THE BOOK OF
COFFEE & TEA

A Guide to the Appreciation of
Fine Coffees, Teas, and Herbal Beverages

JOEL, DAVID, & KARL SCHAPIRA

illustrated by Meri Shardin

2305

St. Martin's Press   New York

Library of Congress Catalog # 73–90585
Manufactured in the United States of America
Designed by Meri Shardin

Library of Congress Cataloging in Publication Data

Schapira, David, 1906—
  The book of coffee and tea.

  Bibliography: p.
  Includes index.
  1. Coffee. 2. Tea   3. Cookery (Coffee)
  4. Cookery (Tea)   I. Schapira, Joel, 1946—
joint author.   II. Schapira, Karl, 1939—
joint author.   III. Title.
  TX415.S28   641.3'37'3   73–90585

Acknowledgements

For access to information we thank the Pan American Coffee Bureau, especially Charles Grebinger, John Adinolfi, and Kenneth W. Burgess; Dan and George Gilbert of U. and J. Lenson; Peter Irwin and Joe Staci of Irwin-Harrisons-Whitney; Mike Margolies of Tea Pack. Thanks also to the publishers of *The Coffee and Tea Trade Journal* and *World Coffee and Tea*.

Thanks to Marcel and Julie Goldenberg for some space and time in peace and quiet.

Thanks to our editor Paul de Angelis, whose patience, support and enthusiasm kept us going and brought us through. With energy, intelligence, and kindness, he guided us on the paths of clarity.

Thanks to Bonnie for typing and support.

Thanks to Diane for sharing.

To Diane, Rosalen, and Bonnie

Contents

The West of which I speak is but another name for the Wild, and what I have been preparing to say is that in Wildness is the preservation of the world. Every tree sends its fibers forth in search of the Wild. The cities import it at any price. Men plow and sail for it. From the forest and wilderness come the tonics and barks which brace mankind.

—Thoreau

Foreword

This book has been two years in the writing but more than seventy years in the making. For three generations our family has provided freshly roasted coffees and carefully selected teas to patrons of our New York shop. Morris Schapira (we called him Schap) founded our family business, and for many years it was his custom to invite his favorite customers to join him for tea at the testing table. With this book, we extend that invitation to all who seek that "cup of infinite pleasure." We are your hosts and your guides. We want you to share with us a world of warmth and flavor—the enjoyments of a delicious cup of coffee, and perfect cup of tea. We want to tell you the story of how these wonderful and bracing beverages are created. They come out of antiquity and from across the wide oceans to delight your senses and invigorate your spirit. We want to share our knowledge, gleaned from long experience and based on a somewhat fanatical devotion to quality. We have tried to answer the questions, solve the problems, correct the misconceptions, and combat the lies about how to get and make good coffee and tea. Most of all, we have tried to give you the know-how to intelligently and confidently select and prepare two of humankind's most cherished refreshments.

The elements of fire, water, air, and earth join forces to give us the coffee bean and the tea leaf. Coffee may be pulped, washed, dried, roasted, ground, and finally brewed. Tea may be withered, dried, rolled, fermented, fired, cut, and also, at last, brewed. But through the metamorphosis, in all their forms, coffee and tea each remains a single thing, manifesting itself in a variety of disguises. The energy put into the beans and leaves by nature is the energy which suffuses our being when we drink.

Ancient myths that proposed to explain the origins and attributes of coffee and tea are fanciful—peopled by ghosts, goatherds, messenger birds, monks.

If these legends and tales are extravagantly imaginative, they have only stretched the truth in order to express the tremendous awe once inspired by these newly discovered plants. Modern coffee and tea myths manufactured on Madison Avenue inspire us with nothing more than well deserved mistrust.

We most heartily recommend that you do some gustatory shun-piking—take the backroads, take your time, and put your money where your mouth is. Use this book as a map—but if you come across some uncharted byway, make the turn, take the chance, and be all the richer for it.

Joel Schapira
June, 1975
New York City

COFFEE

1. The Story of Coffee

THE ORIGINS OF COFFEE

COFFEE WAS FIRST prepared not as a beverage but as a food. African tribes would use stone mortars to crush the ripe cherries from wild coffee trees, mix them with animal fat, and then fashion this exotic blend into round balls which they consumed on their war parties. This food had two advantages: the fat, combined with raw coffee's high protein content (lost when coffee is prepared as a beverage), provided concentrated nourishment; and the considerable caffeine content of the mixture acted as a stimulant to spur the warriors on to heights of savagery.

Coffee as a beverage appeared next—not in the form that we know it, but as a wine made in Africa from the fermented juice of the ripe cherries mixed with cold water. Or in some cases, the aroma of the dried beans was so attractive to early coffee drinkers that they simply immersed them in cold water and drank the resulting beverage; as a later refinement they crushed the beans. It wasn't until 1000 A.D., when the Arabs learned to boil coffee, that it became a hot drink.

From its first discovery the new drink was shrouded in mystery, imbued with magical properties, and surrounded with controversy. Legends link coffee with doctors, priests, poets, and philosophers. The first coffee drinkers experienced sensations ranging from exhilaration to religious ecstasy.

One legend concerns the adventures of the dervish Omar. Condemned by his enemies to wander and die of starvation in a desert outside the Yemenite port of Mocha, Omar is awakened at midnight by an enormous apparition, the spirit of his dead mentor. He is guided to a coffee tree, where he picks the fruit and roasts the seeds. He then tries to soften them in water, and, when this fails, drinks the liquid. Astounded at his physical and mental feeling of well-being, he introduces the beverage to Mocha where its beneficial effects, attested to by his survival, are considered signs from God.

In another legend Kaldi, a young goatherd, sees his flock prancing and cavorting on their hind legs after eating certain cherries. Being of a melancholy disposition, he resolves to try the fruit himself. A passing monk is astonished one day to see herdsman and flock merrily dancing together in a meadow. After learning Kaldi's secret and adding the refinements of drying and boiling the fruit, the monk uses the new drink to keep awake for night-long religious ceremonies.

So the coffee beverage took on a mythical status—somewhere between that of the manna of the Old Testament and the heady wine of Bacchus—and began to spread throughout the Arab world. At first consumed only on the advice of a physician or as an adjunct to a religious ceremony, the beverage rapidly became popularized. More and more doctors accepted coffee as beneficial and prescribed it to their willing patients. Dervishes introduced the drink at night-long religious ceremonies in Aden, Yemen, Cairo, and Mecca, where they passed huge jars of coffee around and chanted prayers until the newly risen sun glinted on the hot, dark liquid. Scholars, lawyers, artists, and those who worked at night discovered the delights and beneficial side-effects of coffee. Doctors no longer had to prescribe the drink; coffee was becoming a permanent part of the civilized Eastern world.

To supply the growing demand for the new drink the Arabs developed a simple but effective form of cultivation, starting their coffee plants in nurseries from seed and transferring the young plants to plantations in the foothills of nearby mountains when they were strong enough. An irrigation system of pebble-lined trenches distributed water from the mountain streams among the young coffee trees, and shade poplars protected them from the sun.

Methods of preparation also became more sophisticated as the popularity of coffee grew. Around 1200 A.D., coffee was being prepared as a decoction from the dried hulls of the bean. Soon someone got the idea of roasting the hulls over a charcoal fire. The roasted hulls and a small amount of the silver skins were thrown into boiling water for half an hour, producing a pale yellow liquid. By the sixteenth century further advances had been introduced: the whole bean was roasted on stone trays, then on metal plates; the roasted beans boiled in water produced a strong liquor. Finally the roasted beans were pulverized with a mortar and pestle and the powder combined with boiling water. This decoction was consumed grounds and all, and was the reigning method of coffee preparation for over 300 years.

At the same time as coffee beans were introduced, the Arabs made changes in coffee preparation that greatly improved its flavor. Powdered coffee was steeped in water for a day, and half the liquor was boiled away and then stored in pots to be reheated and served when needed. The invention of the *ibrik,* or coffee boiler, speeded up the process; powdered coffee, cinnamon, cloves, amber, and sugar were boiled together and the brew was served in tiny china cups. The grounds were allowed to settle and the coffee was sucked up in sips as hot as the human tongue could stand.

When coffee began to lose its purely religious associations, the first coffee houses, or *qahveh khaneh,* sprang up in Mecca to accommodate secular demand for the beverage. The music, gambling, and free-wheeling social, political, and religious discussions that were a part of Levantine coffee-house life threatened rulers of the sixteenth century. At three different times the government, aided by clerics who saw their congregations deserting the temple for the coffee house, and by doctors who were interested in dispensing coffee as a costly medicine, attempted to shut down the *qahveh khaneh.* These persecutions eventually failed; coffee was too delicious to be restricted, and since wine was forbidden, water in the Levant was scarce and brackish, and goat's milk hardly palatable, coffee was the perfect thirst-quencher. Finally, the grand viziers realized that the coffee houses could provide an important source of tax revenue.

The *cafenets* of Constantinople and Damascus were the protoypes of the great Western coffee houses. These Eastern establishments were devoted to enhancing in leisure the sensibilities of the men of the age. Simple and comfortable, with prints and rugs decorating the walls, they were located in cool, pleasant open squares, often with a view onto water or a wide landscape, and represented a welcome refuge from the scorching desert. Friends met here to talk and contemplate life. The excitement of the city was concentrated here; for patrons of the coffee house it was opera and theater combined. Backgammon and chess were played in coffee houses, and it is said the game of bridge originated in the coffee houses of Constantinople.

Once coffee had become popularized in the coffee houses it moved into the home, where the drink took on an ever-increasing importance in the lives of Near Eastern peoples. An elaborate coffee ceremony evolved that rivaled the Japanese Tea Ceremony in complexity, beauty of implements, and decorum, if not in spiritual import. The ceremony took place in the *K'hawah,* or coffee hall, which featured a charcoal-burning fireplace, decorative rugs and cushions, and ornamental copper coffeepots around the place of honor. The host and his guests exchanged salaams along with formal

salutations invoking the blessings of Allah. The host then roasted the green beans, crushed them with a mortar and pestle, and ceremoniously prepared the drink. Dates dipped in butter were served as a refreshment. When the coffee was ready the host poured for everyone and drank the first cup himself, assuring the company there was no "death in the pot."

Coffee touched all aspects of life in the Near East. Arab drivers and laborers had coffee kits in their saddle bags and packs. They would build a fire by the roadside, roast their supply of green beans on an iron plate, pound them in a mortar, and boil the strong, foaming brew in their *ibriks*. Merchants served coffee to their customers before the bargaining began. Barbers gave it to patrons waiting for haircuts. And Turkish wives could legally divorce a husband who failed to supply them with the all-important beverage.

THE SPREAD OF THE COFFEE BEAN

It is probable that Italy, and more specifically Venice, was the first part of Europe to become acquainted with coffee. Venetian fleets plied the waters of the world and had a tremendous trade in silks, spices, perfumes, and dyes with the East; coffee, imported from Constantinople, probably came to Europe as part of this trade. When the drink reached Rome, fanatic priests attacked it with such virulence that it was almost forbidden to the Christian world. The priests maintained that coffee was the drink of the Devil. Since Moslems were forbidden the use of wine—a drink sanctified by Christ and used in the Holy Communion—Satan, leader of the infidels, had invented coffee as a substitute. Were Christians to drink this hellish brew, the priests reasoned, they would risk eternal damnation. Towards the end of the sixteenth century Pope Clement VIII asked that the beverage be brought before him in order to settle the dispute. Attracted by its characteristic pungent aroma, he took a sip and found it delightful. He realized that to allow coffee to be banished from the Christian world would be a sin indeed and, turning the tables on Satan, baptized it on the spot.

The Pope's blessing quickened the flow of coffee throughout Italy and made it possible for that country to open the first western coffee houses. These were at first plain, unadorned, windowless, rather dimly lit rooms. Slowly they became an integral part of Italian life. They were patronized in the mornings by doctors, merchants, and artisans, and in the afternoons and evenings by the leisure classes and the ladies, and soon became vivacious centers of business, politics, and gossip.

The English did not become acquainted wtih coffee in their homeland until nearly a century later, well after their explorers had encountered it on journeys to the East. In 1599 Anthony Sherley, an English adventurer, set sail for Persia to convince the Shah to join forces with the West against the Turks, and to foster British trade interests. An account of the expedition contains the first mention by an Englishman of coffee drinking in the Orient; it tells of "damned infidells drinking a certaine liquor, which they do call Coffe." In following years of the seventeenth century the English seamen Captain John Smith and Francis Bacon described coffee in their travel books. Robert Burton, English philosopher and humorist, painted a pen portrait of Turkish coffee houses, and Sir Henry Blount, "the father of the English coffee house," told of his coffee-drinking experiences in Turkey and Egypt.

When Cyrill, Patriarch of Constantinople, was strangled by the vizier in 1637, his disciple Conopios fled in terror to England. A native of Crete trained in the Greek Church, Conopios was given sanctuary by Archbishop Laud, who made a place for him at Balliol College, Oxford. Every morning he would take coffee, and as the strong fragrant brew passed his lips we may imagine the fugitive cleric offering a silent prayer for his murdered mentor while giving thanks for his own deliverance. Conopios' escape is the earliest reliable date given for coffee's entry into England, although it is probable, given the many previous descriptions of it by writers and travelers, and the vast trade between the Orient and the British Isles, that coffee was introduced into England somewhat earlier.

Coffee became a great favorite with the students who formed the Oxford Coffee Club, which was later to become the Royal Society. The first coffee house in London was opened by Pasqua Rosée in 1652, and other coffee houses were soon to be seen in many cities throughout Great Britain.

Coffee first came to France in 1660, when several merchants of Marseilles, who had acquired the habit of drinking the beverage while living in the Levant, decided they could not forgo the pleasure of having it at home. So they brought beans with them and soon were importing coffee commercially in bales from Egypt. The merchants of Lyons followed a similar pattern. In 1671 the first coffee house was opened in Marseilles. The spread of coffee through France was fought by the wine makers and doctors; the former feared its popularity would change the drinking habits of Frenchmen and cut into their profits, while the latter wanted to retain control over experimentation with and dispensation of the new beverage, thus keeping it at the level of a rare medicine.

The drink's popularity won out, and coffee received its final approbation in the Paris of Louis XIV in 1669, when the Turkish ambassador, Suleiman Aga, began holding flamboyant coffee parties for the French nobility. These elaborate bashes were held in an opulent rented palace and were fueled by Suleiman Aga's enormous personal coffee supply. These exotic affairs are described by Isaac D'Israeli in his *Curiosities of Literature:*

> On bended knee, the black slaves of the Ambassador, arrayed in the most gorgeous Oriental costumes served the choicest Mocha coffee in tiny cups of egg-shell porcelain, hot, strong and fragrant, poured out in saucers of gold and silver, placed on embroidered silk doylies fringed with gold bullion, to the grand dames, who fluttered their fans with many grimaces, bending their piquant faces—be-rouged, be-powdered and be-patched—over the new and steaming beverage.

Captain John Smith, who founded the colony of Virginia at Jamestown in 1607 and who knew of coffee from his Turkish travels, was probably the first to introduce the beverage to North America. The cargo list of the *Mayflower* carried this item: a wooden mortar and pestle used for grinding coffee powder. It is quite likely that Dutch New Amsterdam was familiar with coffee, but not until 1668, when the town was called New York, does the earliest reference to coffee appear. Mention is made of a drink made from roasted beans and flavored with sugar or honey and cinnamon. In 1683 William Penn, founder of Pennsylvania, was aghast at the price he was forced to pay for a pound of coffee from New York: 18 shillings 8 pence, or the equivalent of $4.65. It can readily be seen why the early colonists made do with beverages prepared from herbs, spicewood, sassafras root, and other shrubs.

As coffee cultivation spread and travel to the East increased, coffee drinking came to Europe, spurred by the tales and by samples brought to the continent by enthusiastic returned voyagers. But it wasn't the people like Suleiman Aga, Conopios, and John Smith who popularized coffee as much as the little businessmen—the Italian lemonade vendors who added coffee to their other refreshments; Pascal, an Armenian who first sold coffee in the streets of Paris from a tent in the fair of St. Germain; and countless unnamed peddlers who spread throughout the streets of Europe carrying on their backs the gleaming tools of their trade—coffeepots, trays, cups, spoons and sugar. These men bore the steaming, potent gospel of coffee beyond the boundaries of the East to the as yet uninitiated West.

A colorful story is told of how one of these peddlers got his start and introduced coffee to Vienna. On July 7, 1683, the city of Vienna was surrounded by 300,000 Turkish troops led by Kara Mustafa. The capture of Vienna was to be the first step in the plan of Mohammed IV to annihilate Christendom and occupy Europe. Vienna was completely sealed off from the rest of the world, but Holy Roman Emperor Leopold I had escaped before the final closing of the trap and was waiting nearby with an army of 33,000 Austrians for the promised aid of King John Sobieski of Poland. Count Rüdiger von Starhemberg, commander of the besieged city, called for a volunteer to slip through the Turkish lines with a message to the Emperor: hurry!

Franz George Kolschitzky, a Polish adventurer who had lived for many years among the Turks and spoke their language, stepped up to offer his services. Putting on a Turkish uniform, he started on his perilous journey. Infiltrating enemy lines and swimming the Danube, he reached the friendly forces outside the capital. After receiving assurances of rescue, he returned to Vienna to relay the good news and raise the failing spirits of the defenders. As the siege continued Kolschitzky served as intermediary between city and camp, until finally King John arrived with his supporting troops and the Christian forces were poised for the attack. A final time Kolschitzky returned to Vienna with the signals for the start of the battle. At that instant the Viennese troops were to mount a charge of their own from inside the walls of the town.

The battle was a stunning victory for Christendom. The Turks fled, leaving behind an enormous amount of gold, equipment, and supplies, among which were numerous sacks of an all but unknown substance—green coffee. When the spoils were distributed no one wanted the coffee. Kolschitzky, who had lived among the Turks and so knew the value of the strange beans, offered to take them off the soldiers' hands. Within a short time the enterprising courier was selling the drink in the streets and from house to house. Soon afterward he opened the first coffee house in Vienna, The Blue Bottle.

During the seventeenth century coffee houses proliferated in Vienna. Kolschitzky became known as "great brother-heart" to his patrons, and Vienna came to be called the "mother of cafés" to other central Europeans. The Viennese-style café became extremely popular and spread to other cities in Austria. These coffee houses served good strong coffee, sometimes blended with roasted fig to make a potent liquor, and often accompanied by a *Kipfel*. *Kipfeln* were crescent-shaped rolls first baked in 1683 as a defiant gesture against the Turks who were beseiging the city (the crescent was the Turkish emblem).

Until late in the seventeenth century, almost all coffee came from Arabia. For hundreds of years the Arabs had maintained their monopoly over coffee supply, forbidding seeds to be taken from the country and prohibiting strangers from visiting the plantations. But coffee's increasing popularity made it harder for them to protect their profitable new industry and its expanding market. The tree, living up to its Arabic name *cahuha* (force), would not be denied its destiny. Beans were smuggled into India by Muslim pilgrims who had easy access to the holy city of Mecca. Dutch coffee spies intent on profits finally succeeded in stealing plants from Arabia and cultivating them in Java, thereby giving the Western world its first informal synonym for coffee. Plants from the botanical gardens in Holland were freely distributed by the Dutch throughout Europe. The fruit of one sturdy five-footer that reached the Jardin des Plantes in Paris around 1714 contained the coffee future of all of Latin America.

The plant in question thrived for ten years in France under the hands of the royal botanist Antoine de Jussieu, and brought him considerable fame. In 1723 a young French naval officer serving in Martinique, Gabriel Mathieu de Clieu, had the brainstorm that was to change coffee history. He had heard fabulous stories of the prolific coffee groves of Java, and while in Paris on leave had found coffee houses spreading everywhere. His idea: bring a few seedlings back to Martinique and start cultivation in the French colony. This personal coup could start a flourishing industry in the West Indies and bring glory to France.

But when De Clieu approached Jussieu with his plan the botanist jealously refused, preferring to bask in the acclaim he received from the nobility of Europe, who journeyed to Paris to view the exotic hothouse coffee plant. But De Clieu was not to be put off. The young officer attempted to enlist the aid of M. de Chirac, the royal physician, doubtless counting on the enthusiastic curative claims made for coffee by European doctors to enlist Chirac's support. But the royal physician balked and, as was not uncommon in French intrigues of this period, it was the insistence of a beautiful lady of high rank that broke the impasse. Details are sketchy, but we may imagine the infatuated doctor tête-à-tète one evening with a charming woman in her well-appointed apartments on one of Paris' most exclusive streets. She leans forward, murmuring praises of the drink set before them—a dark, rich brew, steaming in tiny cups. The entrancing aroma wafting toward the doctor is subtly blended with the perfume of her décolletage. The next morning Chirac agrees to help De Clieu, and several nights later a gang of masked men, led by De Clieu, climb the walls of the Jardin des Plantes and escape with their prize—the coffee plant.

De Clieu set sail for Martinique with his precious cargo. Though protected by a glass-sided wooden frame, the plant was beset by dangers from all sides. An enraged fellow passenger—a Dutch agent—tried to destroy the plant, and with it De Clieu's vision of French coffee plantations spreading across the West Indies; he actually succeeded in tearing off a branch in his struggles with the young naval officer. The ship was pursued by a pirate vessel and narrowly escaped capture. A fierce tempest bore down upon the ship, almost destroying her and, in the process, smashing the protective glass around the coffee plant and inundating it with salt water. After surviving all these near catastrophes the hardy plant was subjected to an even graver ordeal: The ship was becalmed, drinking water grew scarce, and the captain imposed a strict rationing system on the ship. Since the captain refused to issue water for the plant, De Clieu was obliged to share his scant portion with it. Things were looking grim indeed when land was sighted at last. De Clieu went ashore carrying the green and flourishing plant in his arms. Upon arriving at his home in Martinique he planted it carefully in his garden, surrounded it with thorn bushes, and set up an armed guard around it. The plant did exceedingly well and in the years that followed De Clieu was to see his dream realized in the thriving, abundant coffee crop of not only Martinique but Santo Domingo, Guadeloupe, and adjacent islands as well.

Coffee spread throughout the West Indies. Brazil, destined to become one of the world's leading producers, had not yet started growing coffee but was actively seeking a way of acquiring the fanatically guarded seeds. In 1727 a boundary dispute arose between two rival coffee-producing colonies who had forbidden export of seedlings under pain of death: Dutch and French Guiana. When the two colonies called upon Brazil to help settle the matter, that country sent word that she would be happy to assist. Brazil's secret motive was to steal some of the closely guarded coffee seedlings and start an industry of her own. For this purpose a lieutenant colonel in the Brazilian army, Francisco de Melo Palheta, was chosen. This worthy, while ignorant of the intricacies of coffee cultivation, had the reputation of being a fine professional soldier, having a good head for business, and enjoying a string of successful romances with the most beautiful ladies of Brazil.

When Palheta arrived in French Guiana, the Governor of that colony welcomed him graciously and the arbitration proceedings were begun. At the same time the Brazilian officer began his seduction of the Governor's attractive wife. After mornings of hearings, surveys, and examination of boundary lines and documents bearing on both sides of the dispute, Palheta spent his afternoons with the Governor's lady. In the end he achieved brilliant success in both suits.

The dispute resolved, the Governor held a lavish banquet in Palheta's honor. In front of hundreds of guests the Governor's wife presented Palheta a bouquet. On the surface a charming gesture applauded by the company, in reality it was a courageous token of gratitude for an amorous interlude. For hidden among the bright garden flowers were the fertile cuttings of a coffee plant. In a few days they were carried back to Brazil by Palheta to start what was to be one of the greatest coffee empires in the world.

THE GOLDEN AGE OF COFFEE

An initial stage in the history of coffee had been reached. The era of cultivation intrigues was over. With the spread of plantations to Brazil and other parts of South America, an age of coffee abundance was started which forever ended the need to traffic in illicit seedlings and plants. Increased supplies of coffee were a reflection of the growing popularity of the dark beverage. The magical desert drink was well on the way to becoming the popular refreshment for the masses of Western Europe. And in the seventeenth and eighteenth centuries, when the West was about to break the centuries old equilibrium with Asian, Indian, and Islamic cultures by its voyages of discovery and advances in science and government, coffee shared in its ascendancy as a democratic symbol and fuel for the thinkers of the day.

Abundant coffee supplies and the intellectual ferment of the Enlightenment ushered in the golden age of the coffee house. The coffee houses of London and Paris were perfect vessels for distilling the strange and mystical relationship between man and coffee. The ceremonial liquid of the East became the beverage served in the centers of social, business, political, and artistic life of London and Paris. This leap points to a unique characteristic of coffee: When it appears it is likely to be linked with an atmosphere of heightened spiritual or mental awareness.

In seventeenth- and eighteenth-century London there was a coffee house to represent every shade of commerce, politics, and literature. These houses generally opened off the street and were furnished at first only with tables and chairs scattered about a sanded floor. Later booths or boxes were added. The walls were adorned with broadsides, newspapers, Rules of the House, playbills, auction notices, and handbills and posters advertising salves and cure-alls—in short, a cross-section of the throbbing life of London.

For the price of a penny you could enter a packed, smoke-filled room and be entertained by the scintillating wit and wisdom of the leading savants of the day—thus the reference to these houses as "penny universities."

Smoke from the roaring, open fireplace, the smell of tobacco, and the aroma of freshly roasted coffee blended together to provide a dense, powerful atmosphere. Perfumes and hair oils of the day mingled with the horsey smells of saddle and coach. Patrons milled around, forming a continuously shifting throng. For two cents the waiters and wenches served a portion of steaming coffee, and brass-bound boxes were set up to receive coins from the customers. The words "To INSURE PROMPTNESS" could be found written on these boxes; this was the origin of the custom and the word "tip."

After the restrictive reign of Puritan Oliver Cromwell men needed centers of social intercourse where they could learn the news and discuss it. The time was shaping a unique and powerful group of men, middle-class in terms of values and wealth, well-educated and with progressive ideas. They had found they could challenge the king and even overthrow him. They saw to it that England was governed the way they wanted, they created a free press, organized trade, and changed English prose radically. The coffee house for them was pulpit, courtroom, stage, and classroom.

Stockbrokers at the end of the seventeenth century left the Royal Exchange for Garraway's coffee house; in today's London Stock Exchange the attendants are still called waiters. At the Turk's Head the ballot-box, known as "our wooden oracle," was first used to settle discussions by vote. Lloyd's of London started out as a coffee house where marine insurers sought each other out and consulted shipping lists. At Will's John Dryden held forth from his reserved seat—nearest the fire in winter and the balcony in summer. Young Man's was famous for duels between the soldiers and gallants who frequented it; a surgeon and a solicitor were in constant attendance. The Tories went to Ozindas, the Whigs to St. James. Barristers traded legal repartee at The George. Candlelight auctions were held for the benefit of estate agents at The London. If you were ill you went to Baston's, where the doctors sharpened their medical skills. Addison and Steele gathered material for the *Tatler* and the *Spectator* in Button's, and Pope, whose *Rape of the Lock* was inspired by coffee-house gossip, was a member.

The gradual introduction of alcoholic beverages into the London coffee house signalled the decline of the golden era. The former patrons sought the seclusion of private clubs as a rowdier and less intellectual segment of society began taking over the coffee houses. Businessmen found it more convenient and efficient to work from offices. Tea became popular at court and the British East India Company, profiting from increasing tea imports from the Far East, did everything possible to encourage consumption of the new beverage. Because it was more easily prepared at home, requiring only boiling water rather than roasting, grinding, and brewing, and because the speedy clipper ships could transport tea more quickly than the slower vessels bringing coffee from Asia and Africa, England became a nation of tea drinkers and the coffee houses a symbol of post-Restoration Britain.

Suleiman Aga's lavish coffee parties, Pascal's waiter boys selling *petit-noirs* from Pont Neuf and le Candiot, and the cripple who sold coffee in the streets of Paris for two sous all helped popularize coffee in Paris. But it was not until 1689, with the opening of the Café de Procope, that the first real Parisian café was born. Before the Procope there were only coffee booths and small coffee houses frequented mainly by the foreigners in Paris.

François Procope was a lemonade vender who had been issued a royal license which permitted him to serve such refreshments as spices, barley water, and ices. He soon added coffee to the menu and began to have fabulous success. He had shrewdly established his café opposite the new Comédie Française, and so it became the natural meeting place of the most renowned French actors, writers, and musicians of the eighteenth century, who were attracted not only by its location, but by its dark, cave-like atmosphere. Voltaire, whose favorite drink was a mixture of coffee and chocolate, was a regular customer. When the Procope closed two centuries later, Vol-

taire's marble table and chair were still there as objects of veneration. Rousseau, Beaumarchais, and Diderot were a few of the scores of famous Frenchmen who were patrons of the café.

When Benjamin Franklin died in 1790 and all France was in mourning for their favorite American, the Procope was entirely draped in black. During the French Revolution Marat, Robespierre, and Danton could be heard at the Procope, holding forth on the explosive issues of the day. An unknown officer named Napoleon Bonaparte played chess at the café and was once forced by François Procope to leave his hat as security while he tried to scrape up some money to pay his bill.

Coffee houses spread rapidly throughout Paris in the early 1700s. One notorious café of this period was the Royal Drummer, established by Jean Ramponaux. While the Procope appealed to artists and intellectuals, the Royal Drummer was known for its vices and excesses. Louis XV was a constant visitor and Marie Antoinette would come to enjoy herself whenever some particularly wild revelry was in progress.

The Café de la Régence, opened in 1718 near the Palais Royal, was a coffee house whose list of patrons reads like a history of French art for two centuries. François Philidor, one of the greatest chess players of all time, fought some of his most brilliant battles here. Robespierre once played chess here with a girl who had disguised herself as a boy to save her lover's life. Victor Hugo, Théophile Gautier, and the Duke of Richelieu all sipped coffee at the Régence. Diderot, whose wife gave him nine sous every day for coffee, worked on his *Encyclopedia* there.

The historian Michelet described the heady atmosphere of the early eighteenth century by likening all Paris to a coffee house intoxicated by the new beverage. He praised coffee as the catalyst for the evanescent flow of spontaneous wit that characterized the time. The cabaret life during the reign of Louis XIV, fueled by wine and liquor and accompanied by ignoble revelry, had given way to a new climate of dazzling lucidity. Michelet divided Parisian history into three ages of coffee drinking. Before 1700 beautiful ladies sipped Arabian coffee and chatted of the seraglio, the *Thousand and One Nights,* and the wonders of the Orient. Beginning around 1710, the cheap, abundant coffee from the island of Bourbon in the Indian Ocean gave rise to the age of Indian coffee. The volcanic soil of Bourbon (or Réunion) provoked through its coffee an explosion of sparkling wit, verse, and books, epitomized by the life and works of Voltaire. Similarly the coffee of Santo Domingo, imported later in the century, transmitted its characteristics: full-bodied, coarse, strong and stimulating to the age of revolution.

Diderot and Rousseau saw at the bottom of their cups the days of 1789. The revolutionary Danton took several cups of coffee before mounting the tribune and proclaiming "The horse must have its oats."

In July, 1789, the coffee houses around the Palais Royal were thronged inside and out with crowds listening to the fiery orators harangue the monarchy. Sentiments of violence against the government were greeted with thunderous applause. On Sunday, July 12, 1789, a young journalist named Camille Desmoulins stepped outside the Café Foy. He jumped up on a table and began a passionate speech that so moved his audience that they marched off frantic with revolutionary fervor. Two days later the Bastille fell.

Magny's was frequented by Gautier, Saint-Victor, and Turgenev. The Trois Frères Provençaux was mentioned by Balzac. Zola took coffee at Venua's. The Tortoni was home to Talleyrand, Rossini, and Manet. The most costly house was the Café de Paris. The Jacobites haunted the Dutch Café. Thackeray described Terre's. The Café Madrid featured Carjat, a Spanish lyric poet. In the Café de la Paix, Second Empire imperialists and their spies intrigued.

Although most of the Parisian coffee houses have passed into history, some are still flourishing at their original locations. Unlike the houses of London, which succumbed to tea and the British East India Company, the cafés of Paris evolved with the times. Most of them had always served wines and liquors along with coffee, and this acted as a stabilizing factor and increased their longevity. Also, a substantial number of cafés served good food and developed into fine restaurants. Finally, coffee and coffee houses seem too much an expression of the French sensibility to ever disappear easily, since behind every Parisian there is a wit, a revolutionary, and a gourmand.

One of Italy's most famous coffee houses, the Florian, was opened in 1720 and still stands in the Piazza San Marco in Venice, where a small band in formal wear entertains the tourists even in the chilliest weather. The Florian's first proprietor, Floriono Francesconi, acted as a confidant, diplomat, matchmaker, postmaster, and source of gossip to his clients, the nobility and prominent people of Venice.

In Padua a poor lemonade vendor, Antonio Pedrocchi, gathered what savings he had and borrowed the rest to finance his dream of building a coffee house for young people and students. He purchased an old house and started to convert it when he was dismayed to find that there were no cellars, necessary for making ice and drinks on the premises. In spite of the crumbling walls and floors he desperately went ahead with his renovations. While attempting to dig the cellar he uncovered, to his surprise and delight, an enormous buried treasure. He built what was to become one of the most luxurious and beautiful coffee houses in all of Italy.

In the eighteenth century the cafés of Vienna had the same reputation for wit and erudition as the "penny universities" of London. Novelists and journalists, called *Zeitungdoktoren* or "newspaper doctors," would hold forth on the weightest of literary and political questions before an audience of acolytes. The Viennese café became so well liked that by 1839 the city boasted 80, with 50 more in the suburbs.

The golden age of the coffee house did not leave America untouched, though its manifestations were naturally somewhat different. Coffee houses gradually began appearing in New York, Boston, Baltimore, and Philadelphia. In reality they were inns or taverns where meals were served and rooms rented to sailors, bachelors, and other travelers. Every beverage from tea, chocolate, and wine to ale, beer, and Vermont applejack competed with coffee. Most of these coffee houses did not live up to their inspired European prototypes because the settlers followed the Puritan ethic of prayer and hard work. They felt that the idle hours spent in a public house were slightly sinful, so they gave Dorothy Jones the first license to sell coffee in Boston in 1670; as a woman she would presumably be on better terms with the Devil. Actually, women opened quite a few of America's early coffee houses, not only because the pious merchants and farmers felt that operating a hostelry was women's work, but because women in the colonies were much more involved in the social and economic life around them than the ladies of Europe. Although women operated coffee houses and served in them, the social code of the age forbade them as patrons.

One of the several American coffee houses that did approach the level of those in Paris and London was Boston's Green Dragon, which dominated Union Street for 135 years, beginning in 1697. Participants in New England's dynamic and colorful history occupied its tables and sipped its coffee: redcoats, governors of the colonies, officers of the crown in powdered wigs, nobility, revolutionaries, conspirators, patriots, and generals of the Revolution. Indeed, Daniel Webster called the Green Dragon "headquarters of the Revolution."

Soon after New Yorkers substituted coffee for beer at breakfast—around 1668—the New York coffee houses started to flourish. While American coffee houses never influenced the arts as did their Continental models, they fulfilled a role entirely missing in the old cafés: they all contained long assembly rooms where court trials and council meetings could be held.

One of the most celebrated of New York coffee houses was the Merchants Coffee House, so named because it was located near the downtown Meal Market, carried lists of arriving and departing ships and their cargo, and so became the meeting place for tradesman and merchants. Citizens were warned here in 1765 to stop rioting against the Stamp Act. The Sons of Liberty met here to plan strategy after the battles of Concord and Lexington. The Bank of New York was planned here in 1784. The governor of New York and the mayor welcomed newly elected President Washington here in 1789. And in 1790 brokers first sold stocks at the Merchants. It lasted from 1737 until 1804, when it burned down.

In 1791 the Tontine Coffee House, one of the most elaborate and pretentious buildings in the city, was an important rival of the Merchants. Each of the original 157 shareholders paid £200, with ownership reverting to the surviving participants upon his death. Great balls and banquets were held here: it also served as the New York Stock exchange. This house was a great tourist attraction; no stranger considered his visit to New York complete without visiting the Tontine.

THE POPULARIZATION OF COFFEE

Since its beginning coffee drinking has been associated with scholars, wits, and artists. Lively ideas and liberal opinions generated around coffee cups from the *cafenets* of Constantinople to the coffee houses of eighteenth-century New England have made rulers from Amurath III to George III fear coffee's influence. Charles II tried to close the London coffee houses in 1675, when he rightly connected them with the progressive political sentiments that were to change the course of the British Empire. Eleven days after his "Proclamation for the Suppression of the Coffee Houses" was issued, he was forced to withdraw the order due to indignant public outcry from all parties. The ideology and leadership of the French Revolution were first tested in Parisian coffee houses. And the Merchants coffee house in New York was the Government headquarters in the days immediately following the outbreak of the American Revolution.

But the golden age of the coffee house faded during the nineteenth century, as successful political revolutionaries consolidated their gains. The dynamic, talented patrons who dreamed of a new age over brimming cups of the robust brew became scions of the changed world they had helped create. The revolutionaries who plotted in the cafés of Paris and the coffee houses of American became heads of government. The writers and artists who haunted the coffee houses of London and Europe had created the classics by which other works would be measured. The traders and merchants who fought for a new economic freedom now ran the stock exchanges and banks and controlled vast mercantile empires.

The coffee-house men were aristocrats of thought, art, and commerce. When their dreams became reality they became the Establishment. Coffee was embraced at the dawn of the Industrial Revolution by the growing middle classes and by the common man.

The history of coffee in Germany points up its peculiar quality as an indicator of social status. Leonard Rauwolf traveled to Aleppo in 1573 and his published account of the voyage makes Germany the first European country to mention coffee in print. Other German adventurers in Persia also mention the drink, but coffee was not introduced into Germany until around 1670. Coffee was served at the court of the Elector of Brandenburg in 1675. A London coffee merchant opened the first coffee house in Hamburg in 1679. Coffee houses spread to Berlin, periodicals were written about the new beverage, and by around 1750 coffee was served in German homes, often replacing flour-soup and warm beer for breakfast.

When Frederick the Great saw how much money was going from Germany to the hands of foreign coffee merchants (English in northern Germany, Italian in southern Germany), he tried to make coffee a drink of the aristocracy at the expense of the middle classes by restricting supplies and raising prices. German doctors, who had maligned coffee for years, supported him by claiming the drink caused sterility in men and prevented women from bearing children. Bach wrote his *Coffee Cantata* in 1732 poking fun at the physicians' campaign of false propaganda. In 1777 Frederick issued a manifesto exhorting the German people to give up coffee and return to the drink of their fathers—beer. Coffee drinking did not stop because of the decree, but beer, which had always been coffee's strongest competitor, supplanted coffee for a while, mainly because coffee supplies and coffee roasting licenses were withheld by Frederick. But by the close of the eighteenth century the German people were clamoring for coffee. A small army of coffee spies, mostly retired soldiers, were employed to track down clandestine roasting by the populace—they were nicknamed "coffee smellers" by the outraged Germans. Even strict Prussian military rule could not keep coffee down and eventually German monarchs gave way to the demands of the increasingly enlightened middle class.

A strong impetus to coffee's spread came from the women of Germany. By 1800 the average housewife was no longer on a farm working beside her husband in the fields; she was a burgher's wife in contact with the townspeople, enjoying leisure time. Epitomizing this new lifestyle was that unique invention of German women, the *kaffeeklatsch*. "Coffee-gossip," a term coined by uneasy husbands, originally referred to the subject matter of these coffee get-togethers, but now has come to mean the gathering itself. No one knows for sure how much of the discussions were about Goethe's latest play and Beethoven's newest symphony and how much about births, deaths and marriages. But the *kaffeeklatsch* enabled the German woman to share a little of the world of new ideas and served as an arena for her new role as a free talker and free thinker. Frederick's past attempts to make coffee an aristocratic beverage made it all the sweeter for the housewife to serve the drink to her friends whenever she pleased.

During the entire nineteenth century Germany held the lead in European coffee consumption. Coffee was quaffed at mealtimes, at the *kaffeeklatsch*, at Sunday afternoon family get-togethers, and at the spacious cafés that could be found in every German city. These cafés featured pastries and magazines, and in big cities like Berlin they catered to specific professions, trades, or sensibilities. The Admiral's Cafe was frequented by chorus girls, acrobats, and jugglers; the Café des Westens appealed to melancholy poets, visionaries, and egotists.

Coffee drinking in America has been seen as an ally of democracy since the Boston Tea Party. On the night of December 16, 1773, Samuel Adams and fifty fellow Bostonians boarded British ships in the harbor and, disguised as Indians, dumped 342 chests of tea overboard in retaliation for harsh taxes imposed by the Crown. The Boston Tea Party created a nation of coffee drinkers practically overnight; two centuries later prejudice against tea has not been completely wiped out. To quench the thirst of the tea-boycotting colonists, French and Dutch coffee merchants supplied them with cheap plentiful beans. Later American merchant fleets returned with cargoes of coffee from Martinique, Puerto Rico, and Haiti. After the eighteenth century coffee moved westward from the coffee houses to the frontiers of the newly expanding nation.

Immigration and annexation of territory helped spread coffee's popularity in the United States. Florida, whose ties with Cuba made her familiar with the drink, brought a state of coffee drinkers to the country when it became American. When the Louisiana Purchase was signed, New Orleans and all the French towns along the Mississippi brought more coffee lovers into the

fold. European coffee drinkers left for America in droves during the nineteenth century, reinforcing an already strong custom in their newly adopted land. Scouts for the covered wagon trains and gold-seekers bound for California would not think of setting forth without their supplies of coffee. Legend has it that the site of Fort Laramie, Wyoming, was traded by the Indians for tools, weapons, riding gear, and several sacks of brown roasted Javas—the native Americans had come to be quite fond of the drink.

American soldiers in the Mexican War were issued green beans, which they roasted over their campfires, as part of their rations. They soon learned to enjoy their coffee Mexican style, or *café con leche:* a mixture of coffee essence and boiled milk. Union soldiers in the Civil War were issued 100 pounds of food and 10 pounds of green beans or 8 pounds of roasted, ground coffee which had to last them 12 days. Coffee was prized highly by the soldiers, as is testified to by the fanatic measures they went through to make sure it was divided fairly. Coffee would be spread out evenly in piles on a rubber mat and the sergeant, with his back turned, would call names at random from the roster.

So coffee became firmly entrenched in the lives of the American settlers, cowboys, scouts, shepherds and soldiers who, above all, liked their brew "hot, black and strong enough to walk by itself."

In the nineteenth century coffee found a new home in the workplaces of America and Europe. As the Industrial Revolution gradually changed the landscape, economics, and social habits of the western world, workers of all kinds took to the stimulating, refreshing beverage that helped see them through sixteen-hour work days. When hundreds of British textile mills closed down in the 1880s and the unemployed workers stopped buying coffee, British coffee merchants found themselves in the unfamiliar position of advocating a more secure economic climate for English labor.

THE GROWTH OF A WORLD COFFEE SUPPLY

The mass consumption of coffee which began in the 1800s went hand in hand with a growing but chaotic world supply. Until 1690 Arabia had supplied all coffee to the world. Then for a century and a half the West Indian colonies of Spain and France—Jamaica, Haiti, Guadeloupe, Puerto Rico, and Cuba—were predominant. By around 1830 the Dutch colonies of Java and Sumatra wrested supremacy from the West Indies, and Amsterdam became the world coffee capital. India and Ceylon, financed by millions of pounds sterling from London, made bids in 1850 to dominate the world coffee market but could not shake Holland loose.

In the middle of the nineteenth century the dreaded disease *Hemileia vastatrix* struck Asia and suddenly changed the source of supply of the much-sought-after commodity. Unaffected by all the sprays and insecticides the planters used, the blight swept over Ceylon, India, Java, Sumatra, Malaya, and all the producing areas of Asia, and within a few years completely wiped out coffee growing there.

This left the field wide open for Brazil, and by the end of the nineteenth century, she achieved the dominant role in world coffee production, a position she still holds today. Her enormous annual increases in production helped shift coffee from a luxury beverage consumed by the aristocracy to the drink of the common man.

When Francisco de Melo Palheta escaped to Brazil in 1727 with his bouquet containing fertile coffee seedlings, he resigned from the Army and started to grow coffee on a riverbank farm. But the progress of coffee cultivation in Brazil was slow during most of the eighteenth century. Sugar for the European market was the major crop until Napoleon planted sugar beets in Europe, ending the Continent's dependency on imported sugar. By this point Europe needed more and more coffee and the United States was beginning to demonstrate the demand which was to make it in time the world's largest consumer of coffee.

Brazil's soil and climate were ideal for coffee cultivation, her government was cooperative, and a horde of slaves gave Brazilian coffee an economic edge over its competitors in Java and India. Planters and their armies of slaves penetrated deep into the untouched forests and chopped them down by the acre, clearing away the underbrush as they went. They waited until the hot, rainless months dried out the cut trees and brush before clearing the land by means of enormous fires. The rich, volcanic soil combined with chemicals in the burned wood ash to make a perfect planting environment. A means of shade for the young plants, usually so vital, was not necessary because of the characteristic moist fog in the air. Since the beans were allowed to dry on the tree, important chemicals returned to the earth in the fallen, unpicked fruit.

The flourishing coffee trees grew in the midst of a favorable political climate also. Pedro II, Emperor of Brazil, the country's last constitutional monarch, was a far-sighted liberal who gathered around himself a band of creative, able advisors. One of his goals was to make Rio de Janeiro the most beautiful city in the world. So as not to insult his followers in the provinces he simultaneously carried out rebuilding plans in the cities of the interior. Pedro had an extensive network of railways and roads constructed that connected the inland plantation areas to the ports. Previously coffee had been subjected to an arduous ox-cart journey to the sea; after the network was completed, the trip took only a few days and Brazilian coffee could compete on a worldwide basis. Pedro was so venerated by planters, traders, and industrialists that in 1871, when he instituted the law of free birth—an act which prevented children from being born into slavery—the slaveholders remained loyal to him in spite of their violent opposition to the liberal new decree. When Pedro was obliged to journey to Europe for medical attention in 1888, he left his beautiful daughter Isabel as regent. Intelligent and as far-seeing as her father but younger and with a more fiery spirit, Isabel, prompted by an act of Parliament, freed Brazil's 700,000 slaves. The planters and army officers rose against the monarchy, and when Pedro II returned in 1889 the monarchy fell. Pedro and his family were forced into exile and thousands of weeping Brazilians lined the harbor to see their ship sail off.

By this point Brazil had stepped in to fill the gap in coffee supplies created by the loss of Asian coffee to *Hemileia vastatrix*. But Brazil's new preeminence also brought troubles of its own. Most of the emancipated slaves gravitated to the cities, and the coffee industry suffered devastating labor shortages for the first few years thereafter. Production dropped 50 percent in many areas. But emigrants from Italy, Germany, Portugal, Spain, and central Europe, encouraged by the Brazilian government, took the place of the former slaves, and probably saved Brazil's coffee industry. These colonists, or *colonos* as they were called, were industrious wage earners who, as soon as they were able, bought some land and started small plantations, or *fincas,* of their own.

The flood of *colonos* continued until 1900, when the world price of coffee fell and the planters could not make good the wages they had promised their workers. When foreign governments threatened to stop the flow of immigrants to Brazil, the Brazilian government was forced to lend enough money to the planters to pay the *colonos*. The decline in the world coffee price also caused the *milreis*, Brazil's unit of currency, to sink to one-third of its previous value. The federal government, aided by the London House of Rothschild, stabilized the *milreis*. But the pattern had been set for a recurring problem of the Brazilian coffee industry, a problem felt even more keenly by a country with a one-crop economy like turn-of-the-century Brazil.

Spurred on by previous years of growth and rising coffee prices, coffee growers had planted vast amounts of new acreage. Ripening fruit burdened the trees. Unpicked, it began to dry on the trees and fall to the ground. Hordes of *colonos*, fed up with the fluctuating nature of the coffee business, fled the plantations for their home countries. The giant warehouses in San Francisco, New Orleans, New York, Liverpool, Hamburg, and Le Havre were filled to overflowing with green coffee. In 1905 the already low price of coffee—5 cents a pound—was poised for a drop to zero should the harvest of 1906, estimated at 20,000,000 bags or over 80 percent of the entire world's production, go to market. With 90 percent of the total wealth of the country invested in coffee, Brazil was hovering on the brink of economic destruction.

An answer to the desperate problem was proposed by Alexandre Siciliano, a merchant and coffee planter from the state of São Paulo. His plan, "valorization," called for every Brazilian state to purchase its entire coffee crop on the trees from the farmers. All new planting would be forbidden. The state would store the coffee until world prices rose, and then sell and recover its investment. A governors' meeting called to discuss the new project ended without resolution, and São Paulo, Brazil's largest coffee-producing state, decided to try valorization alone. Over three-quarters of São Paulo's crop was purchased by the state with loans of more than

$75,000,000 from an association of American and European bankers.

Valorization seemed successful at first. Enormous crops in 1907 and 1908 were purchased and sold in an orderly fashion through 1913. But the planters did not keep their part of the bargain. Instead of following the restrictions against further plantings, new land was planted, and yields were increased on old lands when the planters thought the government could sell everything they grew. In 1925 the federal government realized its error and formed the Permanent Coffee Defense Institute to approach the problem of maintaining stable coffee prices from another angle. Under this new system no coffee could leave the plantations unless there was a foreign order for it. Hundreds of enormous warehouses were built to hold the coffee until it could be matched with import orders. The amount became a carefully guarded state secret, to foil speculators from manipulating prices.

Again, prices artificially maintained at profitable levels encouraged over-planting and led to the appearance of amateur coffee planters who lowered the quality of Brazilian coffee. Finally, the New York stock market crash of 1929 put an end to the loans used by the Institute to purchase crops. The Institute crumbled in 1931, leaving Brazil with 25,000,000 bags of coffee that were unmarketable at any price. To deal with the crisis the federal government created the Departmento Nacional do Cafe, which systematically destroyed millions of sacks of coffee for over ten years, until 1944. The destruction is described by Andres Uribe C. in *Brown Gold:*

> The planters sat upon their shaded patios and the *colonos* stood silent as the *ensaccadores* prepared millions of bags of coffee for the journey to destruction. The crop was handled in the ordinary manner, for few planters could accept the fact that their coffee was worthless. It was picked, cleaned, dried and transported as though destined to bring delight to the dinner tables of the world. But the sacks were hauled to designated locations for prompt destruction rather than to the port cities.
>
> The burning centers were called *pilhars de incineracão*. More than seventy-five of them worked steadily for over eight years. Huge, roof-less sheds, they encompassed burning areas each nearly a half mile square. Thousands of tons of beans were mixed with heavy crude oil and set afire. They burned with a whining moan and exhuded black and reddish flames.

In the wake of this holocaust planters fled the land and *fazendas* went to seed. First weeds, then underbrush, vines, and trees crept over the deserted plantations. Almost 1,500,000,000 coffee trees ceased bearing fruit.

In the midst of World War II coffee prices started rising and slowly, when farmers realized that coffee would once more be in demand after the war, they began returning to the land—clearing, planting, fertilizing and irrigating. The Brazilian Coffee Institute supervised the opening up of new lands for planting and regulated the production on the old. The Instituto Agronomico de Campinas was formed to discover new varieties of hardy, fruitful coffee plants while aiding the farmer in all phases of agricultural production.

The state of São Paulo has been the hub of the Brazilian coffee industry for almost a hundred years. Comprising only 3 percent of Brazilian territory, this state accounts for one-third of the country's gross national product. And in an attempt to avoid the earlier pitfalls of overdependence on the coffee crop, São Paulo has diverted the money it has made from coffee into other fields of activity: industry, science, art, education, and communications. This is the pattern being followed by most modern coffee states in and out of Brazil.

While the history of coffee growing in Brazil has often been one of over-production or "too much of a good thing," the story of Colombian coffee has been one of constant struggle to overcome a hostile topographical ambiance. Colombian beans are richer than many other beans, and they provide a valuable, sought-after addition to any coffee blend. Colombia lies within the coffee belt, between the tropic of Cancer and the tropic of Capricorn, and is favored with high altitude and ample rainfall, conditions necessary for coffee production.

But the Andes mountains, whose slopes are dotted with coffee plantations or *fincas,* present the Colombian coffee grower with some of the most formidable challenges to farming, transportation, and communication in the industry. The steep mountainsides discourage the use of machinery, so that all work must be done by hand, and block one of the prime requisites of commercial farming—easy access to exporting ports. Running in a north-easterly direction across Colombia, this enormous range with fissures, spurs, peaks, and valleys entrap the country in a maze of almost insurmountable barriers. An early Spanish explorer described the land as fit for "madmen, eagles and mules." Nevertheless the Spaniards, who ruled for two centuries, penetrated the interior to search for emeralds and gold, and the present location of Colombia's cities reflects their proximity to the old mineral deposits.

To penetrate the inland barriers two choices were open to the early travelers: muleback or foot. Most chose the latter method, since the treacherous, narrow trails often precipitated animal and man to their deaths in the gorges below. A typical trip involved crossing many rivers, valleys, and ridges. While numerous rivers travel down the slopes of the Andes, all but two flow the wrong way. The Magdalena and Cauca are large rivers flowing to the seacoasts, but only the Magdalena, "the life stream of Colombia," is effective in surmounting the difficulties presented by the Andes. In spite of shallows, sand bars, rapids, rocks, and insects—not to speak of mutineers and pirates—this route along the Magdalena opened up the interior and eventually made possible the establishment of coffee production.

Near the close of the eighteenth century Colombia's first coffee groves were planted around the town of Cúcuta from *Coffea arabica* seeds imported from the French West Indies, a legacy of De Clieu's original plant stolen from the Jardin des Plantes in Paris. Most of the coffee, however, was limited to home use. To transport the coffee from Cúcuta, where it was grown, to Maracaibo, Venezuela, for shipment overseas required an arduous two-week journey by muleback through steaming machete-cleared jungle paths and downriver on flat-bottomed barges.

Despite continued isolation of the coffee regions production slowly increased. Many farmers, unlucky with other crops, switched to coffee. Toward the middle of the nineteenth century three important events coalesced to inject the Colombian coffee industry with a new vitality. World consumption had more than doubled between the beginning and middle of the century. Prices, responding to increased demand, were at their peak, and provided a powerful incentive to grow coffee. And in 1824 the first steamboat toiled up the Magdalena River.

This technological breakthrough triggered a series of related transportation improvements which had the effect of shrinking the awesome Andes. Regular steamboats on the river encouraged a development of trails and roads connecting the villages on the slopes along the river with each other and with the Magdalena. A railroad construction program brought the country even closer together and stimulated trade with Chile, Peru, and Ecuador. Finally, the opening of the Panama Canal brought New York, London, Hamburg, New Orleans, and Le Havre within reach of Buenaventura, located on Colombia's Pacific coast, one of the world's great coffee ports. Colombia could then come into her own as the world's second great coffee producer.

Colombian farmers soon found out that coffee planted in the lowlands grew plentifully and was closer to the ports, but had poor quality and brought low prices on the world markets. This zone, called the *tierra cali-*

ente, they reserved for tropical fruits and vegetables. On the cool land, the *tierra templada,* where the altitude was between 2,000–6,000 ft., conditions for growing coffee were ideal. The cherries were more flavorful, stronger and had more body. These qualities commanded the highest prices in the coffee-drinking countries. Hundreds of thousands of seedlings were planted and by 1890 coffee became Colombia's chief export. The industry flourished and articles and pamphlets abounded with instructions for planting and processing.

At the peak of this boom, in 1899, Colombia became embroiled in a bitter and bloody revolution. Farmers became soldiers and the cherries died on the trees. Overproduction in Brazil glutted the markets and coffee prices tumbled. These conditions led to a wholesale abandonment of the *fincas* by coffeemen. But the revolution was over in 1903 and steps were taken to revitalize the coffee industry.

Since then the industry has strengthened and prospered at a much greater rate than that of Brazil, though accounting for a much smaller proportion of world coffee production. This rise has been paralleled by a constantly improving transportation network: new railroad lines, boats for the smaller streams, highways and roads, aerial railways to cross the gorges, and airline travel.

Colombia's coffee industry is dominated by the small farmer. Over 80 percent of the *fincas* are owned and run by a single family caring for less than 5,000 trees. These small mountainside plantations are usually far from the cities and present an arduous and sometime dangerous life. Tilling the slopes by hand is not easy. Most of the coffee is harvested twice a year with the farmer, his family, and neighbors working as long as there is light. Since harvests occur during the rainy season, drying the beans, which requires the sun, becomes more complicated. In fact this negative agricultural circumstance raises production costs of Colombian coffee by 15 percent. By contrast the Brazilian harvest comes once a year; all cherries, ripe and unripe, are picked at the same time, and the unripe ones mature during the dry season.

Brazil and Colombia still dominate the world's coffee markets and have done so overwhelmingly through the 1950s and 1960s. But some of the old coffee-producing countries are again active, and new countries are making inroads on the supremacy of Brazil and Colombia.

Yemen, the land of coffee legend, has for centuries been eclipsed commercially by the greatest producers of each age. Yet since Arabia's demise as major coffee supplier to East and West, a trickle of the storied Mocha has continued to reach the cups of the most discriminating connoisseurs. Ethiopia, where man discovered the first coffee plants growing wild, has produced coffee for over a thousand years and is still supplying a substantial amount to the world.

The West Indies, the first great coffee area after Arabia and beneficiary of Gabriel de Clieu's efforts to spread the plant throughout the French colonies, still produces coffee. For over a hundred years this crop has been the bulwark of Haiti's economy. Since 1790 Haiti has exported between 40,000,000 and 80,000,000 pounds per year, grown on small farms. In 1881 the Dominican Republic exported 1,400,000 pounds; in 1933 the figure was 26,000,000, and its rate of growth has kept accelerating dramatically. Jamaica has been growing coffee since 1730, and while its crop is tiny, the fabled beans from the Blue Mountains are eagerly sought after as one of the finest tastes in the world. Puerto Rico started growing coffee around 1750 and during the half century preceding 1928, averaged between 30,000-000 and 50,000,000 pounds yearly. In 1926 and 1928 great storms and hurricanes all but decimated the plantations, and now the entire small crop of excellent coffee is consumed domestically. Coffee was introduced into Central America from the West Indies, but Costa Rica, El Salvador, and Guatemala had no significant exports until the last quarter of the nineteenth century.

The success or failure of coffee in Asia has been tied to the fatal coffee disease *Hemileia vastatrix*. The British began cultivating the crop in 1840 in India and by 1872 were exporting almost 56,000,000 pounds. The blight struck in the late 1870s, and in 1933 imports were down to under 20,000,000 pounds. Recently coffee has made a comeback there and India is an important supplier of fine coffee. Java, the prototype of Indonesian coffees and for centuries one of the world's most sought-after drinks, was first exported in the early eighteenth century. It was hit hard by *Hemileia* in the 1870s, and again during World War II. Now part of a small but exquisite crop reaches the outside world, where men still delight in a beverage bearing the name and taste of perhaps the most renowned of all coffees.

Peru, Venezuela, where the famed Maracaibo bean grows, and Ecuador, the three major South American coffee producers after Brazil and Columbia, started growing coffee commercially toward the end of the eighteenth century and play a significant role in today's market.

Hawaii grows the only American coffee. This premium bean, started from imported Brazilian trees in 1825, is produced in small quantities. Complex agricultural techniques are required due to the hard, volcanic soil of the island. Its flavor is excellent and it commands high prices wherever coffee is sold.

Coffee came to Mexico before 1800, but it was not until 1870 that coffee was exported in significant amounts. Proximity to the United States makes America a big customer; the Mexicans themselves consume a large part of their crop.

Domesticated coffee was brought from the island of Réunion, near Mauritius, to Africa by Roman Catholic missionaries in 1893, although coffee had grown wild in Africa for centuries. Most African countries did not start producing commercial coffee crops until the early 1900s. But this newest coffee area, in spite of its late start, today accounts for more than one quarter of the world's crop.

THE COFFEE MARKETPLACE

Any discussion of coffee as a beverage should touch upon coffee as a commodity, since coffee as a trade substance is closest to the consumer in the long chain from seed to cup. Also, how coffee is traded has an immediate effect on its retail price. Adding to the precariousness of coffee as a commodity is its luxury status. Unlike food, metal, or fiber staples, the disappearance of coffee from the marketplace would not affect the human diet or stop the wheels of industry. Furthermore, the four to five years it takes for a coffee plant to reach full producing maturity tends to reinforce the boom-and-bust cycle that has dogged the industry for more than three centuries.

In London bags of coffee were first sold in lots at candle auctions. While a candle stub flickered in front of the auctioneer, bids were accepted. When it sputtered out, the last bidder got the lot. In the New World before the existence of the New York Coffee and Sugar Exchange, merchants roamed the streets in known areas, taking bids and selling to the highest bidder at the end of the day. Until the 1870s speculators could corner the coffee market by buying up all the coffee in the port warehouses. Because no one knew exactly when the next coffee ship would arrive, merchants were forced to pay whatever price was demanded of them. The advent of intercontinental cables, the telephone, and fast sailing ships curtailed artificial manipulation of coffee. Shipping schedules became well known and information about conditions affecting the crops, such as adverse weather or strikes, was at hand. Prices began to reflect conditions in the producing countries, rather than the available supplies in the consuming countries.

For well over twelve decades cycles of overproduction and underproduction, with a full cycle lasting approximately seven years, have dominated coffee merchandising. We can trace the development of a typical cycle by starting at any arbitrary point. Coffee supplies are scant and prices start to rise. The planter, seeing a chance for profit, clears new land for planting more coffee. During the first three years of the five it takes for the new plants to mature, the planter reaps profits from his already producing trees. He reinvests this in clearing still more land. By the fifth, sixth and seventh year, his annual harvests are gigantic. Other planters who have followed the same pattern are producing mammoth crops also. As the warehouses become crammed with coffee, prices start to drop. The planter rips up his coffee trees to plant sugar, cotton, wheat, or rice, or leaves his farm altogether. The vines, weeds, and forests encroach upon the abandoned fields. As the years pass, the supplies in the warehouses are used up. Production is low and prices start rising. The planter starts clearing his land again to plant more coffee.

This cycle has lead to the development of the future delivery contract, a concept as old as commerce itself (it dates back to ancient Egypt), which is the mainstay of modern coffee commerce. To reduce uncertainty caused by future price changes or shortages of goods, merchants pay in advance, to insure delivery. This, in essence, is what goes on on the floor of the New York Coffee and Sugar Exchange. A merchant agrees to buy or sell a lot—250 bags—of coffee of a certain standardized type, as determined by a consensus of the trade (such as Santos Type No. 4 from Brazil) at a set price, on some particular future date. A constant check or barometer of future contract prices are "spot" prices, or what coffee will cost if purchased directly from the warehouse.

Between 1940 and 1972, several international coffee agreements were signed by over a dozen nations of Latin America and the United States. The purpose of these agreements, which contained a complex formula of export and import quotas, crop regulation plans, and price decline guarantees, was to maintain prices at a fair level for producers and consumers, while encouraging the increased consumption of coffee. By 1972 Brazil, long the world's leading producer and the dominant force in the I.C.A., had lost much of its strength as Central America and Africa began playing a much stronger role in world coffee supply. The I.C.A. lost its power base and collapsed.

The abandonment of controls and the gradual disappearance of huge surpluses from Brazil led to wider price fluctuations. This revived a refinement of futures trading: hedging. A typical hedge, the purpose of which is to insure against loss of money by the coffee grower in the face of fluctuating prices, works this way: A green coffee importer, a roaster, buys a shipment of Central American coffee in July, for delivery to New York during August. He thinks prices will fall. So he sells the same quantity of green coffee in the form of September delivery, futures contracts, on the New York Coffee and Sugar Exchange. He has agreed to take delivery at today's price and make delivery at today's price. He is even, no matter what happens. If the market goes down, his coffee from the shipper is worth less, but his contract with the Exchange is worth more. If coffee goes up, the reverse is true.

2. How Coffee Is Grown

Growing up as we did in a family that roasted coffee, we got to know coffee in its raw state, as it comes green into the country. One wall of our shop has always been lined with those huge, heavy sacks of green coffee beans—seven rows of bags, each row stacked seven bags high. We spent many pleasant afternoons perched atop those bags of raw beans. We watched the world go by from there, innocent of everything. We had no idea where those beans, which supported us literally and figuratively, came from. We knew only that until some adult member of the family roasted them, they served no better purpose than to sit on—and that purpose they served very well. Since those days we've learned how those beans come into our possession: of the process that yields the product, of men attending to nature and nature returning the favor.

Most coffee drinkers in the consuming countries know coffee primarily as a beverage, secondarily as a ground or powdered substance which, when mixed with water, will yield that beverage. The coffee that we drink is made from ground roasted beans, but since so much coffee is sold already ground, few people get to see roasted whole bean coffee. Still fewer people are familiar with green unroasted coffee beans, though virtually all coffee comes to the United States in this form. These green beans are the hulled and dried seeds of the coffee tree. The tree flowers and bears a red cherry; the cherry has pits; the pits are the seeds; the seeds are the beans. They are very hard, unperishable, unpalatable, and without coffee flavor or aroma.

While we Americans consume millions of cups of coffee a day, we grow none in the continental United States. (A tiny percentage of the world's coffee is grown in Hawaii.) We depend for our coffee on farmers who cultivate the coffee tree on small farms and large plantations around the world between the latitudes 25 degrees north and 25 degrees south. Their efforts accounted in 1972 for over $3 billion in foreign exchange, nearly one percent of that year's total world trade. Coffee cultivation as a modern agribusiness accounted in six countries for 26–49 percent of their total foreign-exchange receipts. For the innumerable farmers who grow the coffee, it is their livelihood and their lives.

THE CULTIVATION OF COFFEE

The species of coffee which has traditionally provided the world with most of its crop is *Coffea arabica*. Indigenous to Ethiopia, it thrives also in Java, Sumatra, India, Arabia, Equatorial Africa, the Pacific Islands, the West Indies, and of course Latin America. In our discussion of the coffee tree and its cultivation, we will be speaking of this species unless specific reference is made to other types.

While *Coffea arabica* continues to dominate world supplies, in recent years *Coffea robusta* (*Coffea canephora*) has become more and more important. Trees of this type were first found to be growing wild in the Belgian Congo (now Zaire) and began to be cultivated around the turn of the twentieth century. They can be successfully cultivated at lower altitudes than those suitable for *Coffea arabica*. Arabica trees generally do not bear fruit until their fifth year, while yields of Robusta are generally realized two or three years after planting. Robusta is more resistant to disease than Arabica and fares better against the ravages of frost. The flavor of Robusta does not compare favorably with Arabica, but its hardiness, rapid growth, and high yields make it popular with farmers. Groves of Arabica which have been killed by disease or frost have often been replanted with Robusta.

A third species of coffee is *Coffea liberica*. It grows large, sturdy, and is resistant to disease but its product finds little favor outside Liberia, where it grows in the lowlands. This species produces an even smaller crop than the generally favored Arabica. Its flavor makes it unpopular with consumers. Its low yield makes it unattractive to farmers. So far it has not become commercially important.

Whatever the species, wherever they are grown, coffee trees have certain physical characteristics in common and are similarly cultivated. The coffee plant is a small tree—or large shrub, depending on how you look at it—which if allowed to attain its full height would grow to between fourteen and thirty feet. It is, however, usually pruned to a height of between five and twelve feet. The plant has glossy, deep green, simple leaves, opposed to each other in alternating pairs. Though sometimes called an evergreen, it is not; its leaves last only from three to five years. As there are no drastic seasonal changes in the tropical and subtropical climates where coffee grows, the trees bear flowers and fruit at various times during the year. The flowers are small, white, and delicately fragrant. These blossoms, whose perfume has been compared to the scent of orange blossoms and jasmine, fall from the trees after only a few days, to be replaced by tiny clusters of green cherries. As the cherries ripen, they get larger and turn a deeper and deeper red. When the cherries have turned a deep purplish red, they are ripe and ready for picking.

The number of times that a tree flowers and bears fruit in a year depends on the temperature and moisture of its environment. At the higher and cooler semi-dry altitudes flowering and fruiting may occur only once a year. In such cases there is a single, ongoing cycle which repeats itself. In the hotter and wetter lowlands, blooming and fruiting may occur three or four or even five times a year. On such trees ripe fruit, green fruit, open flowers and flower buds may all be seen on the same branch at the same time. Just as the frequency of flowering and fruiting are determined by environment, so is the amount of time it takes for the cherries to mature. High-grown coffees mature in six to seven months, taking two or three months longer than their lowland cousins. As the cherries mature, they turn into red ellipsoidal balls. Each cherry normally contains two locules (chambers); each locule contains a "stone" which is the seed and its parchment covering. The seeds or beans are usually a round-oval shape, flat on one side, and marked longitudinally by a shallow incision. When a cherry has one locule and contains only one stone, that stone is usually round and is called the peaberry or male berry. Cherries containing peaberries are usually found at the extremities of the branches but may occur as botanical freaks anywhere on the tree. Peaberry coffee is favored by some connoisseurs, but this preference may be a holdover from the days of home roasting, when peaberry coffee was prized because the round beans could be shaken around in the pan and were easy to roast evenly. We suggest you try a peaberry coffee and decide for yourself on its merits.

The availability of peaberry coffees is dictated by the grading procedures of the growing countries. It is usually available as such because other grades are not permitted to contain more than a small percentage of peaberries. You may find peaberry coffee from the Republic of Cameroon, Tanzania, Burundi, Zaïre (Kivu), Venezuela, Colombia, Ethiopia (Harrar), and Indonesia.

The cultivation of a coffee tree starts with the seed. The finest seeds, those known to produce hardy trees with high yields of good flavored coffee, are selected for planting. The seed used for planting has its parchment-like covering—stripped of that covering, it becomes the green coffee bean of commerce. Seeds are usually given their starts in a nursery on the plantation. Planting can be done any time during the year. The seedlings are permitted to grow in the nursery for about a year, until they have reached a height of from eighteen to twenty-four inches. They are then transplanted in the coffee grove in rows ten to twelve feet apart, in much the same fashion as apple trees are planted here.

Many different types of seeds such as typica, bourbon, mundo nuevo, caturra, and maragogipe produce trees of the Arabica variety. Important as these specific distinctions are to the agronomist and the farmer, they do not materially affect the general principles of coffee cultivation.

The most suitable climate for coffee growing lies within the tropics, where the mean annual temperature is 70° F. The average minimum temperature should be no lower than 55° F. The average maximum temperature should be no higher than 80° F; higher temperatures cause the beans to mature too quickly and beverage quality suffers.

The altitude at which coffee is grown and the positioning of the groves are important as they affect the temperature and the amount of sunlight that falls on the trees. Coffee grows at all altitudes from sea level to 7,000 ft., the frost line in the tropics. Robusta coffee seems to thrive in the hotter, wetter lowlands (up to 3,000 ft.), while the fine flavored Arabicas come from trees growing at the cooler higher altitudes. It is a botanical oddity that the best coffees are grown where coffee does not grow wild. Coffee cultivated at higher altitudes matures more slowly and develops more and better flavored oils. The coffee plant needs sunshine, but a few hours daily exposure is sufficient. Hilly ground has the advantage of offering the kind of exposure that coffee trees need—sunlight part of the day, shade for the rest. Cloud covers and mists often act to shield high-grown mountain coffees (eg. Colombian, Mexican, Sumatran) from prolonged hot sun. Shade trees are sometimes planted in coffee groves to offer the same kind of protection.

The best earth for growing coffee is composed of decomposed mold, organic matter, and disintegrated volcanic rock. The soil should be rich in potash, nitrogen, and phosphoric acid. Since artificial chemical fertilizers generally have to be imported and are far too costly for the world's average coffee farmer, he must usually content himself with working back into the soil the droppings of the trees themselves, along with weeds, prunings and manure, to replenish these elements. In Hawaii, coffee grows in ground composed of volcanic lava. The trees are actually planted in soil that is imported from other parts of the island. In Brazil, the famous and bountiful *terra roxa* (red earth) nourishes the trees. This land has a topsoil of red clay three to four feet thick and gravelly subsoil. In Java, the Arabica estates consist of rolling terrain. In some areas a loamy topsoil overlies a porous subsoil; in others pockets of rich soil are found to be distributed throughout a rocky soil. In each case, the environment is highly nutritious, the trees are abundantly supplied with much-needed minerals, and the physical makeup of the soil is responsible for the optimum balance between retention of moisture and drainage. The soil should be moist and loose enough to accept rain while allowing excess moisture to drain quickly away. Well drained land is important to the health of the tree; accumulation of too much water in the soil causes development of the wood of the tree at the expense of the flowers and fruit. This is a special problem for coffee trees grown in low-lying regions where rainfall is heavy and drainage is poor. On the other hand, prolonged drought is fatal to coffee trees. An abundant rainfall, about 70 inches annually, equally distributed throughout the year is ideal. Since the best kind of soil for the trees should not store the water, continual rainfall is needed to keep the trees well watered. If only to point out the risky nature of the farmer's job, it's worth noting that if it rains too hard when the trees are in bloom, the blossoms will be washed off the trees and no fruit will develop. Windbreaks are sometimes built to protect the blossoming trees and to prevent erosion of the soil.

But wind and rain are not the only problems. Today's coffee farmer faces the age old enemies of agriculture: frost, pestilence, and disease. Frost kills coffee trees by freezing the sap in the trees. As the sap freezes, it expands, rupturing the tissues of leaf, branch, and root. Warmer temperatures come; the frozen sap melts and runs out of the ruptured tree. The tree dies. There is no prevention; there is no cure. Devastation can be enormous. In July, 1975, what is being called the worst frost of this century struck Brazil's major coffee growing areas. It is estimated that the 1975–76 crop will be only 8,000,000 bags, down from 22,000,000 in 1974–75. Coffee prices have risen sharply and may rise even further. The effects of the frost on the 1976–77 crop cannot be determined until an assessment is made of how severely the trees were damaged.

It is not surprising, given the tremendous quantity of coffee consumed in the United States, that an attempt was made to grow coffee here. At the turn of the century, as coffee was becoming commercially important, numerous farmers tried to cultivate coffee in Florida and Louisiana. The crop was small and of unremarkable quality. The insurmountable impediment to the success of those experiments was the killing frost.

The *broca* or coffee-bean borer, the worst of coffee's insect enemies, is tremendously destructive, since it bores into the bean itself and eats it away. It has resisted all but the most intensive and expensive attempts to control it. Another bug, the coffee leaf-miner, feeds on the tender new leaves of the tree. A host of other bugs and worms must constantly be fought. Those that attack from underground are among the most dreaded enemies of the farmer, since they can sever the roots of the tree before he becomes aware of their existence.

In the 1870s, Ceylon was exporting 120,000,000 pounds of coffee per year. By the turn of the century, not a single living coffee tree was left in the country: a wind-borne, spore-forming fungus called *Hemileia vastatrix* had struck the trees and wiped them out within twenty years. It was unstoppable and still is, though scientists are working to find a defense. One avenue being explored is the development of a strain of tree resistant to the disease. The western hemisphere, while it has lost upward of 400 million pounds per year to other pests and diseases, has not so far been attacked by *Hemileia*. There is no known reason for this. In fact, its imminent arrival in this hemisphere has been recently forecast. While it can and has had far less devastating effects than it did in Ceylon, we certainly hope that the forecasters are in error.

Even when he succeeds in defending himself against these enemies, the coffee farmer must work to increase the efficiency of his farming techniques and thereby increase his yield. Before the advent of national federations, little energy was expended on programs that would increase the quality and quantity of the crop. When prices were low and times were bad, such programs were considered an unaffordable luxury; when times were good, they were thought to be superfluous.

A coffee tree raised from seed generally begins flowering in its third year. A good crop can be expected from the tree in its fifth or sixth year, and it will continue to produce a good crop through its fifteenth year. The yield measured in green beans ranges from half a pound to eight pounds annually; two pounds is considered good, one pound is average. It takes five pounds of cherries to produce that one pound of beans. When the trees get too old to bear profitable yields, they are cut down to twelve inches above the ground and renewed by permitting the strongest two sprouts of the stump to mature.

To permit easy picking, trees are pruned to a height between five and twelve feet. If left to their own devices they would grow as high as thirty feet, and much of the tree's strength would be absorbed by the wood and not by the fruit. The ripe cherries would not only be harder to reach if the trees were not pruned; there would be fewer of them.

HARVESTING THE CROP

As no mechanical means of picking coffee has yet been devised, all coffee is still picked by hand. The method of picking differs depending on whether the coffee is to be processed by the dry method or the wet method. The purpose of either of these methods is to remove the outer skin, the fruit pulp, the inner "silver skin," and the parchment of the cherries from the green beans. The result is the green coffee bean of commerce. If the dry method is to be used, all the cherries are stripped from the branches at once—green, partially ripe, ripe, and over-ripe. If the wet method is to be used, only ripe cherries are picked.

Whether on the owner-operated *fincas* of Colombia or the great *fazendas* of Brazil, when it's time to harvest the cherries, everyone picks. In Colombia the farmer, his family, his friends and neighbors come out for the harvest. Since all the cherries don't ripen at once, and since only the ripe fruit is picked to be washed, the pickers must return three to five times to clean a tree. During the months of October through March the peak harvest coincides with the rainy season, making picking even more difficult. Regardless of which cleaning method is used, the cherries may be "winnowed" or sifted, and are then washed to free them of leaves, twigs, small stones, gravel, and other foreign matter.

In Brazil, the main harvest is from April to September, in the dry season. On the large plantations workers are hired to strip the trees of cherries that will be processed by the dry method. While this method of picking is simpler and easier, the subsequent task of sun-drying the cherries is a painstaking and arduous one. Coffee is a harsh taskmaster, but the farmer who picks his own crop reaps the rewards of the harvest. The worker who picks the crop on large plantations suffers the low status and low standard of living of farm laborers the world over. Where other ways of making a living have presented themselves, the pickers have abandoned the coffee groves for more secure, less seasonal, and less backbreaking work. In Puerto Rico and Hawaii, the growth of the tourist industry has been not the least of the causes of decreased coffee production.

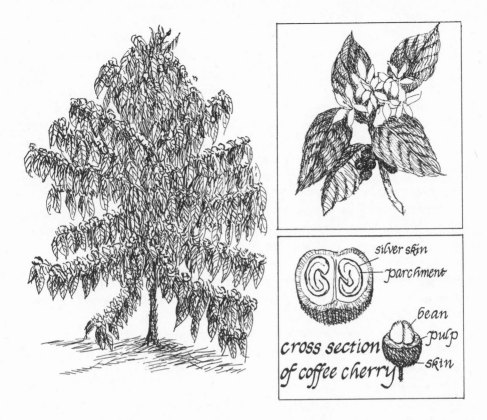

silver skin
parchment
bean
pulp
skin

cross section
of coffee cherry

The dry method is the oldest method of coffee preparation. It was used by the Arabs in Yemen, where they allowed the sun to shrivel the fruit on the tree, and then shook the dried beans into cloths spread on the ground. Sixty-five percent of the world's coffee is still prepared by the dry method. In Yemen and Ethiopia much coffee is still permitted to dry on the tree, but almost everywhere else the dry method now works like this: After the initial washing, the coffee cherries are drained and spread on drying grounds in thin layers, usually for a period of two to three weeks. During this time, fermentation occurs. They are turned by rakes several times a day during the drying period to insure even drying, and heaped and covered at night to protect them from moisture. When thoroughly dry, they are transferred to milling machines for removal of the dried husk, parchment, and thin, inner silver skin. The result is the green coffee bean.

The wet method, used where water is abundant, works like this: After the initial washing, the cherries are put into machines to remove the outside fruit pulp, exposing a sticky substance which surrounds the parchment. The berries are then placed in large, clean concrete tanks to ferment, usually for twelve to twenty-four hours, to facilitate removal of this sticky substance, then poured into concrete sluiceways or washing machines to be thoroughly washed in constantly changing clear water. After washing they are drained and spread out to dry as in the dry method, although usually for a shorter time period. On some plantations, machines are used to shorten the drying process. The dried beans are transferred to hulling machines for removal of the tough parchment-like skin and the silver skin. The final product is the same as in the dry process: the green coffee bean. Improperly dried coffee will result in rancid beans and a hide-flavored brew.

Washed coffees, or coffees processed by the wet method, generally bring higher prices in world markets. Such coffees tend to be more finely flavored for several reasons: generally, the better coffees are prepared by the more costly wet method; only ripe cherries are picked for preparation by the wet method whereas coffee prepared by the dry method often includes immature and over-ripe cherries; also, allowing the beans to ferment for a short time after the pulp has been removed is said to enhance their flavor.

In the wet method, the fermentation process is controlled. In the dry method, little control is possible, and the risk of overfermentation is high. Washed coffee may also be spoiled by over fermentation if it is left in the fermenting tanks too long or if incompletely washed upon removal from the tanks. Carelessness can negate the potential benefit of the wet process.

Some of the fine washed coffees are Colombian, Costa Rican, Guatemalan, Venezuelan, Mexican, Kenyan, Tanzanian, Kona from Hawaii and Kivu from Zaïre. Most Brazilian coffee is processed by the dry method. Mocha coffee from Yemen and Djimmah from Ethiopia are coffees which are often left to dry on the trees. It appears that the flavor of these coffees is enhanced rather than hurt by tree drying. The air is so dry that over-fermentation does not occur.

Coffee processed by either the wet or dry method is then graded for size, type and quality, by hand or by machine; sorted by hand to remove impurities and defective beans, and packed in bags of about 132 pounds each and transported to the nearest port.

COFFEE CROPS AND COFFEE PRICES

In 1972, the United States imported 20,800,000 bags of green coffee and the equivalent of an additional 1,500,000 bags of roasted or soluble coffee. Each "bag" denotes a bag of 60 kilos or 132.276 pounds. These 2,646 million pounds accounted for 37 percent of the world's imports. Americans ten years and older drank an average of 2.4 cups per person per day. Coffee drinkers drank an average of 3.6 cups a day. Per capita consumption was 13.8 pounds a year. Coffee-producing countries of the Western Hemisphere provided 65 percent of our coffee, African producers gave us 30 percent, and the remainder came from Asia and Oceania.

The economies of many of the larger coffee-producing nations rest somewhat precariously on the successful cultivation of the coffee tree. As the tree or the crop's value is threatened, so is the livelihood of the coffee farmer. In the past few decades, national federations have taken up the task of preventing and combatting the diseases which threaten the economic well-being of their countries. They not only conduct programs of research and education, but also provide the farmers with seeds and seedlings, fertilizer, low-interest loans, health care, and even plumbing.

These federations also act on the farmers' behalf in the world markets to stabilize prices at the highest possible levels, by regulating plantings so that overproduction does not force prices downward. Should prices fall below a certain minimum level, these federations save the farmer from ruin by buying his crop and reselling it at a time when a higher price may be obtained. At present, however, we are seeing this procedure used not as a safety valve to protect the farmer from falling prices, but to force prices up on the world market. Since the lapse, in 1973, of the price and quota provisions of the International Coffee Agreement, a trade agreement which for ten years established export and import quotas, the producing countries have formed international corporations that are buying huge quantities of coffee. The governments of the coffee-growing countries hope that by thus decreasing supplies in the face of constant demand prices can be forced higher and higher. In the past, speculators who tried similar tactics failed because they did not have the financial resources to corner the market. Whether coffee-producing countries will succeed where the speculators did not remains to be seen. Their attempt must certainly be viewed as part of a growing trend, that of the poorer nations trying to increase their wealth by selling their products to the wealthier ones at the highest prices they can get. If the age of cheap oil is over, so may the age of cheap coffee be drawing to a close.

The crucial difference between coffee and oil, however, is one which has in the past always made high coffee prices go down again. Coffee is cherished by many, but it is not a necessity. When prices go way up, consumption goes way down. Unlike the famed peanut shell and the wine grape, coffee beans have no secondary uses. They have no by-products and serve only as the material from which an appealing beverage—of no nutritional value—can be made. If, as has happened in the past, high coffee prices send consumers to other beverages, the decreased demand may spell doom for the producing countries' attempts to maintain high prices. They would probably not be willing to either severely cut back production or to buy "surpluses" in ever increasing amounts.

The pressure coffee producers are exerting may only be short term; they may wish to negotiate a new international agreement, but to do so from a position of strength. If, however, they indeed intend to push prices to high levels and keep them there indefinitely, there are some indications that they might succeed where speculators failed before. American consumers may view increased coffee prices as just another part of the higher cost of everything. If so, they would not boycott coffee as they did in 1953, when coffee prices rose unilaterally. Even if demand did drop, coffee-producing countries that are already more highly diversified might indeed be willing to put up with decreased demand, as long as they could sell their smaller output at a premium price. The worldwide demand for soybeans, for example, is high and farmers may choose to plant this crop instead of coffee. Soybeans require less care than coffee and yields can be realized in one-fifth the time. Free of the necessity to buy huge quantities of coffee from its farmers, the government of a producing country could then hold out for a high price for its crop.

3. Brown Gold:
The Roasting Process

HOW COFFEE IS ROASTED

THE BEANS have developed an exquisite chemistry engendered by the sun's energy, the soil's nutrients, the rain's caress. Time was needed and time taken for the beans to listen to the sun's secrets, the earth's tales, the rain's music. There was time to listen, to grow in wisdom. What the beans learn from sun, soil and rain is their treasure, and this treasure is revealed when we roast. The green beans which, before processing on the plantation, could have been the seeds of a new generation of trees, are ressurected to a new life of flavor by the roaster. Said Jabez Burns in the first issue of *The Spice Mill* (1878); "You do not give to pepper or ginger or cinnamon or cloves strength or quality, pungency, or aroma—but coffee you develop and by skill and judgement change from caterpiller to butterfly. You bring out the hidden treasure." Development is the key. Under the farmer's hand the beans develop their unique characteristics on the *fazendas* of Latin America, on the ancient hills of Arabia, on the mountainous slopes circling the world between the tropics of Cancer and Capricorn. The person who roasts coffee should continue their development not only with "skill and judgement" but with a measure of love and devotion.

The renowned coffee economist Andres Uribe C. titled his classic work on coffee *Brown Gold*. Coffee is surely brown gold to the economies of countries where it is a major crop. The high value that millions of coffee lovers accord the beverage again makes it worthy of the name. But coffee is also brown gold as it calls to mind the strivings of alchemists to transform base metals into precious ones. The coffee roaster turns alchemist when he transforms an unappetizing seed into the makings of a delicious, invigorating drink. His magic is genuine; he must interpret the beans' secrets and reveal them to our senses. No sleight of hand will do the trick. The roaster's hand must be only as quick as his eye, never quicker.

Unroasted coffee gives no clue as to what it might become. The beans do not have the characteristic look, smell or taste of coffee. Most people do not even recognize the contents of the freshly-imported bags. To understand this situation, think what it would be like if all our bread came from a plastic bag; we might not know what to do with flour.

A controlled application of heat brings about both physical and chemical changes in coffee beans. When coffee is roasted it shrinks about 16 percent in weight (up to 20 percent for the darkest Italian roast), doubles in volume, turns from a pale green to a rich brown in color, and develops characteristic coffee taste and aroma. A complex series of reactions is set up, including decompositions and interchanges. The resulting chemical composition differs radically from that of the green beans. At varying rates and to various extents the constituent elements of green coffee are decomposed. Those elements include water, oil, protein, caffeine, chlorogenic acid, trigonelline, tannin, caffetannin, caffeic acid, starch, sugars, fibrous material, ash, and traces of vitamins. The weight loss is attributable to loss of moisture and of volatile decomposition products. The remarkable increase in volume results from the beans popping and expanding in response to heat: the higher (darker) the roast, the greater the volume of any given weight of coffee. The color change is caused by carmelization of the sugars. In darker roasts carbonization occurs and is responsible for the distinctive flavor of such coffees.

The physical and chemical changes that contribute to the creation of coffee taste and aroma are not fully understood. The caffeine component is quite stable, showing a slight decrease only in the highest roasts. A large volume of carbon dioxide is produced, some of it expelled into the atmosphere, some held within the fibrous structure of the beans, where it is instrumental in maintaining the aroma and flavor of the coffee for up to a few weeks. Carmelized carbohydrates also contribute to flavor, as do the many organic substances created and partially destroyed during roasting.

Chlorogenic acids, a class of the taste-stimulating phenolic acids, are produced during roasting by the decomposition of aromatic hydrocarbons. They and caffeine contribute to the pleasantly bitter taste in coffee. The true tannins provide astringency. Trigonelline, a nitrogen-containing compound, is found in about the same amounts as caffeine, but its effect is not yet understood. Other organic acids abound. The acidity of coffee is highest when treated to a fairly light roast—light-roasted coffee is more acid than either green or dark-roasted coffee. This is because acids are both created and destroyed during roasting, and in the light roast more acids have been created than destroyed. The true tannins and the chlorogenic acids, for example, are decreased by half in a heavy roast. Acids form only part of the flavor picture, however, so it would be wrong to think that since light roasts are highly acid, they are the most flavorful.

If the chemicals of taste are hard to pin down, the aromatics are even more elusive. Extremely volatile aromatics are produced during roasting and seventy distinct compounds have been identified in a distillate of these substances. No single one is responsible for what every coffee drinker recognizes and appreciates as coffee aroma. The mystery remains. We do not as yet know what combination of what constituents makes coffee aroma. We know only slightly more about what constitutes the taste of coffee. Though the art of coffee is old, the science of coffee is an infant.

How does a coffee roaster judge the development of his coffee, that is, how does he know when the required chemical changes have taken place? Here's where the physical changes come in. The roaster hears the beans popping as they expand; he sees the beans turn a rich brown color; he smells that smell that smells like . . . coffee. When a roast is just finished, when it's just ready to be "taken off," the aroma promises something wonderful. All that planting and shading and hoping and picking and cleaning and sorting and shipping and selecting and now, just at that moment when he cuts off the heat and pulls the lever to let the beans down into the cooling drum, he knows he's done those beans proud. When people come into our shop and the aroma of just roasted coffee hits them, they inhale deeply and smile. They know they're onto something.

The fragrance of freshly roasted coffee is at once tantalizing and satisfying, like a promise made and kept. Unlike purely sweet smells like chocolate, perfume, or incense, the aroma of coffee is neither monotonous nor overbearing. Like the beverage itself, the smell of coffee is refreshing; it treats the nose to a stimulating sharpness, a pungency, that offsets and complements the sweetness. Sometimes in the shop we are asked if we ever tire of the smell or grow insensitive to it. Neither has been the case; through each day and over the years the aroma continues to delight us.

The basic principles for roasting a batch of unroasted coffee beans are:
1. Heat should be applied to the beans so that each bean and every part of each bean from the center to the surface is equally treated by that heat.
2. The heat should be applied at both the lowest temperature possible and for the shortest possible amount of time.

The second principle presents a sticky problem, but is essential to the proper development of the coffee. Roasting at too high a temperature will produce scorched or "tipped" coffee; the tender tips of the beans get burnt, while the centers are not sufficiently developed. Surface oils may be decomposed, rendering the coffee defenseless against the ravages of oxidation, and chaff produced by roasting may get burned into the surface of the beans. Roasting too slowly at low temperatures will produce "baked" coffee, underdeveloped beans lacking in zest and sparkle. The beans are dried out and color doesn't develop quickly enough; the crucial chemical and physical changes do not take place. The coffee falls victim to what the food chemists call inadequate structural expansion—the beans don't swell, and poor extraction becomes inevitable. Proper development demands that a sufficient quantity of heat be applied to the beans and that that heat be absorbed rapidly and thoroughly.

THE DEVELOPMENT OF ROASTING MACHINERY

Until a bit more than a century ago most coffee roasting was still done in the home. In 1662, the following recipe for the roasting of coffee was published:

> The coffee berries are to be bought at any druggist, about three shillings the pound; take what quantity you please and, over a charcoal fire, in an old pudding pan or frying pan, keep them always stirring until they be quite black; and when you crack one with your teeth that it is black within as it is without. Yet if you exceed then do you waste the oyl, which only makes the drink; and if you should continue fire till it be white, it will then make no coffee but only give you its salt. The Berry prepared as above, beaten and forced through a lawn sive is then fit for use.

Not until the middle of the nineteenth century was there any marked change from this method of roasting. True, as coffee gained in popularity and availability, the pudding pan gradually gave way to specialized utensils for the "parching" of coffee. Some were not unlike the old-fashioned bed warmers. These, in fully enclosing the batch of beans, kept the coffee's precious aroma from being entirely lost to air. Another improvement was the cylinder roaster, which permitted a small batch of beans to be rotated over the fire, insuring even exposure to heat. The recipe set forth by our seventeenth-century forebears could certainly have benefited from technological advances but, although primitive, it was not unsound. The roaster was wisely cautioned against excessive roasting, which would only drive off the oils that give the drink. He was also exhorted to roast the beans so that they were cooked inside and out, that is to say fully developed. Probably the beans prepared by that recipe were charred, and some aroma was driven off, but it was good advice for the times.

The roasting of coffee moved out of the kitchen and into the factory in the nineteenth century—not because better methods were inherent in large batch roasting, but rather in response to the growing demand for coffee in urban centers. Since it didn't go stale or spoil, green coffee could be distributed through the smallest general stores in the most sparsely populated areas. The beans could take a long time in transit and could remain in the grocers' stocks without deteriorating until they were sold. Perishable roasted coffee could not have survived such a long journey to the cup. Not until the demand for coffee was concentrated in the cities and distribution time shortened was factory roasting feasible.

As coffee roasting gained the stature of an industry, the eyes and hands of inventors, engineers, and later, chemists turned toward the improvement of coffee-roasting technique and machinery. Roasting technology had to meet two distinct demands, the demand for quantity and the demand for quality. As consumers required more coffee, coffee roasters needed efficient means to handle larger and larger quantities. Mechanization and later automation made for greater efficiency, as did the switch from coal to oil or gas, from manpower or horsepower to electric power.

The demand for quality was met with no less zeal. Machinery of greater and greater sophistication was developed, machinery that could help the roaster to make more precise judgments and more easily exercise control over the process. It did the coffee no good if a roaster with a sharp eye and a quick hand had to depend on equipment which could not respond to his intelligence and muscle. When a roast is done it should be taken off quickly and quickly cooled. The early factory roasters of the mid-nineteenth century were known as Carter pull-outs, because the roasting cylinders were pulled out of the furnace for charging and discharging. They used coal fires, were hand-cranked, and were very cumbersome—too cumbersome to provide very accurate control at the end of a roast.

Even these crude monsters did the coffee a better turn than the frying pans at home, but the real breakthrough came when Jabez Burns patented the forerunner of the modern coffee roaster in 1864. The incorporation of an ingenious system of helical flanges within the roasting cylinder served

old style "Royal" roaster

not only to mix and agitate the coffee so that it was uniformly heated, but also discharged the beans when a door was opened. The cylinder did not have to be stopped or removed from the fire for charging and discharging the beans, and samples could be taken even as the roast was in progress. This type of bricked-up coal-fired roaster was refined from time to time, and continued to be used by the majority of United States roasters until around the turn of the century. They were two-bag roasters; each roast took half an hour and 6.6 pounds of coal. One man could tend four roasters at once.

In the early 1900s, the quality of the roast was further enhanced by two major innovations. Gas replaced coal as a fuel, so that heat could be more accurately controlled. And roasting cylinders were perforated, so that the transfer of heat depended more on the hot gasses themselves and less on the hot metal of the cylinder. A major cause of scorching was thus eliminated.

The first gas-fired roasters were converted coal burners, but they soon gave way to internally-fired gas roasters. The roasting time was cut to eighteen minutes, but huge amounts of cold air had to be drawn through the cylinder to prevent the beans from burning. The genius of Jabez Burns arose again in 1914 to produce a refined internally-fired gas roaster. The coffee in his Jubilee roaster never came in contact with the flame, so the need for tempering by cold air was eliminated. Heat was transferred entirely by the heated gasses. A roast still took eighteen minutes but the process was efficient and almost all dangers to the beans had been eliminated.

In 1935, Burns outdid himself. He invented the Thermalo process, a process in which the quantity of heat applied to the beans is greatly magnified while the temperature of that heat is halved. This is achieved by considerably increasing the volume of the heating medium (hot air), and by having it blown at high speed through the roasting cylinder. The speed at which the hot air is drawn across the beans contributes to the efficiency and rapidity of heat transfer, since each bean is normally insulated against heat by a thin envelope of cool air, and the fast moving hot air literally washes this envelope away. Today much coffee is roasted by this method; Burns Thermalo equipment is used by more than 130 coffee roasters around the world.

One of the latest improvements in roasting technology is the "continuous roaster" which allows very large quantities of coffee to be roasted a little bit at a time. Each bit is roasted only about five minutes, at about 500° F. The success of this method is based on the fact that it takes less time to provide sufficient heat to a five-pound batch than it does to a 500-pound batch, the capacity of most four-bag Thermalo roasters.

Both batch and continuous roaster installations are in use today. Many plants employ a combination of batch and continuous roasting systems tailored to their needs. Continuous roasting, as a rule, is best suited to high volume roasting of one blend, while batch roasting is better for many low volume blends.

The coffee roaster takes off a roast when he judges the beans to be fully developed. He makes his judgment primarily on the basis of surface color. He has made careful adjustments of heat source and draft and assumes that his machine has caused similar development to occur throughout each and every bean. Except in very sophisticated automated roasting plants, the operator of a roasting machine makes his judgment against a previously roasted standard. As the roasting cylinder whirls the beans around over the heat, he will insert his tryer (a long, narrow scoop) and catch a few. Satisfied that the color is right, that full development has occurred, he will turn the heat off and open the gate allowing the beans to spill into the cooling cylinder or pan. This cooling stops further, at this point unwanted, development. In large roasters with capacities of four or five hundred pounds, a spray of water may be used to help quickly cool the huge mass of beans.

The roaster in our shop is a one-bag (132 lb.) Jabez Burns that we've been using for forty years and three generations. Ron Bowen, who's been in the business for more than ten years, shares the roasting duties with us and has become a master of the art. The machine has developed a few squeaks and a couple of clanks, but it still turns out several beautiful roasts a day. We roast about 100 pounds green (yields 86 pounds roasted) at a time. This relatively small batch makes it possible for us to achieve fully developed roasts at low temperatures in about eighteen minutes. Larger batches in the

same kind of roaster would require more heat and therefore either higher temperatures or longer roasting times. Since neither change would be good for the coffee, we keep the batches small and avoid the need for more sophisticated equipment.

The early pioneers of the coffee industry saw that there was a profit to be made in providing the urbanized masses with pre-roasted coffee. The lure of profit also engendered the development of machinery that could roast large quantities of coffee, and do it better than the cook at home. A handbill for Arbuckle's coffee in 1873 stated uncategorically that "You can not roast coffee properly yourself." This pronouncement may have overstated the case for pre-roasted coffee, but considering the state of home roasting in those days, it was probably more true than not. Still, we suspect that such a newfangled notion took some selling and that it took more than a few handbills. It took good, untainted coffee, properly roasted and distributed with great dispatch. In the nineteenth century roasted coffee was indeed a "convenience item," but it provided convenience without sacrificing quality. The product was in fact better than what people could provide themselves with the hard way. The beverage's popularity steadily increased.

Since those early pioneering days, roasting technology has been perfected. Modern mass roasting has the potential to provide the beans with better treatment than ever before. The product of mass roasters does indeed tend to be uniformly roasted, not underdeveloped or charred, and delivered to the consumer pure and fresh in vacuum tins. Why then has coffee consumption in the United States steadily declined over the past ten years? People would not be drinking less coffee if they were enjoying it more. We are convinced that consumers are not getting what they want from coffee and so they are using less of it. Why is it that so much coffee is such a dismal mediocrity?

The answer is not just in the roasting, of course. No matter how well coffee is roasted, the roasting process cannot bring out flavor if it isn't in the beans. The blends roasted by major packers are generally not of good quality. Low grade, low price filler coffees are too much in use.

And the roasting does play a part. While mass-roasted coffee is fully and uniformly roasted, most brands are a shade or two lighter than what we feel provides really robust flavor. The lighter the roast, the less the coffee shrinks, therefore the less money lost through shrinkage. There are even roasters who cut down on shrinkage either by leaving part of the beans undeveloped or by "soaking" the coffee as it is taken off. It's fine to use a small amount of water to cool down a finished roast so that overdevelopment doesn't occur. It's another matter entirely to use so much water that it is absorbed into the beans, adding weight and harming flavor. A roaster who uses either of these methods is cutting his shrinkage from the normal 16 percent to 15 percent, and can make a lot of money at the expense of flavor.

Now, we're not going to start knocking the profit motive *per se*. The profit motive was responsible for the birth of coffee roasting as an industry. That industry, in its infancy, provided Americans with better coffee than they had been able to obtain before. But under present conditions of severe competition the same profit motive is causing the deterioration of beverage quality and the slow erosion of the market as a whole. The fine art of roasting coffee is in need of a renaissance.

THE VARIETY OF ROASTS

The roasting of coffee turns the beans brown; the longer they're roasted, the darker they get. Coffee roasted too light won't have much of a coffee taste at all. Coffee can also be roasted so dark that it tastes burnt. Between these two extremes are a variety of roasts all tasting like coffee, each appealing to particular tastes.

Simply put, the darker coffee is roasted, the darker it tastes. Is any one roast the optimum? No, just as it would be silly to say that steak should only be broiled "medium." Is dark-roasted coffee stronger? No. It is common to credit dark-roasted coffee with producing a very, very strong beverage, but this is not accurate. It would be best to say that dark-roasted coffee has a characteristic "dark-roasted" taste, even if that may seem to be begging the question. The strength of coffee is directly dependent on the amount of soluble solids in the brew, that is, the solution of coffee in water. If coffee is "strong" it should be because more coffee is used, resulting in a stronger solution, not because of the roast itself. Espresso is in fact usually brewed with twice the amount of coffee normally recommended.

Not only does coffee get darker in color the longer it is roasted, but it also loses more weight and swells more in size. Oils held within the beans of a lighter roast are driven to the surface in a dark roast. Dark-roasted beans appear shiny. They have very slightly less caffeine and are somewhat less acidic than light-roasted beans. They are slightly more susceptible to becoming stale because surface waxes that remain intact on light-roasted beans are destroyed by more prolonged heating. The characteristic dark-roasted flavor tends to overshadow the more subtle flavors produced by lighter roasting. Some of the more delicate flavor oils and aromatics are in fact destroyed by dark roasting. What dark-roasted coffee may lack in subtlety, it more than makes up for in force. A thick syrupy decoction of dark-roasted beans is the choice, nay, the passion of coffee lovers throughout Europe and Latin America. We Americans should treat ourselves more often to the pleasures offered by this vigorous brew.

If the measurement of roasted coffee color were left to those with a scientific bent, we might find our customers ordering a pound of #6 roast. As it is, we are called on to provide a pound of American or French or Italian, Spanish, Viennese, Cuban or New Orleans. The nomenclature of coffees derives not only from where they grow, but also from the various degrees to which they are roasted. Because very dark-roasted coffee is the national preferance of Italy, any coffee so roasted, whether Columbian or an African Robusta, is "Italian Coffee." (Coffee doesn't grow in Italy.) A coffee labeled Mexican French would be (certainly should be) coffee grown in Mexico roasted to the French taste.

It has been suggested that the use of place names to designate roast color be abandoned in favor of a numerical scale. Such numbers would correspond to the amount of light reflected by coffees roasted to different degrees. Measurement would be made on samples of the various coffees similarly ground and compressed to equal depths. (Comparing ground coffees rather than beans would eliminate the difficulties in judging differences between dark-roast coffees, whose surfaces are usually so shiny they glare.) The darker the roast of any sample, the less light it would reflect, therefore the lower the number it would be assigned. The lighter the roast, the more light it would reflect, and the higher the number it would be assigned.

With this method we might end up labeling Italian roasted coffee #1, and Viennese #5. If widely used and generally understood, such standards of roast color might reveal the overly light roasting of many standard brands. The consumer would certainly benefit from this information. If such a standard is ever accepted by the industry, we hope that it is used in conjunction with the traditional place-name designations. We would rather drink *vin rouge* (or even red wine) than Wine No. 103.768.

Out of coffee-roasting history and from around the globe has emerged a charming, if somewhat unwieldy, array of names that are meant to designate roast color. We have heard of French, Italian, Greek, Spanish, Viennese, Cuban, and New York. Such terms as regular city, full city, normal, regular, full, heavy, whole, special, standard, high, and cinnamon are also used. Below is a list of some of the coffees you may encounter, from lightest to darkest, with our descriptions and comments.

Even within the categories listed, there can exist very fine shades of difference. A roaster may treat all his coffees to the full city roast but judge that certain growths require, within this range, just a bit more development than others. He is of course guided by his cup testing experience, as he is constrained by the fact that all coffees do not develop in exactly the same way. He must know the particular color that indicates full development for each type of coffee being roasted. He wants to achieve the degree of roast that will most enhance the flavor and aromatic constituents characteristic of each type. Commercial blends are generally roasted as blends to make handling easier, but it is hard to say whether the coffees they use warrant the special treatment of roasting by type. Martinson's coffee advertises that their beans are roasted by type, but then tells the consumer that because of this he can use 25 percent less coffee—thus negating whatever benefit he might have got from the special roasting! We feel that the different types of coffee should be treated as individuals, but such treatment is valuable only if the highest standards are adhered to in all other aspects of preparation.

Light city roast: In sections of the West, this is the standard. The bean is not fully developed, the color more cinnamon-like than brown, the flavor thin.

City roast: The most widely used style in this country. Also called brown roast or American roast, it is the preference of most consumers here. This roast yields a beverage that may lack brilliance and come up on the flat side.

Full city roast: Favored by some regional roasters in cosmopolitan centers, particularly New York City. Slightly longer roasted, the bean is dark brown, shows no oil on the surface, and gives a deeper heartier cup. The American roasts of specialty shops are likely to be full city rather than city.

Brazilian: Don't confuse this with the name given to coffee grown in Brazil. Just darker than full city, this roast has the faintest hint of dark-roast flavor. A trace of oil shows on the bean.

Viennese roast: There seems to be the least consensus on what this roast is, probably because there are many variations, even in Vienna. It falls midway between full city and French roasts. Mix half and half of these two roasts.

French roast (New Orleans roast): With this roast oiliness is quite apparent on the bean's surface and the color is burnt umber, the color of semi-sweet chocolate. The flavor is remarkably different from any of the lighter roasts. It approaches Espresso flavor but remains smooth. It is French-roasted coffee to which chicory is added for Louisiana style coffee. Two commercially prepared examples of this coffee/chicory mixture are Luzi-anne and French Market.

Spanish/Cuban/French-Italian roast: Darker than French but not quite Italian, this coffee is great for those who want Espresso without the bite. Mix French and Italian roasts, if this happy medium is not available, and you'll get very close to the flavor. Commercially prepared versions of this roast are Bustelo and El Pico. Some A&P stores have coffee in this roast in the bean.

Italian/Espresso roast: This roast is the highest, heaviest, darkest. Almost to carbonization. The bean surface is shiny and oily, the color black, the flavor Italian. Medaglia D'Oro is a commercially prepared example of this roast.

unblended coffee. Really fine coffee establishes its own following. We feel a responsibility to have on hand those coffees for which people develop a taste. It is also true that since many of the finer coffees tend to be consistently excellent, it makes very good sense to consistently offer them.

The marketplace, always in a state of flux, makes some very fine coffees available on a catch-as-catch-can basis. Some, such as Costa Ricans and Kenyas, traditionally go to Europe. When these coffees find their way to the United States, the coffee merchant should avail himself of the opportunity to offer his customers a treat. The coffees we select should have real flavor appeal. We stay away from run-of-the-mill-price coffees like the low-grown, neutral Robustas. We seek out coffees that offer distinct if subtle taste differences. No coffee can be all things to all people, but each should evidence the characteristics of its kind. Each should be evaluated for use unblended or in combination with complementary coffees. No coffee is acceptable that comes up unpleasant because it is harsh or hidey, groundy or thin. An Ethiopian Djimmah, for example, should be of piquant aroma, winy and acidy in flavor, with light body. In bean style it is small and somewhat unattractive; it tends to roast unevenly, as is characteristic of Mocha-type coffees. If our cupping of a Djimmah shows it to yield the kind of cup for which it is valued, it passes the first test. It is judged to be a worthy representative of the type. If we feel that it not only lives up to its own reputation, but also lives up to our idea of a good cup of coffee, we would offer it to our customers.

The method we use in selecting coffees is cup-testing, a wonderful ritual of looking, smelling, and tasting. Before we purchase any coffee, we receive both green and roasted samples. The green and roasted beans are placed in separate sample pans, one beside the other, on a testing table.

First we examine the green beans for imperfections, namely broken beans and quakers, which are unripe, blighted, or underdeveloped coffee beans that roast lighter than sound coffee. A large number of these will adversely affect cup quality; the resultant brew will taste more like boiled straw than coffee. Broken beans, or those that were cracked in the process of curing or cleaning, will roast darker than undamaged beans and impart a burnt taste to the brewed coffee. The merchant of whole bean coffees is likely to reject a sample containing many brokens, while a roaster who sells only ground coffee may pay little attention to these defects. Next, we judge and note down the appearance or "style" of the roasted beans. Does the bean develop well? Is the color uniform or spotty and has the bean swelled sufficiently?

Before the beginning of the twentieth century, practically all coffees bought and sold in the United States were judged only on appearance, in the way mentioned above. This "looking" test is useful, but only in conjunction with the most telling of tests—the test for flavor, aroma and body, qualities which are best evaluated by the human senses of smell and taste. The experienced palate of a coffee man can detect as little as one part in several billion of one or another volatile essence, elusive taste components no food research chemist has yet been able to isolate.

In cup-testing, it's aroma first, then taste. Drip-ground coffee equal to the weight of a nickel is placed in a six-ounce white china cup. Boiling water is poured on, forming a crust of wetted grounds that floats on the surface of the brew. Before the crust is broken, the tester sniffs the aroma; this is called the wet smell or crust test. If several samples are being tested, the revolving table top will be turned to bring each sample under the nose of the tester. Two or more samples would be tested simultaneously if, for example, a coffee dealer could no longer buy one particular kind of coffee and is seeking a replacement lot. While the coffee is cooling down to sipping temperature, the tester stirs each sample, breaking the crust, and sniffs a few more times. The sniffing is like an introduction or prelude to the tasting which follows: a spoonful of each sample is noisily sucked up, held in the back of the mouth, rolled on the tongue, then spit out (hopefully into a nearby cuspidor).

In cup-testing, the brew is made without any device; the only ingredients are clean white cups, measured amounts of coffee, and freshly boiled water. This uncomplicated method provides control: there is no apparatus to detract from or enhance the coffee's cup qualities, which are made immediately available to the tester's senses. Sucking the coffee up aerates it somewhat, maximizing the flavor, for good or ill; and since the brew is sprayed directly on the palate, it is at first undiluted by saliva. The coffee man's palate tells him much about a coffee brew: if the drink has body and is smooth, rich, acidy, or mellow; if it's winy, neutral, or harsh; or if it has the definitely undesirable attributes of being rank, hidey, sour, muddy or bitter. The coffee tester spits out the coffee after tasting simply to avoid getting bloated by one too many mouthfuls.

UNBLENDED COFFEE

In our section on the cultivation of coffee we discussed some of the differences among coffees. Botanically, we have the species of Arabica, Robusta,

Liberica. Libericas are of virtually no significance to the American consumer, representing only about 5 per cent of Liberia's crop, wihch itself recently totaled less than 100,000 bags annually. Libericas are similar to the Robustas, which make up the balance of Liberia's crop. Libericas that come to the United States find their way into commercial blends.

As a rule Arabicas are better than Robustas. Robustas, valued for high yields and resistance to disease are widely used in commercial blends, but they are neutral in the cup as compared with Arabicas, which possess finer aroma, flavor, and body. As a rule, coffee merchants worth their beans offer only Arabica coffees. Shun the merchant who includes in his selection of "gourmet coffees" African Robusta at a price anywhere near the other growths.

Besides botanical classifications, there are classifications of commerce used for marketing purposes: Brazils, Milds, and Robustas. Brazils are Arabica coffees grown in Brazil; Milds are Arabicas grown anywhere outside of Brazil; Robustas are Robustas. These designations are significant to green coffee merchants who have contractual obligations to fulfill, but they have no real significance for the consumer. The names have little practical bearing on quality or flavor. Within each category, the actual coffee may range from the ridiculous to the sublime. Milds are not necessarily mild in flavor; they may be terribly bitter. Brazils can apply to any quality coffee as long as it's grown in Brazil.

These botanical and commercial classifications are so general as to offer minimal guidance in your selection of coffees. We mention them here not so much for your use as to guard against your being misled by their misuse.

The most telling and therefore useful sort of classifications for coffee are geographical; different kinds of coffee are named according to where they are grown and called growths. Growths are often further classified by the names of the ports from which they are shipped. A growth is designated by the country and sometimes also by the region in which it grows (*e.g.*, Colombian Armenia, Mexican Coatepec, Jamaican Blue Mountain). For the consumer as for the importer, these names only indicate qualities that are generally characteristic of coffees from particular areas. There can be vast differences among the crops of a given country depending on the region or climate, fertilization methods, and shading procedures of a particular year. The port from which a coffee is shipped serves a variety of growing regions, and it also is only indicative of type, but not definitive. For example, in Venezuela the port of Maracaibo serves the growing regions of Táchira, Caracas, Trujillo, etc. The cup-testing ability of your coffee supplier, his integrity, and of course your own taste must be the final judges.

The importer has learned that even coffees similarly designated are never exactly the same from one lot (chop) to the next. However, the exporting organizations of the producing countries try to ensure that consistency within type is maintained as far as possible. Aware that no importer or consumer will seek out a particular coffee if he finds that coffee to fluctuate wildly from one encounter to the next, they maintain a careful watch on coffee set to leave their countries. They have their own expert cup-testers, as well as rigorous grading procedures. The coffees we get reflect a balance between the changes wrought by nature and checks maintained by coffee producers. The alert coffee man seeks out the growths that either live up to an established standard of excellence or promise to build, on the basis of their cup characteristics, a reputation of their own. As long as there are people who have taste, as long as they can't fool all the people all the time (no matter how much they spend in the attempt), the test of flavor will remain, as will the value of a good coffee man.

Labeling according to geographical place names is undeniably confusing. The very same coffee may be sold as Venezuelan, for the country, Maracaibo for the port, or Táchira for the growing region. Two genuine Maracaibos may cup very differently from each other. Some labels are misleading; others are boldfaced lies. Jamaican Blue Mountain coffee is excellent, but other Jamaican growths may be quite unremarkable. The merchant who sells ordinary Jamaican coffee because the name suggests excellence is taking unfair advantage of the consumer. The merchant who puts a Jamaican Blue Mountain label on coffee from El Salvador is a thief.

The demand for coffee by type is evidence of people's disenchantment with "nothing much" blends and of their desire to experience the distinctive qualities of the world's great variety of types. The response of coffee merchants to this growing interest in fine unblended coffees is mostly praiseworthy, but some abuses should be pointed out. We have noticed, shall we say, a lack of candor in some of the merchandising techniques of coffee merchants.

A coffee merchant in San Francisco or New York may feel he has to sell Kona coffee because his customers are asking for it or because his competitor across town does. The merchant, if he can't obtain Kona coffee, might decide to sell something else—and call it Kona coffee. Whether or not his competitor was selling genuine Kona in the first place is open to question. Outrageous but not inconceivable is the phenomena that ten different merchants may be selling ten different coffees as "Mocha" when in fact none of them are. The more notable the coffee (*e.g.*, Mocha, Java, Kona, Blue Mountain), the more notorious the abuses. Consumer beware.

What coffee connoisseur does not hear magic in such names as Kona, Jamaican, Mocha, and Java? What merchant would not be proud to be able to offer these prized coffees to his customers? The merchant who is able to acquire these coffees knows that even his willingness to pay the premium prices they command does not mean he'll be able to get more. Only small amounts of these coffees are produced, simply because the regions in which they are grown are tiny. These coffees are scarce; not only is the supply extremely limited but the demand is very great. The coffee man may be tempted to make his name coffees go further by using them in blends and offering his creations as Kona Blend, Jamaican Blend, etc. It's possible that in stretching the supply of a scarce coffee, the merchant may also be stretching the truth. Are a few beans of the "name" variety being thrown in to justify such labeling? Or is the named type predominant in the blend so that the name is indicative of the blend's characteristics? Can there be any justification for offering a Kona Blend in which Kona is not the major component? There is a canned specialty coffee whose label reads "JAMAI-CAN" in big letters but the fine print says "and other Arabica coffees." If one mass-produced coffee has more Colombian beans than another, is that difference as significant as it sounds? It is not, if the coffee with more is 5 percent Colombian rather than 2 percent. Blended coffees can be excellent, but we suggest that if you're tempted to try a coffee because of its name, you should establish whether the coffee itself is likely to be as attractive as its label.

There follows a catalog of coffees arranged by continent and country of origin. Some you may have heard of. Some you will probably run into as you search for the cup that suits you. A coffee's name should and almost always does include the name of the country in which it was grown. The name of the country, like a person's surname, identifies coffee in a general way. But just as Smith is modified by John, so Colombia is modified by Armenia, Brazil by Santos, Costa Rica by "hard bean," Venezuela by Maracaibo. These modifiers derive variously from the name of the growing district, the altitude at which the coffee is grown, the port from which it is shipped, the method by which the cherries are prepared, or the quality, size, or shape of the bean. All indicate, however obliquely, the cup qualities to be expected. It is our hope that the descriptions in this catalog will help you to find what you're looking for by making you more knowledgeable about the names that coffees go by.

Remember that any coffee can be roasted to any degree of darkness, ground to any degree of fineness, and prepared by any number of brewing methods. While there are indeed such things as Italian coffee, drip coffee, and Turkish coffee, here we are concerned with the differences that arise from the various circumstances affecting the green bean. All our descriptions and evaluations are based, in each case, on coffee treated to the full city roast and prepared by the cup-testing method. The dark-roasted versions of the finer coffees will cup better than their poorer counterparts similarly treated. However, since dark-roast flavor tends to predominate, the subtler differences are blurred.

We have included in the catalog those growing countries whose product is either imported in large quantities or known for its excellence or at least its interesting cup qualities. No country has been left out just because it provides a small crop, but where the crop is both small and unremarkable, we have excluded it. We have tried to point out that in many areas, coffees of significantly different quality are produced. The larger the area, the greater the differences are likely to be. Brazil gives us the smooth Santos and the harsh Rio coffees. Africa, where the great bulk of the crop is composed of neutral cupping Robustas, gives us also some of the finest coffees in the world.

Coffees do not always live up to their labels. The labels may be innaccurate or the particular crop used may not be an excellent example of the type. Whatever your choice, make sure the coffee you buy is fresh. We want to emphasize the importance of buying coffee that's freshly roasted. The finest coffee gone stale has lost its valuable aroma to the air. It won't show up in your cup so it's no good to you at all. Make sure you store your coffee properly, and make very sure you brew it with the care it deserves.

THE AMERICAS

BRAZIL   Brazil is the giant, the monarch of the coffee world whose reign has so far lasted for more than a century. Her export production runs between two and three times that of Colombia, the world's second largest exporter. In the 1950s that figure averaged fifteen million bags, in the 1960s, 17,000,000. In 1971–72, Brazil exported over 19,000,000 bags. In that year, Brazilians drank more coffee than any other country even produced (nearly 9,000,000 bags).

Over the past five years Brazil has experienced considerable frost and drought-related damage, culminating in the disastrous frost of July, 1975 (see

Santa Marta
Barranquilla
Cartagena
Maracaibo
TRUJILLO
VENEZUELA
TÁCHIRA
MÉRIDA
Medellín
Manizales
Armenia
COLOMBIA
Buenaventura
ECUADOR
CUMBAYA
Manta
Guayaquil
PIURA
CAJAMARCA
LAMBAYEQUE
SAN
MARTIN
PERU
Chanchamayo
Valley
Amazon   River
BRAZIL
MINAS
GERAIS
Vitória
SÃO
PAULO
ESPÍRITO
SANTO
Río de Janeiro
Santos
PARANÁ
Paranaguá
PACIFIC
OCEAN
ANDES   MOUNTAINS
CHILE
ARGENTINA
ATLANTIC   OCEAN

N

SOUTH AMERICA

SCALE OF MILES
0   200   400
MAJOR COFFEE
PRODUCING COUNTRY

GROWING DISTRICT
OF NOTE

page 40). She has had to dip into her coffee reserves to continue to meet the world's tremendous demand. It was expected that stocks would be practically wiped out in 1974, even with recent plantings coming to bearing age. Short supply is causing high prices in the short run, but if Brazil loses customers (and blends are modified) she may have a hard time getting them back.

It's been estimated that about one-third of Brazil's 3,288,000 square miles, or 650 million acres, is suitable for coffee growing. This region extends from the Amazon in the north to the southern borders of the states of Paraná and São Paulo, and from the Atlantic coast to the western boundary of the state of Mato Grosso. Actually only 10 percent of this area is under cultivation. Recent plantings have been selectively made in areas found to be least often hit by frost. Brazil's economic policy of diversification (not to mention that of supporting coffee prices) has in fact resulted in the destruction of billions of trees. While coffee is grown in seventeen of Brazil's twenty-one states, four states are responsible for about 98 percent of the total crop. The two major producing states are Paraná (over 50 percent) and São Paulo, followed by Minas Gerais and Espírito Santo. These are followed in importance by Rio de Janeiro, Mato Grosso, Pernambuco, Bahia, Goiás, and Santa Catarina.

Because Brazil is so large, there exists an especially wide spectrum of growing conditions and consequently a great variety of types of coffee. To tell the consumer that a coffee is 100 percent Brazilian is almost worse than telling him nothing at all about the origin of the coffee. It suggests truthfulness without being the whole truth; the label suggests quality that the product may in no way live up to. We would be willing signatories to a treaty banning the proliferation of such non-information. The unwary consumer might incorrectly presume that 100 percent of a known, indeed promoted, type must be superior to the blends whose formulas are well-kept secrets. While we have little enthusiasm for most mass-marketed blends, we are even less favorably inclined toward inferior coffees with pretensions.

Is Brazilian coffee good, bad, or indifferent? In a word, yes. Actually, we hope we have made clear that the designation is too all-encompassing for any one answer to suffice. All Brazilian coffees are Arabicas and almost all are prepared by the dry method. The farms—about 300,000 of them—are located at altitudes of 1,800–4,000 ft., high on rolling plateaus.

The coffees of Brazil are, for purposes of trade, described as "Brazils" to distinguish them from the "Milds" of other countries. They bear the names of the states in which they are grown or the ports through which they are shipped. A correlation exists between the quality of the coffee and the port of embarkation; coffees grown in certain regions are shipped from particular ports. Thus Santos is the designation for the finer coffees of Brazil, grown in São Paulo, Paraná, and southern Minas Gerais. Bourbon Santos (Bourbon denotes a type of seed, a kind of tree) is the best of Santos coffees, yielding a cup smooth, sweet and very palatable. Such Brazils are characterized as soft-drinking. Aging these coffees causes them to develop sharp acidity.

The hard-drinking coffees from northern Paraná are shipped through the port of Paranaguá. These coffees (Paranás) are clearly harsh in the cup but not unpleasantly so if grown at higher altitudes. The term "hard-drinking" should not be confused with hard-bean, which denotes coffees of excellent body and acidity. Rioy coffees, grown in Espírito Santo and Zona de Mato in Minas Gerais, are shipped through Vitória and Rio de Janeiro. Rioy coffees possess a harsh pungency which to most tastes is unpleasant. History tells us, however, that in bygone days this coffee had a small but devoted band of adherents.

We suggest that if you want to try Brazilian coffee, get a good Bourbon Santos and expect only a solidly acceptable brew. It seems that in recent years, even such modest expectations are not always realized. Perhaps extensive crop damage has forced the Brazilians to scrounge for coffee and we are experiencing a "bottom-of-the-barrel" phenomenon. Lately, even Santos, the best, has not always been its old self.

COLOMBIA Colombia's annual export production of well over 6,000,000 bags makes her the second largest exporter of coffee in the world. Almost all of this tremendous quantity of coffee (over 12 percent of the world's supply) is of very good quality. The best is virtually unsurpassed. All respect is due this magnificent land where over 2,000,000,000 trees provide the world with an abundance of truly delicious coffee. About half the crop comes to the United States.

Most Colombian coffee is high-grown. The farms, located on the slopes of the three cordilleras (chains) of the Andes, are usually small and owner-operated. All Colombian coffee is of the Arabica type and all is prepared by the wet method. The major origin classifications are Manizales, Armenia, and Medellín, the names of cities in the major growing regions. Coffee bearing the latter two marks is most highly regarded. MAMs, an acronym derived from these three classifications, is a term of trade. Buyers and sellers of green coffee often contract for coffee so designated rather than for the specific growth. The lesser growths of Colombia are Bucaramanga, Cúcuta, Santa Marta, and Bogotá.

Colombian coffee is graded before shipment according to bean size. These gradations are not indicative of cup quality. The greatest volume of exported coffee is Excelso, a grade which includes good- to large-size flat beans and some peaberries. Supremo, the "top grade," includes bold to extra large size beans. Small quantities of Peaberry (Caracoli) and large bean (Maragogype) coffee are also exported. Not exported is Pasilla, the coffee left when exportable grades have been sorted out. All exported grades are free from foreign matter and characterized by fine body, rich mild flavor, and good acidity. The generally high standards applied to the grading of Colombian coffee are responsible for the fact that the standard grade, Excelso, is as excellent as it is.

Since Colombian coffee well deserves its excellent reputation, why then may some "100 percent Colombian coffees" be disappointing? Some so-called pure Colombian coffee may not be what it's represented to be. Then too, among an annual crop of over 6,000,000 bags, even some genuine Colombian coffee must fall short of our great expectations. Remember that the even best quality control can't affect sunlight, rainfall, and temperature. Some coffee that has had the best from nature may have been carelessly tended in the process of washing and fermenting. Finally, even a great coffee will not yield its great treasure if it is improperly roasted, stale, or incorrectly brewed.

COSTA RICA Costa Rican coffee is grown at altitudes ranging from 1,600 to 5,400 ft. on both the Atlantic and Pacific slopes. All are Arabicas and most is washed. Costa Rican coffees are highly favored by Europeans. In 1971–72 Europe imported almost 900,000 bags, as against United States imports of just over 250,000. Total exports were just over 1,200,000 bags.

The most famous coffee-growing region is known as the central plateau (*meseta central*) covering a radius of about ten miles around San José. Some of the district names are Cartago, San José, Heredia, and Alajuela— but Costa Rica is unusual in using a classification system which makes little use of these designations.

The Pacific growths of Costa Rican coffee are typed according to the hardness of the bean. The higher the altitude, the harder the bean, and the finer the coffee. Atlantic growths are not classified according to the hardness of the bean but according to altitude. The hard-bean classifications are significant in that high-grown coffees from the Pacific slopes are finer than similarly high-grown Atlantics. We can see from this that altitude is an important, but not definitive determinant in quality.

Following are the types of Costa Rican coffee listed from finest quality to poorest. Costa Rica is a good example of how geographic labeling can mislead the consumer. Sixty-five per cent of the coffee exported from Costa Rica falls into the two highest categories—no wonder that this mark has and deserves the reputation of representing one of the world's finest coffees. However, as we go down the list, we note that some quantity of medium- and even low-grade coffee is produced here. We have evidence, then, that even coffee correctly labelled "Costa Rican" may not live up to our expectations. It would be foolish to assume that coffee labelled simply "Costa Rican," without further specification, is a poor grade, but it would also be foolhardy to presume that coffee so labelled could not be a disappointment.

Strictly Hard Bean (SHB): produced on the Pacific slopes from 3,900–5,400 ft. Noted for high acidity, fine body, and good aroma. Bold to extra large bean.

Good Hard Bean (GHB): produced on the Pacific slopes from 3,300–3,900 ft. Very good acidity, good body and aroma. Bold to large bean.

Hard Bean (HB): also grown on the Pacific slopes, but from 2,600–3,300 ft. Good acidity, body, and aroma. Bold to large bean size.

Medium Hard Bean (MHB): Grown in the zone between Atlantic and Pacific slopes at altitudes from 1,600–3,300 ft. Good acidity, body and aroma with a winy cup quality (similar to Táchira from Venezuela).

High Grown Atlantic (HGA): Grown on the Atlantic side at altitudes above 3,000 ft. Good acidity but less body and aroma than Pacific growths. Also a very large size bean.

Medium Growth Atlantic (MGA): Grown on the Atlantic side at altitudes of 2,000 to 2,900 ft. Another few hundred feet down the slopes and the quality of the yield is correspondingly lower. Still a good cup but limited.

Low Grown Atlantic (LGA): Grown on the Atlantic side from 500–2,000 ft. Undesirable, grassy cup quality. Little body or aroma.

Costa Rican coffee is carefully graded for particular markets. The "European Preparation" calls for large beans with all imperfections removed by hand. "U.S.A. Preparation" calls for large and small beans with defects removed by machine cleaning.

Of the approximately 30,000 coffee farms in Costa Rica, half are under 85 acres in size. However, coffee is big business to some Costa Ricans. More than 2,000 farms are larger than 1,200 acres. Strict government control limits new plantings and keeps prices up. Costa Rica has recently recovered from a series of disasters (including widespread insect damage) which had reduced the exportable crop.

DOMINICAN REPUBLIC   About 85 percent of this country's export crop comes to the United States; this has recently amounted to over 350,000 bags annually. Coffees are known as Santo Domingos. The three main types classified according to region are Barahona, Ocoa, and Baní. All are Arabicas; either washed (*lavados*) or naturals (*corriente*). The Barahonas are the most desireable, being of good body and pleasantly sweet; but even the better examples of this country's crop are not great, so don't expect to see them offered as straight coffees. Even the high-grown coffees (up to 5,000 ft.), though sound, are not remarkable.

ECUADOR   Probably the world's highest Arabica plantation in the world is located here at 9,000 ft., in Cumbaya, but most coffees from Ecuador are low-grown Arabicas. Called simply Ecuadors, they are characterized by a sharp woody flavor, and have only fair body. They are rarely offered unblended.

EL SALVADOR   The coffee of El Salvador is cultivated on the volcanic slopes of a central range at altitudes from 1,500–5,500 ft. All coffees from here are Arabicas; 94 percent of them washed, only 6 percent unwashed. Salvadors account for about 4.5 percent of the world's total export production. Her best customer has recently been West Germany, but the United States does get about 500,000 bags a year.

Coffee grows in all fourteen departments of El Salvador, but Salvadors are not marketed by region or port name. They are classified as Central Strictly High Grown, High Grown, and Central Standard and make up 15 percent, 30 percent, and 55 percent of the crop, respectively. The top two grades have good acidity and body; they are mild in flavor and not particularly aromatic. Most of this coffee goes to Europe while the Central Standard type comes to the United States. This type, grown below 3,000 ft., is slight in body but has nice acidity and a winy taste.

GUATEMALA   Half of Guatemala's 2,000,000-bag annual crop is produced on 30,000 small farms, each having a yield of forty bags or less. Coffee is grown mainly in the central and southern regions of the country on mountain slopes where altitudes range from 1,000–5,500 ft. All are washed Arabicas, classified, like Costa Ricans, according to altitude. Growing districts are seldom referred to; quality in Guatemalans is a function of altitude rather than latitude and longitude. All are flavory with zest and snap. Aroma is on the dry side—straight and narrow. The high-grown Guatemalans, classified as Extra Prime (3,000–3,500 ft.) Semi Hard Bean (3,500–4,000 ft.), Hard Bean (4,000–4,500 ft.), and Strictly Hard Bean (above 4,500 ft.), are acidy and heavy bodied. Those growths designated Extra Good Washed (2,000–2,500 ft.) and Prime (2,500–3,000 ft.), are somewhat thin but are mild cupping and not without good flavor. Coffees grown below 2,000 ft., designated as Good Washed, are neutral cupping but inoffensive. Two place names that do come up in connection with Guatemalan coffee are Antigua and Cobán. Both are districts from which come the finest, highly acid, heavy bodied coffees of this country. Very little of these particular types is grown and most of it is spoken for by Europeans. If you come across the genuine article, don't miss the chance to try it—either one can be quite a treat. The Cobán in particular can be quite sharp, almost bitter . . . but nice bitter.

HAITI Haitian coffee is of the Arabica variety and processed by both wet and dry methods. A third classification is called Triage and may be either washed or unwashed—the important point about it is that it may contain many spoiled beans. Most coffee is grown at altitudes of 1,000–1,500 ft. with some lower-grown. Obviously, High-Grown Haitian and High-Grown Costa Rican mean two different things. On the other hand, West Indian growths are finer than coffees grown at similar altitudes in the Central American countries. Farming is done on small holdings in the districts of St-Marc, Port-au-Prince, Petit Goâve, Jacmel, Cayes, Gonaïves and Jérémie, all in the mountainous areas. Haitian coffee is very mellow, having a pleasant mild sweetness when prepared by either the washed or unwashed method. Naturals tend to be a bit pungent. The higher-grown Haitian coffees possess good body and some acidity. The Haitians roast their coffee dark as do the French, who value this type highly. The United States takes from one-quarter to one-third of Haiti's export. France, Italy, Belgium, and the Netherlands take about one-half.

HAWAII Coffee is grown in ony one place in the United States—on the slopes of the active volcano Mauna Loa in the Kona district of the island of Hawaii. At altitudes of only 1,500–2,000 ft. (below the snowfields), the trees that bear Kona coffee enjoy some of the most ideal growing conditions in the world. The "soil" actually consists of broken chunks of well-packed volcanic lava; holes have to be dug with a pick-axe to permit planting.

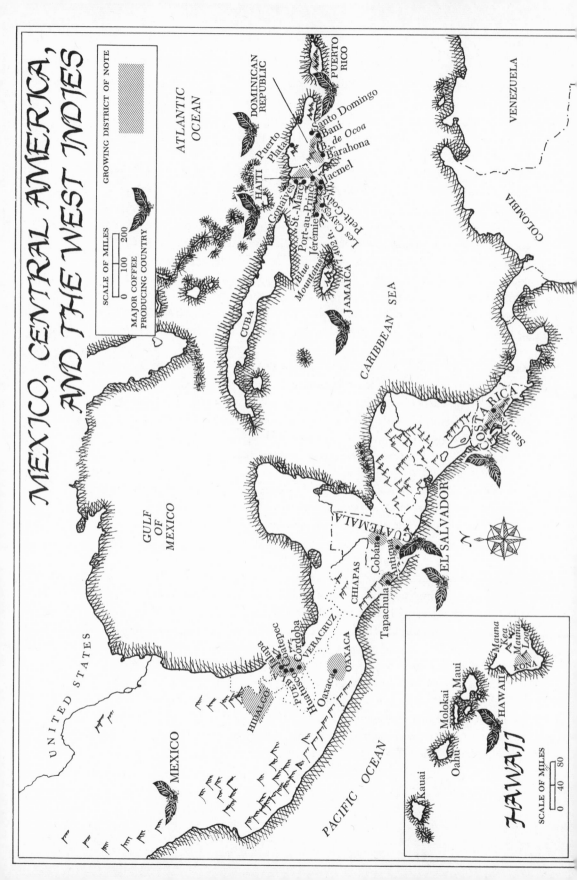

MEXICO, CENTRAL AMERICA, AND THE WEST INDIES

SCALE OF MILES

0   100   200

MAJOR COFFEE PRODUCING COUNTRY

GROWING DISTRICT OF NOTE

ATLANTIC OCEAN

UNITED STATES

GULF OF MEXICO

MEXICO

HIDALGO
Jalapa
Coatepec
Córdoba
PUEBLO
Huatusco
VERACRUZ
Oaxaca
OAXACA

CHIAPAS
Tapachula

GUATEMALA
Cobán
Antigua

EL SALVADOR

PACIFIC OCEAN

COSTA RICA
San José

CUBA

JAMAICA
Blue Mountains
7,402 ft.

HAITI
Gonaïves
St.-Marc
Port-au-Prince
Jérémie
Les Cayes
Petit-Goâve

DOMINICAN REPUBLIC
Puerto Plata
Santo Domingo
Baní
B. de Ocoa
Barahona
Jacmel

PUERTO RICO

CARIBBEAN SEA

VENEZUELA

COLOMBIA

HAWAII

Kauai
Oahu
Molokai
Maui
HAWAII
Mauna Kea
Mauna Loa
KONA

SCALE OF MILES

0   40   80

Before planting, the trees' roots actually have to be packed in soil from other parts of the island. Fertilization must be provided throughout the year. Nature provides continual gentle rainfall, bright sunny mornings, and a protective mist that rolls in from the sea like clockwork every afternoon. The trees are sheltered from the prevailing winds by Mauna Loa and a neighboring extinct volcano, Mauna Kea. Coffee grown on Hawaii is, for reasons scientists can't explain, completely untroubled by disease. These conditions combine to produce not only a coffee of fine quality but also the highest per-acre yield of Arabica in the world. While the average Latin American farm produces 500–800 pounds of green coffee per acre, a crop of 2,000 pounds per acre is not unusual in Hawaii. Since, however, only about 3,600 acres (about 720 farms of five acres each) are under cultivation, the total crop is tiny when considered on the scale of worldwide production. The Chicago-based company who has owned exclusive marketing rights to Kona coffee since 1970 claims there is an annual crop of 3,000,000–3,500,000 *pounds* (about 23,000 bags).

Kona coffee is very flavorful and full bodied, a rich coffee with a mellow straightforward character. It is offered as whole bean, "all purpose" grind, and instant by the Chicago-based Superior Tea and Coffee Company. It is rarely available as a fresh roasted unblended offering in specialty shops, but should a few bags come your merchant's way, get it while you can. Hope that it isn't squandered in a "Kona Blend" that's 90 percent something else.

JAMAICA Jamaican coffee is grown on the slopes of a mountainous ridge that runs the length of the island from east to west. The Jamaica Blue Mountains, which reach a height of over 7,000 ft., are the home of one of the world's most famous coffees. Each year, about 800 bags, or just over 100,000 pounds of this Jamaican Blue Mountain Coffee is produced, much of it grown on the Wallenford Estate. This coffee is extremely mellow, sweet-tasting and delightfully aromatic. As is true of all exported Jamaican coffee, it makes a very attractive roast, the beans being free of defects and of a uniformly bold size.

The two other grades of exported Jamaican coffee are High Mountain Supreme and Prime Jamaican Washed. Together they account for about 15,000 bags. These coffees are shipped in the usual burlap sacks, while the Blue Mountain variety is exported in barrels which contain 260–275 pounds of coffee. These two growths are generally soft-drinking, that is without any unpleasant characteristics, but are not comparable to Blue Mountain. The High Mountain Supreme has medium to sharp acidity with good body.

Prime Jamaican Washed has medium acidity and only fair body. Both are more in the class of good Central American growths than that of the very special Blue Mountain.

Because Jamaican coffee is famous, because the crop is small, and because only a tiny amount of that crop reaches the United States, the price of the genuine article is usually very high. Blue Mountain has sold in New York for $4.50 per pound. Jamaican "blends," whole bean and vacuum packed, sell for over $2.25. More coffee is sold as Jamaican than is actually imported. About 98 percent of the exported crop goes to Japan; about 2 percent comes to the United States. If you can locate genuine Jamaican coffee and don't mind paying the price, by all means buy it. If you can't, don't settle for Taster's Choice in the meantime. Try Maracaibo from Venezuela, or Kona from Hawaii, or one of the high-grown coffees from Kenya, Tanzania, or Cameroon. These are of course not Jamaicans, but they are among the fanciest, most mellow, and most interesting coffees in the world.

MEXICO   Mexico in the last twenty-five years has tripled its yield from about 1,000,000 to 3,000,000 bags. The fact that Mexico is a large country with a big population affects its exportable crop dramatically. Half the coffee produced in Mexico is consumed there, partly due to heavy promotion by the Mexican Coffee Institute. The coffee that is exported, because it comes from a fairly wide-ranging area, is quite variable—less so than Brazilian, but more so than Guatemalan or Costa Rican.

Mexicans are all washed Arabicas, 70 percent of the crop coming from the states of Veracruz and Chiapas. Ten percent comes from Puebla; the remainder comes from the neighboring southern states. The three exportable grades of Mexican coffees are Altura (High-Grown), Prima Lavada (Prime Washed), and Bueno Lavado (Good Washed). A fourth grade, called "Specials," is not exportable. (If it were, we imagine some enterprising merchant would have a field day.) Most of the finer coffees coming from Mexico fall into the Prime Washed category, but are best known by the names of the districts in which they grow: Coatepec, Jalapa, Huatusco, Oaxaca, Tapachula, Córdoba, and Pluma Hidalgo. (Altura grades of these types are also available. Remember that Altura means High-Grown and High-Grown means so much the better.) These Mexicans possess a wonderful bouquet, nice gutsy liquor, and fine acidity. Córdobas and Tapachulas tend to be lighter, smoother; Oaxacas and Plumas shade toward sharpness. Other Mexicans are risky. Ninety-five percent of the farms in Mexico are under twenty-five acres. The United States gets more than three-fourths of

Mexican coffee, while Europe takes more than half of many of the other Central American growths.

PERU Peruvian coffee is a comer in the world coffee market, having recently achieved an export production of about 800,000 bags. The United States takes over half of Peru's exports, all of which are washed Arabicas and known as Peru coffees. One of the principal growing regions is the centrally located Chanchamayo Valley, which produces 40 percent of the total crop. The fine growths, however, come from the northern part of Peru, where coffee is cultivated on the western and eastern slopes of the Andes at altitudes ranging from 3,000–5,000 ft. This coffee is mild in flavor, with good acidity and excellent body. It is not generally to be found among the offerings of specialty coffee merchants, but as imports increase with increased production, this may change. The regional marks to look for will be those of the northern high-grown types: Piura, Lambayeque, San Martín, and Cajamarca. About 70 percent of Peru's crop is cultivated on agricultural cooperatives; the government is active in promoting both the quantity and quality of coffee culture.

PUERTO RICO What can we say about a delicious coffee that isn't exported? Since 1971–72 the only coffee to come out of Puerto Rico has been a tiny quantity of soluble or instant coffee. The Puerto Ricans drink all their own crop of nearly 200,000 bags, and have to supplement it with imports of almost 100,000 bags, mostly from the Dominican Republic. The coffee is not particularly high-grown (1,000–3,000 ft.), but excellent soil with 60 percent slope, consistent rainfall, and cool nights conspire to produce a sweet rich bean. If you've had the coffee in Puerto Rico and want to approximate it when you get home, try a good French roast or a blend of French and Italian. They roast their coffee dark down there, and that could be the taste you're looking for.

VENEZUELA Venezuelan coffees are all Arabicas, most of them washed. This country's coffee farms are to be found from 1,000 to 5,000 ft., but growths are classified by region rather than altitude. The finer coffees come from the mountainous districts of Táchira, Mérida and Trujillo. These coffees, which account for about half of Venezuela's crop, are sometimes marketed as Maracaibo, the name of the country's major port. Also shipped from Maracaibo is Cúcuta, grown in Colombia and comparable in cup quality to the other Maracaibos. Maracaibos are flavory, rich and delicately winy in the cup. They are somewhat light-bodied coffees, mellow, on the sweet side —delightfully aromatic, and a good choice for those who like a smooth cup with little acidity. We like these growths very well for blending with French and Italian roasted coffee. Venezuela's crop has remained fairly constant at 1,000,000 bags over the past ten years. Increasing local consumption has cut into the export crop—Venezuelans drink more than half the coffee they produce. The United States gets about two-thirds of exported Venezuelan coffee.

AFRICA

While total world production of coffee has doubled in the past three decades, African coffee has increased by a factor of six. Where African coffee accounted for only about 10 percent of the world's crop in 1945, today that continent's share is over 25 percent. In 1951, the United States depended on Africa for less than 5 percent of its coffee imports. By 1971, that figure had reached over 30 percent. For the past five years Africa has produced close to 20,000,000 bags; her role promises to become more important as demand increases and as the traditionally major producers (Brazil, Colombia, *et al.*) approach the limits of their supply capabilities. The recent trouble in Brazil with frosts and rains has emphasized to the world's growing number of coffee consumers the importance of alternative suppliers. The Colombian crop, though not plagued by natural disasters, has been curtailed as a matter of economic policy; because of economic diversification coffee now, for the first time in Colombia's history, accounts for less than half her world trade credits.

Three-quarters of the current crop of African coffee is Robusta; one quarter is Arabica. In some countries only Robusta is grown, in others only Arabica; many produce coffees of both varieties. If the consumer is to select wisely from among African coffees he should continue to be guided by regional classifications, but only after ascertaining that it is Arabica coffee he is considering. Zaïre, for example, produces both types, but while a good Robusta from this country is merely acceptable for mass-produced blends, the Kivu (Arabica) is delicious unblended, and worthy to be offered as such by any specialty merchant.

ANGOLA Angola is the fourth largest exporter of coffee in the world, with a crop of 3,500,000 bags per year, much of it grown on very large plantations. Arabicas account for only about 1.5 percent of this amount, these being

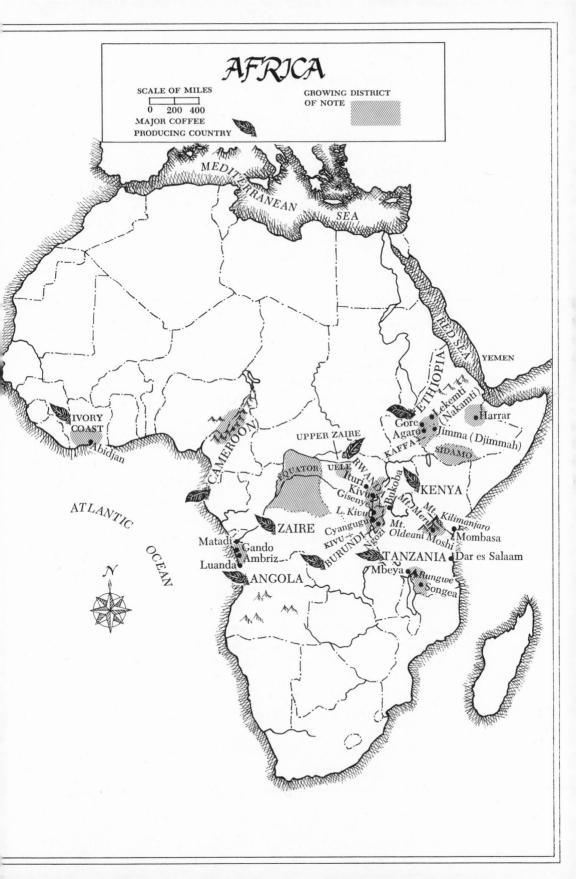

grown in the Gando and Andulo regions in the south. They are unspectacular but pleasant enough coffees, similar to Brazilian Santos, and like Santos good for use in blends. Since the Arabica output is only about 50,000 bags, and since it is not inexpensive compared to better Central American growths, little importance can be attached to it at this time. Angola Robustas, two-thirds of which come from Ambriz, are apparently of considerable importance to United States blenders, who took half of Angola's exports in 1971 and 1972. Ambriz is valued for its neutrality, for the fact that it can be used as filler without harmful effects on the cup quality. More stringent truth in advertising laws might someday lead a major packer who uses Ambriz as a base to tout his blend as containing less downright awful coffee than his competitor's.

BURUNDI   About 95 percent of Burundi's average annual crop of 300,000 bags is of the Arabica variety. About 80 percent of the crop, grown on farms having only 60–300 trees, comes to the United States. Cultivation is particularly widespread on the high plateaus in the interior. In Ngozi coffee is grown at altitudes of 4,000–7,500 ft. All Burundi Arabicas are prepared by the wet method and graded from AAA down to BBB. The high grade, which accounts for about 80 percent of exported Arabicas, is rich in the cup and has high acidity, good body, and strong flavor. The low grade, BBB, contains many defects and cup quality is poor.

CAMEROON   The Republic of Cameroon in 1941 exported less than 2,000 bags of coffee, but for the past five years has exported over 1,000,000 bags. This country ranks twelfth among the coffee-exporting countries, accounting for 2.3 percent of the world total. Only about 30 percent of this crop is of the Arabica variety, but this is well up from 16 percent just fifteen years ago.

The Arabicas are grown on the high slopes and plateaus of the northwest. All are washed and graded for bean size, as well as defects per 300-gram sample. Since Elephant beans and Peaberry coffees are sorted out from the standard size grades, it is not unusual for these coffees to appear on the market as such. The Arabicas from Cameroon are mellow, sweet-drinking coffees. It is interesting to note that while the United States has imported nearly half of Cameroon's Robusta crop, she has in the same years (1971–72) taken only 13 percent of that country's Arabicas.

ETHIOPIA   Coffee of the Arabica variety originated in Ethiopia, where it has been growing wild since before the ninth century. It is from the Ethiopian town of Kaffa that coffee may have received its name. Ethiopia produces an annual crop of over 2,000,000 bags, but since annual per capita consumption is unusually high (7.2 pounds), more than half that quantity is retained for domestic use. Recently the United States has been taking two-thirds to three-quarters of Ethiopia's exports. Much of the coffee grows wild, and so much goes unpicked because there are no access roads to many of the wild stands that it is estimated that the total output of this oldest of coffee-producing nations could be tripled without planting new trees. Even so, coffee currenly accounts for over 60 per cent of Ethiopia's total export value.

Ethiopian coffee is still entirely of the Arabica variety and is all processed by the dry method. Around the towns of Agaro, Gore, Gimbi, and Lekemti in the district of Jimma (Djimmah), coffee grows wild at altitudes of 4,000–6,000 ft. In southwestern Ethiopia, in the Sidamo regions, coffee grows wild and is harvested, as is Djimmah coffee, by the natives. Around Harrar (Harer), in east-central Ethiopia, coffee is cultivated at altitudes of 5,000–7,000 ft. Harrars, the only type under cultivation in Ethiopia, account for only 13 percent of this country's crop.

Ethiopian coffee is characterized by a winy pungency, an exquisitely piquant aroma, and a wildness that harks back to the hillsides on which it grows. It lacks the depth of Colombian and the fancier Milds, but as its spicy flavor plays hide and seek with your palate, an altogether delightful complexity is created. In the human family wildness is the province of youth, and so it is with coffee. The sprightly, somewhat frivolous character of new-crop Ethiopian coffee quickly fades with age. Past-crop (old-crop) Ethiopian exhibits a loss of that very character which makes it an interesting coffee. Aging tends to tame this coffee, to "normalize" it. The result is a coffee not mellowed, but dulled with age.

Harrar coffee is the finest of Ethiopian coffees. Being the highest grown, it possesses the greatest body, highest acidity, and most winyness of all the country's growths. Of the two varieties of Harrar, Shortberry and Longberry, the latter is more highly regarded. Harrar accounts for only 13 percent of Ethiopia's crop, and it is uncertain how much of this amount is exported. Very little seems to reach the United States, but the best chances of obtaining it appear to be on the West Coast.

The Djimmahs and Sidamos might well be called the "ugly ducklings" of the coffee world. Their diminutive, somewhat awkward appearance belies a heart of gold. The bean is small, even scrawny, and makes an unattractive roast; but the cup, while not as fine as Harrar nor as complete as Colombian, is exciting and unique. Djimmahs and Sidamos are great for blending with richer, heavier coffees such as Colombian or Java, and their pungency make them an excellent choice for blends that include dark-roasted coffee. Experience this type of coffee unblended and you'll see why it's not likely to get lost in a blend.

Ethiopian coffee may properly be considered a "Mocha-style" coffee. By virtue of geography, climate, and preparation, it has many of Mocha's characteristics. It is not generally as fine as genuine Mocha (see Yemen), since it rarely possesses the depth of that famous aristocrat, but it is similar enough to be a worthy substitute where Arabian Mocha is unobtainable.

IVORY COAST The Ivory Coast produces only Robustas and therefore is of no interest to the consumer searching for fine coffee. What persuades us to include this country in our catalog of African coffee producers while other countries producing only Robustas have been excluded? It is the very simple but nonetheless astounding fact that the Ivory Coast is the third largest producer of coffee in the world. Her annual export crop of about 3,500,000 bags accounts for over 8 percent of the world's total. Only Brazil and Colombia are bigger suppliers. In recent years the United States and France have each imported over 1,000,000 bags of coffee from the Ivory Coast. Close to 1,000,000,000 trees are cultivated on nearly 2,000,000 acres. The farms are small, but over 95 percent of them are controlled by the native population. Now consider this: in 1931, only 12,000 bags were produced here. In the Ivory Coast we have dramatic evidence that Africa is emerging very rapidly as a coffee-producing region of great importance.

KENYA Kenya's crop, entirely of the Arabica variety, is about 1,000,000 bags a year. This mild coffee, characterized by a delicately acid flavor, has, like Colombian coffee, wonderful smoothness and roundness in the cup. Demand for Kenya coffee has always been high in Europe, especially in West Germany, the Netherlands, Sweden, and the United Kingdom, who together took over half the crop in 1972. In the same year, the United States took less than 10 percent. All coffees exported from Kenya are classified by cup quality, from AA down, by the Liquoring Department of the Kenya Coffee Board. The A grades are indeed quite excellent. The Bs are not bad, but tend to be a bit sharp, a quality you wouldn't be after in Kenya coffee.

RWANDA Rwanda's annual crop is only about 250,000 bags per year, but production is entirely of washed Arabicas. Cultivation is particularly concentrated on the high interior plateaus. The highest-grown coffee comes from the regions of Gisenye and Cyangugu, which border on Lake Kivu. Coffees are prepared by both the "fully washed" (FWAAA, FWAA, FWA) and "washed" processes (1, 2, 3a, 3b, 4, 5). The United States imports more than half the crop, primarily the washed 2's and 3a's. These grades account for about 85 percent or the total crop. Most of the fancier FW grades go to Europe.

Rwanda Arabicas are comparable to the best Milds. They have good body, high acidity, strong flavor, and produce a rich cup.

TANZANIA About two-thirds of Tanzania's crop (600–800,000 bags) is of the Arabica variety. This coffee grows on the slopes of Mt. Kilimanjaro in Moshi and other slopes including Mt. Meru and Mt. Oldeani. In the southern highlands of Songea, Rungwe, Mbozi, and Mbeya, mild Arabicas are also grown. Plantation Bukobas are Arabicas processed by the dry method. Like Kenyan coffee and Colombian, Tanzanians are rich and mellow with delicate acidity. A peaberry grade is exported.

The Robusta coffee grows mainly in the Bukoba and Karagwe districts. It is a neutral-cupping filler coffee. If you purchase Tanzanian coffee, make sure it's of Arabica variety. The United States imports about 40 percent of this country's annual crop.

ZAIRE Zaire (formerly the Belgian Congo) produces for export more than 1,000,000 bags annually. While the bulk of Zaire's crop is of the Robusta variety, a significant amount of very fine Arabica is grown and exported. The Robustas are grown primarily on European-owned plantations in the central lowlands of Upper Zaire and Equator Provinces and in the northeast district of Uele. The Arabica coffees are grown at altitudes of 4,000–7,500 ft. in the districts of Kivu and Ituri in Upper Zaire (formerly Eastern) Province. Arabicas are known by the district in which they are grown. Both Kivus and Ituris are fine, strongly flavored coffees, comparable to the growths of Kenya and Tanzania. Kivus, which are better known in the United States, are not unlike the higher-grown Costa Ricans. Kivu yields a cup both rich and highly acid. We experience this combination of qualities as a pleasant sharpness and value the contribution that Kivu can make in a blend containing other more mildly flavored coffees.

ASIA

Three Asian coffee-producing countries are of interest to the western consumer: India, Indonesia, and Yemen.

INDIA India's annual coffee production fluctuates between 1,000,000–2,000,000 bags, while exports remain fairly stable at between 600,000–700,000 bags. About 60 percent of India's crop is of the Arabica variety. The United States takes about 20 percent of India's exports; the U.S.S.R. takes 40 percent, or an average of 250,000 bags.

Three-quarters of the Arabica crop is classified Arabica Plantation; the main export grades in descending order of quality are A, B, and T (for Triage); these are washed coffees. The remainder of the Arabicas are the so-called "cherry" or "native cherry" coffees. These are coffees processed by the dry method and are graded Arabica Cherry AB or Arabica Cherry T. The Plantation coffees are generally superior to the Cherry coffees.

The Nilgiris from the state of Tamil Nadu are known for the delicately acid and very rich cup they yield. Tellicherry coffee and Malabar coffee, both from the State of Kerala, are similar to the Nilgiris. (*Note:* don't confuse Tellicherry with Arabica Cherry. This resemblance is purely coincidental). Eighty-four percent of the Arabica crop is from the state of Karnataka (formerly called Mysore), where mountain-grown, heavy-bodied coffee is grown. This coffee is almost equal in cup quality to the famed Nilgiris and is fortunately in great abundance.

INDONESIA   The Indonesian island of Java was one of the first and greatest of the world's coffee producers. Java coffee was world-renowned, so much so that to this day "Java" is a synonym for coffee. During World War II, however, production dropped; many plantations were destroyed in the war. Indonesia has since re-attained its production of 1941 (over 1,000,000 bags), but now the crop is mainly Robusta, since this type of tree, chosen for sturdiness and high yield, was replanted after the devastation of the war. Java Robustas may not be sold as Java coffee—it's against the law—but let the buyer beware in any case, since the cup is thin and neutral.

This was actually the second major replanting in Indonesia's history; the first was instituted after the crop was ravaged, in 1878, by the dread *Hemileia vastatrix*—only a few years after Ceylon and India had been similarly devastated. The first replanting consisted of Arabica coffee trees. At that time Robusta coffee trees were planted as shade for young rubber trees—a strange switch. When the rubber boom collapsed and planters again turned to coffee as a money crop, Robusta was there for the picking.

Origin designations are used for Indonesian coffee, and some of the most superb offerings will be found to come from this area. Coffee from Indonesia is known for its magnificent heavy body and almost syrupy richness. Wonderfully sturdy, direct, with fine acidity, this coffee comes from Java, Sumatra (Mandheling and Ankola from the area around Padang), Celebes, also called Sulawesi (Kalosi, Rantepao), Bali, Flores, and (Portuguese) Timor.

Good Java coffee is hard to come by these days, as are any of the finer Indonesian Arabica growths. The crops are relatively small. These coffees are available, however, and when they're good, they are excellent. What is gone forever are the Javas that made Java coffee famous in the United States. When coffee was transported in wooden sailing ships, that coffee

underwent a sweating over the four to five month passage which changed its color, aroma, and flavor. Ship captains were paid a premium for delivering coffee in this condition. After the age of long sea voyages in wooden ships had passed, a system developed under which the Indonesian government bought coffee and held it in "godowns" for from eighteeen months to two years, in an effort to simulate the old method of aging. Coffee resulting from this method was known as "Old Government Java." Eventually sweated coffees lost in popularity and the system was abandoned.

Because Java is so famous, its reputation may be unscrupulously exploited. The merchant who sells, as Java, only Arabica coffee from the island of Java is doing the most correct thing. The merchant who applies the name Java to those finer Arabica growths from the other Indonesian islands (Sumatra, Celebes, Bali, Flores) is doing so within the bounds of propriety. He is exploiting the name Java, but he is not exploiting his customer. Neither is he in this case departing from established practice; as far back as 1712, when the first shipment (894 lbs.) of Java was sold in Amsterdam, it was understood that Javas were coffese originating somewhere in the Indonesian Archipelago. Charge him with oversimplification if you must, but not with the sin of duplicity. But watch out for the marketing magician who with the flick of his pen transforms some respectable Salvador into "Java." Mocha-Java, by the way, is *not* a type of Java coffee. Genuine Mocha-Java is a blend of coffee from Java and coffee from Yemen. Next best would be a blend of Java and the Mocha-like Ethiopian.

We have already cautioned you that the names of coffees, even when accurate, are only *guides* to cup quality and to intelligent purchasing. A case in point is an Indonesian Arabica we were offered a few years ago that smelled and tasted more like freshly dug earth than coffee. We rejected it, but you can bet your percolator that it wound up in somebody's cup.

YEMEN One of the world's oldest, most famous, and probably most misunderstood coffees comes from Yemen. The novice coffee connoisseur who's decided there's more to life than being a Maxwell Housewife is likely to seek this coffee as an alternative to mediocrity. The coffee is Mocha, long and justly considered to be one of the world's greatest, uniquely delicious coffees. The legends of Omar and Kaldi attribute to this Arabian coffee the power of life itself. Once the subject of myth, Mocha as a type of coffee has become the object of misunderstanding and misrepresentation.

Mocha was, until just over one hundred years ago, a small port in Yemen on the Red Sea. Some four centuries ago, a small quantity of fine flavored

YEMEN

coffee, grown on the hillsides surrounding the town, was exported from there. It was the first coffee enjoyed by Europeans, and soon after, all imports from Arabia were classified as Mochas. In the seventeenth and early eighteenth centuries even coffees grown in the West Indies were marketed as Mochas. One might think this a case of unscrupulous mislabeling; in fact, the growths of Haiti, Guadeloupe, *et al.* were very much the same as those from Yemen. The coffee trees growing in the West Indies were at that time the grandchildren of the trees in Yemen; the beans produced in both locales were, to the taste, indistinguishable. Since place names were intended primarily as guides to flavor, the labeling was, if literally inaccurate, effectively true.

Were the growths of Arabia and Haiti compared today, the difference in flavors would be easily recognized. An attempt to classify these growths as Mochas in the modern marketplace would be deceptive and confusing and foolish. How did what was true become a lie? The soil, altitude, and climate of any given coffee-growing area contribute unique characteristics of body, flavor, and aroma to the beans produced in that area. It has been centuries since the Arabian seed was transplanted to the West Indies, and Caribbean coffee has taken on the character of its new home. For better or worse it must live up to the merits of its new name—not the name of its ancestors.

What of Mocha today? For more than a century that small port has been unimportant. The tiny crop is now shipped through the ports of Aden and Hodeida. Coffee itself has become less important to Yemen recently. In 1972, 3,784 bags of green coffee were imported to the United States from Yemen. The year before, the number was 4,179. Both figures were so small as to be considered zero percent of total U.S. imports.

Mocha is not only the origin designation for a type of coffee. The term has established itself, in common usage, to mean either the flavor of coffee or the flavor of coffee and chocolate in combination. Enjoy the mocha flavor of coffee and chocolate together? Certainly, but understand that no coffee without the addition of chocolate will provide that flavor.

Mocha coffee is cultivated and processed today much as it has been for centuries. Seedlings, grown in nurseries, are transplanted to terraced farms (from 3,000–7,000 ft.), which have been carved out of the steep hillsides. Lack of rain necessitates the maintenance of irrigation systems designed to provide the trees with controlled constant moisture. The relative dryness of the soil and air results in the production of a bean that's small and extremely hard. All of Yemen's tiny crop is processed by the dry method and much of it, in fact, is permitted to dry on the tree *before* picking and hulling. (Much coffee from Ethiopia is similarly processed.) Again, it is the dry hot air which permits this unusual but in this case advantageous technique.

To the taste Mocha coffee has tremendous character, wonderful complexity. Its uniquely acid cup makes this coffee simultaneously smooth and piquant. It possesses very heavy body, a characteristic usually lacking in its nearest cousin, the Ethiopians. This coffee is smooth with a sharpness that never wounds.

DECAFFEINATED COFFEE

George Gilbert, a coffee merchant for more than fifty years, tells this story: "At a party, a big coffee importer is asked whether or not coffee keeps him awake at night. He replies that it most certainly does. The surprised questioner asks, 'Well, then, why do you drink it?' 'Oh,' the coffee man responds, 'it's not the coffee I drink that keeps me awake; it's the 2,000 bags in my warehouse.'"

Some people are made uncomfortable by coffee's stimulation. Some complain that coffee keeps them awake, while others are made equally unhappy by being deprived of it. Certainly, coffee affects the way we feel, and just as certainly, it does not have exactly the same effect on everyone. Most people find that the stimulation produced by the caffeine in one or two cups of coffee is pleasant to them; they experience no unpleasant side effects. People who find coffee too stimulating for them are not neurotic, but neither are those who miss their coffee caffeine-crazed addicts. The real crackpots in the millennium-old caffeine controversy may be those who have laid at coffee's feet all the ills of man, from stunted growth to sterility. In our time we have seen the headlines shout warnings against caffeine and its capacity to produce anxiety, irritability, etc. In smaller print it is explained that the person in distress had been consuming *fifty cups of coffee per day*. How well, we wonder, would a person feel if he were consuming fifty glasses of orange juice per day, of fifty glasses of milk?

If you enjoy drinking coffee for its flavor and warmth but not for its caffeine, you may choose one of the decaffeinated coffees on the market. Species of coffee trees which produce caffeine-free beans have been discovered, but these beans have such poor flavor that they are not commercially produced. Decaffeinated coffee is not made from such beans. Experiments are being conducted to see if cross-breeding them with other varieties will produce a caffeine-free or low-caffeine bean with good flavor.

Meanwhile, decaffeinated coffee remains the result of a chemical process, the forerunner of which was invented about 1900. The contemporary version of the decaffeination process works something like this: The green, unroasted beans are softened by steam and water. Once softened, they are flushed with a solvent, usually containing chlorine, which soaks through to all parts of the beans. When the softened beans are agitated in the solvent, caffeine from the beans is drawn into combination with the chlorine. After about an hour, the solvent is drained off and the beans are heated and blown with steam, evaporating all traces of solvent. To get a product which will be 97 percent caffeine-free this process must be repeated up to twenty-four times. The caffeine is removed from the solvent, purified, and used in soft drinks, as a pharmaceutical, etc. The solvent may be re-used.

All 97 percent caffeine-free coffees will not have the same caffeine content. Robustas may have up to twice the caffeine content of Arabicas, so decaffeinated Robustas may have twice the caffeine content of decaffeinated Arabicas. Since the total caffeine content of any decaffeinated product is so small, the difference between them may be hardly worth mentioning. Perhaps even those very sensitive to caffeine would find such differences imperceptible. The higher caffeine content of Robustas may, however, be very significant in another respect. Total per-capita coffee consumption has decreased over the past ten years; at the same time, there has been a marked increase in the uses of Robustas in blends. The downgrading of blends may easily be held accountable for the decline in total consumption. During the same ten-year period consumption of decaffeinated coffee has more than doubled, but the tremendous amount of cola consumed is evidence enough that people are not turning away from caffeinated beverages. Is it possible, though, that the increased use of decaffeinated coffee is a reaction against the higher levels of caffeine in regular coffees containing higher percentages of Robustas?

The flavor of coffee is affected by the decaffeinating process but not, as some ridiculous advertisements imply, because caffeine is bitter. In well made regular coffee, the flavor contribution of caffeine is small and its slightly bitter taste is a tiny and not unpleasant component of coffee's complex flavor. Decaffeination does remove some of coffee's oils and waxes; the structure of the bean is altered. These beans develop differently in the roasting process and in fact for full development should be roasted darker than untreated beans.

While we've found no decaffeinated coffee to have the wonderful flavor of the real thing, good decaffeinated isn't bad. For a long time, there was only one mass-marketed decaffeinated coffee but now there are quite a few. Some companies even put out two and say that one is better than the other. Many specialty shops now carry a better grade of decaffeinated coffee and some roast it fresh. There are some good, but very expensive, imported decaffeinated coffees. You may have a good reason to switch to decaffeinated coffee but if you don't, don't switch. If you and your regular coffee are having disagreements, try to work it out. Make sure the coffee you use is fresh and make sure you don't boil it or reheat it. The results of rancidity or reheating are always unpleasant, but you should not attribute this unpleasantness to caffeine. Finally, decaffeinated is more expensive. The process costs money (although the by-product is then sold) and the green coffee itself shrinks about 12–13 percent. The net result is that when you buy a pound of decaffeinated coffee, you pay more for less.

We know that caffeine is responsible for coffee's stimulating effect and that this stimulation has been coffee's attraction ever since it was discovered. Coffee has been praised and criticized, blessed and damned, loved and hated, sought out and shunned. The controversy has raged on for one millennium and it will probably continue unabated for at least another. We certainly aren't going to settle the issue here whether caffeine is good or bad. People may be saints or sinners, but clearly they are not one or the other because of what they drink for breakfast. We side with Voltaire who said of coffee, "It is a poison, certainly—but a slow poison, for I've been drinking it these eighty-four years."

CHICORY

Although chicory is commonly used with coffee to reduce the cost, some people become accustomed to the flavor and continue to use it even when money is easier. If you would like to experiment, use about 20 percent chicory with your coffee brewed your usual method. The flavor will be a little bitter, heavier, and the color a bit darker.

The United States imports chicory from Central Europe, and some also comes from Michigan. It is the turnip-shaped root of the vegetable whose top is commonly used as a salad green. The root is kiln dried, then roasted and ground. It then looks like ground coffee but does not have its flavor.

In New Orleans chicory is well liked and can easily be purchased already mixed. The Creole influence is still strong in all of Louisiana, resulting in the widespread use of the chicory blend. One favorite is called Luzianne.

In New York, where many European immigrants learned to use chicory to economize, some did not switch to pure coffee because they came to prefer the flavor of the additive. Grandfather often told the story of his mother-in-law who insisted on adding chicory to the coffee he supplied her gratis. He never considered its use except to save money, and it seemed absurd to him to drink impure coffee when the need to save had disappeared.

THE PRECARIOUS ART OF COFFEE BLENDING

Almost all of the 2,500,000,000 pounds of coffee brought into the United States annually finds its way into the blends of the major packers. Most of this coffee is sold vacuum packed by grocers. Another large segment is processed by the major institutional packers and reaches the consumer by the cup in restaurants, office services, hospitals, etc. It is said that only forty men actually control the blending, roasting, and grinding of these billions of pounds of coffee. This fact of coffee life is not unique to America. While there are proportionately more stores selling unblended coffees in other countries, the sale of blended coffee is predominant throughout the world.

The average consumer generally chooses from among a wide array of these coffee blends, each identified only by brand name. In the early days of mass-produced coffee, different brands were often described in terms of the types of coffees included in the blends. Folgers included in its advertisements a map of Central America and attributed the unique character of its blend to the high-grown coffees from areas pinpointed on that map. Chain stores often offered three blends—low-, medium-, and high-priced. It was common practice for the blends to be described by type(s) included. Disclosure by the large coffee packers was made on the basis of their customers' acquaintance with the meaning of such appellations as Santos,

Mocha, and high-grown. As time went on, facts about the blends ceased to be forthcoming; the brand names were intended to stand on their own and for the blend's quality. The coffee drinker today is told that one brand is richer, another is coffee-er, while yet another is "good to the last drop." He is given virtually no information by which to judge the validity or at least the probable validity of these claims. The trend, it seems, has been to keep the consumer in the dark, to limit his ability to make intelligent choices and to assault him with slogans instead. The consumer should not be impressed by a brand touted as a blend of "hand-picked coffees." All coffees are picked by hand.

The first New York coffee merchants imported green coffee from nearby Jamaica and Haiti. Imports from the Dutch East Indies (Java and Sumatra) and Arabia soon followed, and in 1809, the first shipment of Brazils arrived at Salem, Massachusetts. A tiny proportion of this coffee was sold roasted in some major cities, but until the 1800s, when mass roasted coffee emerged on a large scale, most coffee for home consumption was sold unroasted, and at first without particular regard to type. To the consumer, all beans appeared to be pretty much the same. Since he roasted his bean very dark in those days, the more subtle flavor differences among coffees were not noticeable. However, the finer flavor and aroma of coffees such as Mocha survived any but the harshest mistreatment. Merchants who recognized some coffees to be more desirable than others, saw the advantage of marketing coffees by type.

Blending began when more sophisticated roasting machinery made possible the fully developed brown roast. The ability to distinguish differences among the many coffees of the world led people to seek out those possessing the most pleasing cup qualities. But just as the positive attributes of coffees were brought to light, so were the weaknesses or deficiencies characteristic of particular types. Combining various types of coffee was the response to a quest for a coffee containing a combination of positive attributes.

Treated to the brown roast, all the nuances of flavor characteristic of any particular type of coffee can be tasted. The winyness of Maracaibo is revealed, the verve and sparkle of Guatemalan, the richness of Colombian. The art of blending was born because coffee men found that they could create, by blending various coffees, a single coffee with an aggregate of delightful traits. Nature provides the basic elements, beans possessing taste, aroma, and body in varying degrees; but individual coffees rarely possess these qualities in the finest proportions. The qualities of particular coffees came to be known and valued, and the blender, by his art, sought to create a balanced composition. The smooth, sweet-drinking Santos from Brazil could be given depth and richness by the addition of Colombians. The lively Guatemalan is flavory but light. It could be combined with a Costa Rican or a Java to yield a coffee with spark *and* substance. Djimmah from Ethiopia possesses an interesting pugency but alone may lack richness. The straightforward, heavy-bodied Java can lend support and stability to this somewhat flighty growth.

Unfortunately, the practice of selling coffee only by growth (generic names such as Colombian, Brazilian, etc.) is not a completely satisfactory marketing solution, even for small specialty merchants. Coffee growths are often quite variable. After all, they are grown on thousands of plantations in countries all around the globe between the tropic of Capricorn and the tropic of Cancer. They are shipped from hundreds of ports, each port serving some group of growing districts in a given country. Growths may change from one season to the next. They may come up either better or worse, or just different. A coffee merchant, and especially a coffee blender, must know how to respond to the vagaries of nature. A specialty blender can usually do this while maintaining the highest standards, the standards of taste. A commercial blender is under the pressure of money as well.

The blender of commercial coffee must from month to month be able to find suitable replacements for coffees that cease to satisfy the requirements of his blend. To achieve uniformity most simply and to reach the widest market at a competitive price, he is likely to select less interesting, more neutral, lower-price coffees. The highest quality coffees are not abundant, are hard to replace, and could force a major packer to price his coffee out of range of his competition. Some major packers, in order to cope with this situation, offer a premium blend as well as a standard.

The coffee blender has always had to serve two masters, his customers who demand certain cup qualities, and the marketplace, which establishes the price and availability of the scores of possible types. As the coffee industry has grown, as it has attempted to serve a wider and wider market, it has become more and more competitive, and blending for quality has been forced to take a back seat. It is easier to mass produce, distribute, and advertise one blend than it would be to offer five or six different coffees. Commercial considerations have induced the blender of mass-marketed coffee to succumb to the rules of marketplace rather than follow the dictates of his craft—at the expense of his customers' enjoyment of coffee. Not only do the major packers offer little choice, but the single offering is often cheapened so that a competitive price may be maintained. Neither high-handed marketing techniques nor underhanded blending techniques serve the interests of the consumer. The primary goal of the blender should be a quality product at a fair (appropriate) price, but this seems not to be the goal of the mass producers. The consumer is indeed responding to the erosion of quality; he has been drinking less and less coffee over the past ten years. We may see a realignment of priorities if the downward trend in coffee consumption continues. Or perhaps we will only see more commercials.

What you pay for coffee is of course up to you. Keep in mind that when you buy canned or supermarket coffee, the price has been artificially depressed. Using coffee as a "loss leader," large stores are willing to lose or break even on coffee while they make money on other sales. Mass-marketed coffees are with few exceptions inexpensive coffees having, at best, neutral cup quality. The operator of a specialty coffee store can provide you with high-quality coffees only as long as he is making a living. His unblended coffees are expensive; his blends are composed of more costly coffees; his expert advice is valuable to your coffee-drinking pleasure.

HOUSE BLENDS

The coffee blender in a specialty store is likely to create a "house blend" of excellent quality. He is of course affected by considerations of price and availability, but he will not sacrifice quality. His reputation and livelihood depend on his maintaining the highest standards in his selection of coffees. His customers make a special trip to him and pay a premium only so long as what he provides is truly superior. If a particular coffee is in short supply, and shows an unwarranted rise in price, he will find a substitute that permits him to maintain both price and quality. If superior coffees show a general price increase, he will raise the price of his blend sooner than resort to cheap, low-quality coffees. He is not competing with a dozen other "brands"; he is catering to the tastes of a discerning clientele who will not (and should not) pay any price at all, but will pay what good coffee has to cost. The coffee man in a specialty store can afford to keep his priorities straight because he isn't supporting El Exigente or the Maxwell Housewife.

However, the operator of a specialty coffee shop finds himself in a predicament. Because of his size, he is very rarely in a position to import coffee on his own. He must skim the cream off the top of the world's supplies before they become the minutest parts of major blends, there to be all but lost in the confusion. He hasn't the volume, and hence the buying power of major packers, to obtain any coffee he may have an interest in. He must be alert to take advantage of offerings as they become available, and must enlist the cooperation of his suppliers to insure that his requirements and those of his customers are met. If he roasts his own, he has greater flexibility in purchasing, since he can lay in a good supply of green coffee and roast it as he needs it.

Try the house blend offered by your coffee merchant. It's the backbone of his business. He depends on it and your trying it is a good way to find out if you can depend on him. His biggest seller should certainly be fresh and pleasing. If it doesn't suit you perfectly, you have at least established a common basis from which you can proceed to make adjustments. Perhaps you'll have him add a little dark roast or a coffee with heavier body. Perhaps one of his unblended coffees will be more to your taste. Our point is that trying the house blend, his pride and joy, is a good way to get acquainted. If you find it just plain unpleasant, you may as well look elsewhere. His other offerings are not likely to satisfy.

A merchant's house blend, like the restaurateur's house wine, is likely to be democratic, that is, pleasing to a broad range of tastes. The merchant of a specialty shop may rely heavily on a pleasant but unremarkable Santos from Brazil if he wants to offer a very moderately priced blend. Passable Central Americans, such as the ordinary coffees from Salvador, Mexico, or Guatemala may be used in such a blend. The finer and more expensive house blend would be based on a good Colombian or Costa Rican and "spiced" with the fancier Centrals, such as the high-grown coffees of Mexico, Guatemala, or Venezuela. The high-grown Arabicas from Africa such as the Kivus of Zaire, the finer Kenyas and Tanzanias, and the Blue Mountain coffee of Cameroon, would all be suitable components of such a blend. Arabian Mochas or Ethiopians might be used to spike the blend, to give it piquancy.

The "nothing special" coffees have no place in a coffee specialist's offering. He must not downgrade his blend with neutral "price coffees," for while a house blend should appeal to a wide variety of tastes, it must do so on the basis of taste, not cost. The coffee merchant may offer unblended and custom blended coffees to suit individual tastes. In so doing, he diverges most sharply from the practice of the mass producers who often blend for the lowest common denominator of taste. The proper market for the specialist's house blend is the highest common denominator.

The coffee man may make his choices from literally hundreds of types to create a successful blend. But a blend is not simply a mixture. It is a combination of the desired coffee characteristics, and it cannot be maintained by always adhering to a formula. No two coffee crops have the exact same characteristics; even two shipments from the same plantation will not be identical. The blender measures uniformity by the effect of the whole rather than by the quantities of the component parts. A light-bodied aromatic blend might include Santos, Haitian, and Maracaibo. A blend with similar characteristics could be achieved with entirely different coffees such as a mixture of Guatemalan, Plantation Bukoba from Tanzania, and a Central Standard Salvador.

A house blend will surely be offered in an American roast (preferably full city). It may be offered also in a dark roast or even two. If a single dark roast is offered, it will probably be the darkest, Italian. An additional dark roast would probably be French—darker than American, lighter than Italian. The French or Italian coffees are likely to be, but are not necessarily, dark-roasted versions of the house blend.

Knowing the relative merits of the many different types of coffee, you may want to know what coffees make up a particular house blend. Ask your merchant—but don't be put off if he won't tell. The merchant usually has nothing to hide, but he guards the secret of his blend, as an artist would the formulas of his colors. Federal legislation may indeed someday require that the components of coffee blends be enumerated on the label. Should full disclosure of the types used become required by law (there is consumer pressure in this direction), the coffee man would comply reluctantly, but unashamedly. The mass producers might have some explaining to do.

Whether your merchant tells all, some, or nothing at all about his blend, his answers to other questions are probably more important to your getting the coffee you want. Does he roast? How often? If not, when was the coffee you're buying roasted? Is he sure that each coffee on his list is the type it is represented to be? How is he sure of this? Does he seem knowledgeable about the characteristics of the coffees he offers? Does he seem aware of the importance of freshness? Of the need to grind coffee properly for each brewing method? Of the best way to store coffee? Or the best brewing methods?

The consumer ultimately puts his faith—not to mention his money—in the taste of a skillful blender who selects good coffee wherever it is to be found. Your coffee supplier must be someone you can trust, someone who knows enough about coffee to know what he is selling you and how to help you suit your tastes. Coffee men should realize that the consumer depends on them for their skill in selecting and blending. The trust should not be betrayed.

BLENDING YOUR OWN

When you blend your own coffee, you do it to suit yourself, and taste— how your concoctions taste to you—is the only test. Following are some suggestions—and they're only guidelines—to help you on your way. Remember that while no mixture of good coffees will be bad, the virtue of a good blend is that it goes beyond the values of individual types.

People often enjoy a blend of light- and dark-roasted coffees. If you're used to American coffee but want some of that dark-roasted continental flavor in your cup, try three-fourths American with one-fourth French. The light-roasted coffee could be your merchant's house blend or one of the more aromatic growths such as Mocha, Djimmah, or Maracaibo. The pronounced flavor of these coffees shows through very well under the burnt taste of the dark roast. Viennese coffee is a blend of half brown and half French. You can mix Italian roast with American roast, but in such a blend the dark roast flavor tends to dominate. This quality is desirable in a blend used for Turkish coffee. You can mix French and Italian together for a lighter espresso blend.

You may, of course, want to create blends which consist of only brown-roasted coffees. Remember that the fully developed brown roast permits the individual varieties to express their own personalities. Among the world's growths, some are neutral, some possess a balance of desirable cup qualities, some are distinguished by a particular cup quality, and some are downright eccentric. Shun the neutral-cupping coffees which are flat and uninteresting. Choosing your coffees from one or more of the other categories, you may employ one of several blending strategies.

A coffee such as Santos from Brazil is well balanced and may be used as the base of a blend. When a single growth is simply smooth it tends to lack brilliance, the keenly pleasurable highlights of taste and aroma. You can "season" the base coffee with one or more of the many Milds, each of which has some predominant cup quality. Winy Maracaibo may flavor the blend while Java can contribute body. A high-grown Kivu or Tanzanian offers to provide any blend with pleasant sharpness. Each of these coffees may be enjoyed unblended, but what is outstanding in each will stand up in a blend.

You can create a blend by combining complementary coffees without using a balanced coffee as a base. This blending strategy requires skillful selection, for success depends on your ability to bring divergent elements into harmony. Bring the flighty Djimmah or Mocha down to earth by blending it with Java. A flavory favorite of ours may be achieved by combining Maracaibo or Costa Rican with these two.

A third blending strategy is in a sense a corollary of the first. A list of the world's finest coffees, the great self-drinkers, would include a superior Colombian, a Strictly Hard Bean Costa Rican, an Altura Coatepec, a Kenya AA, a Strictly Hard Bean Guatemalan. These highly prized high-grown wonders possess balance *and* brilliance. Combine any of these. The melody will be rich and deep while exquisite harmonies delight you. Alternately, season one with a coffee from Haiti or Ethiopia. The idiosyncrasies of either the sweet-drinking Haitian or the piquant Ethiopian will be brought into line by any of these stout hearted growths. Plunge into the uncharted waters of creating your own blends and enjoy the voyage.

5. Making Coffee

A COFFEE IDEAL

LIKE A THOUSAND and one Arabian nights, the pleasure of coffee comes from once upon a time, from long ago and far away. Coffee is the legacy of Omar who, guided by the ghost of his dead teacher, found the tree, harvested the fruit and prepared the beverage which saved him from exile and eventually earned him sainthood. Coffee is also the symbol of communion. Coffee linked Kaldi, the goatherd, with his goats. The wonderful fruit dissolved the distinction between master and flock; they became partners in an extravagant pastoral dance. And for the monk who chanced one day to spy the dancers at their revelry, coffee was a means to quite a different end; coffee's stimulation chased sleep away so that he could more diligently apply himself to his prayers.

We succeed to a long tradition in which coffee is associated with not only sustenance, but enjoyment and devotion; with not only the body, but with the mind and the soul. Man is adventuresome as De Clieu, cunning as Palheta, daring as Kolschitzky. He has had the imagination to discover coffee, the perseverance to cultivate it, the inventiveness to devise a technology which serves to reveal its hidden secrets. When we partake of coffee for refreshment we partake of its history, which is our own history as well. How shall we know coffee? Our coffee culture is great in scope; a rich and varied heritage has been provided us. Our coffee should be as great as this heritage can make it, but generally it is not. Our techniques of selecting, blending, roasting, and brewing coffee are indeed often marked by the absence of good taste and a conspicuous lack of intelligence.

The Chinese and Japanese have had their tea ideals. Shouldn't we as a nation of coffee drinkers have our coffee ideals? Shouldn't our ideal be to participate in this magical process of transformation, to joyfully avail ourselves of coffee's stimulation, to know coffee as *cahuha* (force)? Granted, there is many a slip between the cup and the lip. At one or more of the stages of coffee production, by carelessness or by design, the beans are not given their due, the ideal is not achieved, our opportunity for participation diminished. But if we find that much coffee falls short of the ideal, we also recognize coffee's potential to delight. The pleasure we get from good coffee urges us to seek the delights of great coffee.

In making a cup of coffee you add your efforts to those of the grower, the shipper, the roaster. The grower by his careful attention engenders in the beans their potential for flavor, body and aroma. The shipper insures that the beans arrive regularly and unspoiled from points all over the globe. The roaster by his skill reveals the hidden treasure of coffee, and brings its wonders within your grasp. The retailer recommends a blend or a single variety and provides fresh, pure beans. To you remains the task and also the pleasure of completing the chain. Brew the coffee and become partners with Omar, Kaldi, De Clieu, with the great wits of England and France. Sip the brew and finally give meaning to the work, the patience, and the skill of many people in many places.

People look to coffee as a pick-me-up, a break in the day's harried pace, fortification against the worst the world can offer, a way to reinforce and share a good moment. They call most often for coffee that's strong but not bitter, a brew that invigorates without being harsh or biting. The desired coffee will have full body, rich flavor, and an enticing aroma. Coffee drinking should be a sensual experience, a stimulating adventure in taste, touch, and smell. Too often it is not. Why is there this discrepancy between the great gift that has been passed down and the great disaster that is commonly passed off as coffee? Has someone been stealing from our inheritance while we weren't looking, or, more terrible, have we been watching them do it?

The myths of old have the power to inspire but not to educate. The myth makers of modern America are the copywriters on Madison Avenue, and their myths purposefully mislead us. No matter how many times we are told that "freeze-dried tastes just like fresh-perked," it remains untrue. The implication that percolated coffee is a standard of excellence compounds the insidiousness of this particular message.

Advertisements for pre-measured filter bags of percolator ground coffee that talk about their "mistake-proof product" are also obnoxious. It is insulting to insinuate that the consumer cannot measure the proper amount of coffee into the pot. If you are incapable of measuring out the coffee, how in the name of Kaldi are you going to figure out how much water to use? Whether or not the manufacturers of pre-measured filter bags truly believe that portion packaging will help the consumer make good coffee, it is important to point out that this type of pre-packaging for home consumption has built-in pitfalls which work against, not for, a better drink. Since the packages are of one size, you must make the same amount of coffee each time one is used, or else the brew will be too strong or too weak. If you want less coffee, you must either throw out what's left over—a waste, especially since the product costs more to begin with—or save the rest for later. The quality of the coffee will deteriorate if it's reheated or if it's kept warm for more than an hour. What if you use a package only occasionally, only when the specified quantity is needed? Once a vacuum can is opened, the coffee in it begins to stale, and if it sits around for more than ten days, the brew will suffer. Finally, a word about the usefulness of the filtering performed by this package: It does make cleaning the pot easier, and a clean pot is essential to good brewing. However, the filtering of percolated coffee does not in our opinion significantly counteract the adverse effects of such a brewing method.

We have detailed the faults of this product not because it is particularly evil, but because it highlights the wide gulf between popular practice and sound coffee-brewing principles. The marketing of products which sacrifice quality to convenience is the trend in contemporary coffee culture. That culture is being bankrupted, its principles misappropriated.

If our coffee culture has been made an unreliable source of information, should we turn instead to tradition? Could we get great coffee by returning to the methods of yesteryear? We could not. They made some bad old coffee in the good old days. Here's a typical recipe; quoted in Ukers' *All About Coffee:*

Coffee should be put in an iron pot and dried near a moderate fire for several hours before roasting (in pot over hot coals and stirring constantly). It is sufficiently roasted when biting one of the lightest colored kernels—if brittle the whole is done. A coffee roaster is better than an open pot. Use a tablespoonful ground to a pint of boiling water. Boil in tin pot twenty to twenty-five minutes. If boiled longer it will not taste fresh and lively. Let stand four or five minutes to settle, pour off grounds into a coffee pot or urn. Put fish skin or isinglass size of a nine pence in pot when put on to boil or else the white and shell of half an egg to a couple of quarts of coffee.

A brew made according to these instructions would be objectionable even by today's low standards. Such a stingy amount of coffee could only result in an impoverished brew. Twenty minutes of boiling must drive out the fragile aromatics while bitter elements, better left in the grounds, are driven into the beverage. Nostalgia is nice, but not at the price of good coffee. Our senses, which form the gateway to our dreams, are gently stimulated by flavorful coffee. A bitter, boiled-to-death brew can only be a rude awakening.

The recipe we've included to illustrate "good ol' fashioned" brewing technique indicates how coffee was made here in the nineteenth century. There had been even worse recipes which recommended that as little as a dram (1/16 ounce or about 1/6 standard coffee measure) of ground coffee be used for each cup. To be sure, earlier brewing methods had included boiling the coffee/water mixture for not a mere twenty-five minutes but for an entire day.

Better advice on how to make coffee was being published contemporaneously with the recipe quoted above. A fashionable magazine exhorted its readers to prepare coffee only by "the most modern and approved Parisian methods." The French were filtering their coffee and this was indeed a method to emulate. A handful of Francophiles interested in doing the chic thing may have heeded this sound advice, but by and large we remained a nation of coffee boilers. Our penchant for percolating derives from this unsavory past. The pumping percolator became the preferred method of making coffee even though better methods (e.g., filtration) were known.

The percolator wasn't just a coffee maker—it was progress, a technological wonder. It even provided entertainment. You could see and hear the coffee being made. If the taste of percolator coffee wasn't good, it certainly wasn't worse than boiled coffee; and at least the other senses got a treat. The brew was piping hot, and dyed-in-the-wool coffee boilers didn't have to forgo the pleasure of a houseful of coffee aroma. The percolator obliged by pumping that aroma out of the brew and into the air. While its mechanical performance instilled the kind of confidence that gadgets do, this infernal machine was dissipating coffee's precious volatile oils. As the percolator chugged and chortled along, its users succumbed to its dubious "musical" charms. The stove-top percolator begat the automatic electric percolator, a device which was to prove irresistible to generations of coffee makers. Technology, not taste, had dictated the choice.

Of course the percolator did not achieve its success because people perversely chose the pot that would have the least salutary effects on their coffee. Knowledge of better methods was not widespread. Communications were bad and habits, both good and bad, die hard. If the more fashion-conscious urbanites were up on the latest from the Continent, those in the provinces clung to tradition. Americans could have adopted the method of filtration more than a century ago; ceramic and metal drip pots were available. The Chemex coffee pot, invented over 25 years ago, could have caused widespread defection from the percolator camp, but no sweeping change in coffee-making practice occurred. More recently, the products of the Melitta Company have attracted a relatively large number of adherents to the filter method. But it is a very current phenomena, the automatic electric drip, which promises to transform coffee-making practice in the American home. This device doesn't produce a better beverage than its more humble non-electric cousins, but it does offer the coffee drinker a way to get the flavor of dripped coffee without sacrificing the convenience of the percolator.

Freed from mistreatment by the percolator, the characteristic flavors of various coffees and coffee blends can be produced more accurately and more consistently. Perhaps we will see commercial coffee men upgrading their offerings if the drip method becomes more and more widely used. (Some mass-produced blends have been touted as being particularly suited for use in electric percolators. This claim has always seemed to us to be empty if not perverse—are we to understand that, since the percolator is incapable of yielding up the goodness of fine coffee, fine coffees are not included?)

The following pages will initiate you into the not-so-mysterious mysteries of coffee's chemistry. You'll see what coffee is made of and how it reacts to water, air, and heat. Knowing the way coffee is, you will need only your common sense to understand how it needs to be treated to yield up its delicious secrets.

A master carpenter who taught us as much as we could learn about wood-working had a wonderful way of explaining the right way to do a job. He would say, for instance, that "the wood wants to be cut this way," or "the hammer wants to be held like this." He made our materials and our tools live, and so we learned to be considerate of them. We learned to see into what we wanted to accomplish. It's said that imitation is the highest form of flattery. We hope that Bob is flattered by our borrowing his lesson. Coffee, no less than wood, coffeepot no less than hammer, demand your respect. Follow your nose, your taste buds, and brewing instructions that derive from the nature of coffee. Get into the spirit of coffee and enjoy.

The creators of a good pound of coffee have all been guided by this principle: "Take the best . . . leave the rest."

Their adherence to that principle of controlled selectivity will have put the makings of delicious coffee in your hands. As you continue the process, as you make coffee, you should take that principle as your own. You will get what you want in the cup and leave the rest out.

The only two ingredients you need to make coffee are roasted ground coffee and water. During the few minutes that they come together, the beverage is born. This moment in coffee's long journey from seed to cup must be carefully orchestrated. It is here that you will determine what of coffee's flavor and stimulation will become part of the brew and part of your pleasure. Also, by carefully controlling the variables, you will exclude from your cup that which if extracted from the ground roasted beans would make the coffee unpleasant.

THE IMPORTANCE OF FRESHNESS

One part of coffee's journey must not last too long—the trip from the roaster to the coffee pot. Not to say that there are no dangers before roasting: condensation of moisture on the metal holds of cargo ships threatens to ruin the green beans as they make their way to consuming countries. Elaborate umbrellas of bamboo and burlap and mechanical ventilators are needed to protect the coffee from dampness and keep away disagreeable odors. But with proper protection green coffee may be stored without any markedly adverse affect on quality for a few years. Some connoisseurs claim that the cup quality of certain growths is enhanced by aging. We feel that usually the best flavor is obtained when fresh or new crop green coffees are used.

But what of roasted coffee—which is, after all, the form in which you'll likely purchase it? Once coffee is roasted, it becomes perishable and its freshness must be carefully guarded. If freshness and purity are not protected, the world's finest growth, roasted to perfection, may yield a most unsatisfying, if not downright revolting brew. While dampness and foreign odors are the only natural enemies of unroasted coffee, the air itself threatens to rob coffee of its delightful flavor.

Your coffee should be stored in a tightly covered glass jar in the refrigerator. Cool temperatures retard staling. Glass imparts no flavor and is easy to clean; the tight seal keeps other flavors out. Roasted coffee beans, stored in this manner, will keep well for about three weeks to one month *from the time the coffee was roasted*. Refrigeration will not, of course, restore flavor to already stale beans; so it is crucial that your source of coffee should be able to supply freshly roasted beans. Ground coffee stored in this manner will keep well for a period of seven to ten days.

If you buy vacuum-packed coffee, you can be fairly confident that the coffee is fresh when you buy it. The vacuum pack, if properly prepared, is effective in keeping coffee fresh for many, many months without refrigeration. However, once you open the can, the seven-to-ten-day figure applies. Transfer the coffee to a glass jar with a good seal and put it into the refrigerator. Think twice about buying economy size cans of vacuum-packed ground coffee. There is no economy in ending up with two-thirds of a three-pound can of coffee that is no longer at peak flavor.

Coffee beans can, with great success, be kept in your home freezer for several months. Just make sure that they are kept dry and sealed away from other flavors. Freezing coffee beans can be of much use to those who order a few pounds at a time by mail, or from a shop too far away to visit often. Coffee stored in this manner need not be thawed before grinding and brewing. Ground coffee may also be stored in the freezer, but not for more than one month. Again, this coffee need not be thawed before brewing.

If you store coffee in the freezer, leave it there till you need it. Don't keep taking it out and putting it back. When you take coffee from the container moisture in the air gets into the container. If you put the container back in the freezer, the moisture condenses and spoils the coffee. The coffee that you're actually using from day to day should be stored in the refrigerator.

You should consider the advantages of buying coffee in the bean to grind as you need it. Bean coffee keeps well for three times as long as ground coffee. We can see from the graph below that on the tenth day, when the freshness of ground coffee has hit bottom, bean coffee has about two to two and a half weeks to go. What may be even more important, if you don't keep coffee around that long anyway, is that the difference in flavor becomes apparent almost immediately.

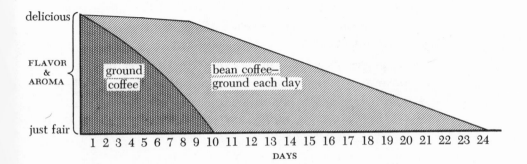

If you enjoy brewing different kinds of coffee from different blends and roasts, grinding your own is even more important; if you keep a variety of ground coffees around, they'll probably all go stale before you use them up. Also, a grinder will give you the flexibility of suiting the grind to the brewing method.

Let's see why coffee is best when it's freshest—that is, when it's just been roasted—and why it becomes less desirable as times goes on. Roasting develops the valued flavor oils and aromatics in coffee. Roasting also induces a chemical reaction in the beans that in time may lead to loss of freshness, staling, and rancidification. Roasted coffee, exposed to the air, loses its powerful characteristic aroma. The aromatics are dissipated: volatilization occurs. Such volatilization occurs most slowly from whole bean coffee, more rapidly from ground coffee, extremely rapidly when the ground coffee comes in contact with water.

Stale coffee is a result of the oxidation of coffee aromatics, accompanied by the development of non-aromatic oxidation products. During roasting, carbon dioxide is created within the coffee beans. Bean coffee stales more slowly than ground because the carbon dioxide held within the beans protects against oxidation. As the carbon dioxide content of coffee decreases, there is an increasing opportunity for oxygen to attack the aromatics. The grinding of coffee causes the loss of a great deal of the protective carbon dioxide and simultaneously exposes much more of the coffee's surface area to oxidation. The more finely coffee is ground, the more susceptible it is.

Rancidity occurs when the coffee oils have been made unpalatable by the long-term effects of oxygen. While staleness may occur within two weeks, coffee does not turn rancid for many months. Coffee must be terribly abused for a long time before it will turn rankly disgusting. However, mere carelessness in storing and protecting the beans will, in a relatively short time, leave you with beans devoid of life. The beverage extracted from this coffee will be a pale and ghostly shade.

Well balanced flavor in brewed coffee is the result of the interaction of taste and aroma. If the aromatic component has been lost or changed prior to brewing, cup quality will suffer. Coffee that has lost its freshness will produce a brew noticeably flat and slightly bitter. A beverage made from stale coffee will be very flat and even more bitter. Remember that where these is less aroma, the basically bitter taste profile of coffee will dominate the flavor. Rancid coffee yields a bitter, sour, unpalatable cup, barely recognizable as coffee.

How do you know if you're buying fresh coffee? If you buy canned coffee, it's probably been kept fresh by the vacuum, but make your own judgment on the basis of your experience with particular brands. If you buy bulk bean coffee, you'll want its aroma to have some spark, some piquancy. It's easy to detect the sour odor of rancid beans, but very difficult to detect, by smelling the beans, whether they were roasted yesterday or a month ago. The strong aroma of fresh-roasted coffee is perceptible for only a few hours since, fortunately, most of the aroma is held within the bean. When you have the coffee ground for you or when you grind it yourself, you'll get a better idea of whether it's fresh or not. If the coffee is fresh, grinding will release the aroma that's been held within the bean. If the coffee is not fresh, there will be little or no aroma for you to smell. It is, in fact, an irony that the wonderful aroma you get from freshly ground, freshly roasted coffee is aroma lost to the air. But do not worry. If the aroma is there to smell, the grounds are reserving plenty for your cup.

As important as maintaining the freshness of coffee is protecting it from foreign flavors and odors. Coffee is very susceptible to such contamination. Allowing roasted coffee to absorb air is bad enough, but if that air is carrying the odor of onion, cheese, herring, and the like, those odors will stick to the coffee until you brew it and then will be extracted right along with coffee flavor. We recommend keeping coffee in the refrigerator, but you can see why half-measures are worse than none at all: if you store an open bag or can of coffee in your refrigerator, your coffee will taste more like whatever else is in the refrigerator than it will taste like itself.

Next to pure, fresh, properly ground coffee, you must have equally pure, freshly drawn water. Water should be coffee's only partner in the brewing process. It represents 98.75 percent of an average cup and its vitality is essential to quality. You want to start with cold water. Hot tap water is made flat by the effects of heat and standing. Naturally soft water yields the best brew, artificially softened water the worst. Because overly long infusion or contact time increases bitterness, any water treatment, such as the water-softening process, that unduly increases this time should be avoided. The water should of course be free from any undesirable tastes or odors. Humphrey Broadbent, a coffee merchant who in 1722 wrote a treatise on *The True Way of Preparing and Making Coffee*, made this comment on the importance of water to the brew: "Some make coffee with spring water, but it is not so good as river, or Thames-water, because the former makes it hard, and distasteful, and the other makes it smooth and pleasant, lying soft on the stomach."

THE PERFECT CUP OF COFFEE

When water comes into contact with ground coffee, extraction always takes place, but the manner in which it takes place will determine the quality of the brew. The perfect cup is one in which taste, aroma, body, color, and stimulation are present in pleasing proportions. Conscious of coffee's composition and of how we may control extraction, we can set out to create that perfect cup.

What we perceive as flavor is the combined effect of what we taste and what we smell, the composite of taste and aroma. Our taste alone cannot distinguish between an apple and an onion, between coffee and quinine. The taste of coffee, which is basically bitter and astringent, is attributable to extractable, non-volatile materials such as the phenolic acids (chlorogenic, caffeic, quinic, isochlorogenic, etc.), carbohydrates (*e.g.*, mannose), trigonelline, and caffeine. The aroma of coffee, an essential and in some ways *the* essential component of flavor, is due to a complex of more than three hundred volatile chemicals, including such classes of compounds as alcohols, ketones, aldehydes, and esters. The extraction of this aromatic component is crucial to our perception of coffee flavor. To get good coffee you must insure that aroma is not lost before, during, or after brewing. Good brewing practice is designed to preserve coffee aroma not only because it is delightful in itself, but because, as part of flavor, it modifies taste.

The body of coffee is an adjunct to taste. It is a richness or heaviness associated with the underlying bitter profile of coffee. Our perception of coffee as heavy-bodied depends on the ratio of aromatic to taste components. All things being equal, less aromatic coffees are perceived as more heavy-bodied. Of course, a coffee that has no taste will have no body either.

Flavor and body are the real criteria of quality in a cup of coffee; they depend on the quality of coffee used and how well that coffee is extracted. The *strength* of coffee depends only on how much coffee ends up in the brew, not how it got there, and not whether what's there represents the best or worst components of the bean. Strength may be defined as the percentage of soluble solids (dissolved or extracted coffee) in a given amount of water. A stronger coffee beverage will have a higher percentage of soluble solids whereas a weaker brew will have a lower percentage. Strength may be varied according to personal preference without adversely affecting the quality of the cup, providing the extraction process itself is carefully controlled. (We will discuss ways to vary the strength of your coffee a little later on in this section.) You will want to remember that you do not get a stronger cup of coffee by changing the type of coffee you use. All types of coffee, whatever the species or country of origin, will yield equally strong, if not equally desirable, cups of coffee.

Certain types of coffee (*e.g.*, Colombian) may be characterized as strongly flavored, and dark-roasted coffee is almost always described as strong. Strongly flavored means the brew is not mild, not bland, but a coffee can be strongly flavored without being particularly strong in the correct sense of the term. Dark-roasted coffee is strongly flavored, but it is also almost always prepared at a greater strength than normal American coffee. Oddly enough, a greater amount of dark-roasted coffee is needed to produce a brew as strong as that made from a lesser quantity of brown-roasted coffee, because dark-roasted coffees have less available soluble solids.

Expert coffee tasters agree that an excellent cup of coffee is one in which 19 percent of the weight of the coffee grounds has been extracted into the coffee brew. They also agree that a good strength for a cup of coffee (and one that will appeal to the American taste) is 1.25 percent soluble solids, or 98.75 percent water. You can get this cup of coffee (1.25 percent soluble solids at 19 percent extraction) from a formula of 2.18 gallons of water per pound of coffee, or six ounces of water per two level tablespoons (one Approved Coffee Measure) of coffee. If you follow proper brewing procedures, this ratio will hold for any quantity of coffee, from one cup to 600 cups. The soluble solids extracted from a given quantity of coffee depends on the quantity, composition, and temperature of the water; on how the water is made to come in contact with the coffee; on the grind (particle size) of the coffee; and finally, on the extraction time. Of course a good coffee will produce a better flavored cup than a poor coffee; but this formula will maximize the flavor whatever the coffee.

Extraction must be controlled so that the desirable portions of the coffee are mixed with the desirable amount of water. It is possible to extract five ounces of material from a pound of coffee, or 30 percent of its weight. But the tasty cup of coffee is one which contains soluble solids at 19 percent extraction. Even espresso, properly brewed, does not exceed the 19 percent figure, since it is simply using the good elements in greater concentration.

When conditions are fixed so that 19 percent of the coffee is extracted, then virtually all of this extracted material will be comprised of non-volatile chemicals responsible for taste, and none of the more bitter, woody elements. The aromatic complex, almost negligible in weight contributing mightily to flavor, is fully extracted at 19 percent.

Less than 19 percent extraction produces weak, light-bodied coffee. Any extraction above 19 percent increases the bitterness of the brew. Complete extration (30 percent) would be disastrously bitter. The lighter aromatic component is extracted from (or in improper brewing driven out of) ground coffee immediately upon its contact with hot water. Taste is extracted more slowly, and body develops along with taste.

There are two more components to the perfect cup which we haven't yet discussed: color and stimulation. Luckily you will have little problem getting them into your cup in the proper amount. Both color and caffeine are very soluble in hot water; all brewing methods, properly applied, fully extract them.

The quantity of caffeine in green and roasted coffee ranges from 1 to 2 percent of the bean's weight. Robustas generally have a higher caffeine content than Arabicas. No caffeine is lost in grinding, and a cup of full-strength coffee generally has a caffeine content of from one and one-half to one and three-quarters grains of caffeine (one grain = 0.002285 ounce). In its pure form, caffeine appears as tiny white crystals which have no odor and are faintly bitter to the taste. It is one of a class of chemicals known as xanthines and is known to chemists as trimethyexanthine. In a typical cup of coffee, caffeine contributes minimally to taste.

In the preceding discussions we have expressed our commitment to a coffee ideal based on cup quality alone, but it would be disingenuous of us to pretend that it is only balanced flavor that coffee drinkers are after. Coffee has survived centuries of abominable roasting and preparation practices not simply because of its flavor, which is an acquired taste, but because of its stimulative effect. All the more reason to cultivate taste, as far as we're concerned. Discriminating wine drinkers appreciate the stimulation of wine, but will not sacrifice bouquet or aroma for its sake. There is no reason coffee drinkers should be any different. Perhaps we can take a cue from John Ernest McCann, who in Arthur Gray's 1902 coffee "almanac" *Over the Black Coffee,* characterized coffee in this way:

> Coffee makes a sad man cheerful; a languourous man, active; a cold man, warm; a warm man, glowing; a debilitated man, strong. It intoxicates, without inviting the police; it excites a flow of spirits, and awakens mental powers thought to be dead. . . . When coffee is bad, it is the wickedest thing in town; when good, the most glorious. When it has lost its aromatic flavor and appeals no more to the eye, smell, or taste, it is fierie; but when left in a sick room, with the lid off, it fills the room with a fragrance only jacqueminots can rival. The very smell of coffee in a sick room terrorizes death.

We have dwelt at some length on the importance of 19 percent extraction. If there is one rule in proper coffee brewing, it is this one. It is the prerequisite for full flavor, no matter what strength you like your coffee. To achieve the 19 percent figure it is crucial to find the proper relationship between grind size and length of brew.

It would take hours to brew coffee from whole roasted beans, and the beverage would taste flat. Ground coffee permits rapid absorption of water and extraction of the soluble components (solids and volatiles) that comprise flavor. Absorption of water and extraction take place at a rate inversely proportional to particle size. Particle size must be carefully controlled and custom-fitted to equipment specifically designed to provide optimum extraction. Actually all "grinds" (e.g. drip, percolator, vacuum, etc.) are really mixtures of particles of various sizes. A mixture containing a high percentage of smaller particles will be designated "fine." A mixture containing a high percentage of larger particles will be designated "coarse" or "regular."

The desirable 19 percent extraction is obtained with the following grind/time combinations. The grind is fitted to the brewing cycles:

GRIND	BREWING CYCLE
Fine	1 – 4 minutes
Drip	4 – 6 minutes
Regular	6 – 8 minutes

The finer the grind, the greater the surface area exposed to the water, and therefore the more rapid the rate of extraction. A coarse grind exposing relatively little surface area is appropriate for the longer brewing cycle. The grind should provide particle sizes that will assure proper extraction during the normal brewing period of the coffeemaker being used. The longer the brewing cycle of any coffeemaker, the coarser the grind it will require for optimum extraction. Too fine a grind for too long a time causes overextraction. The shorter the brewing cycle, the finer the grind needed. Too coarse a grind for too short a time causes underextraction.

An unfortunate fact of physics complicates the task of fitting the grind to the brewing cycle. We have said that a short brewing cycle necessitates the greater surface area provided by a finer grind, so that optimum extraction will be achieved. But the fineness of the grind is actually a determinant in the length of the brewing cycle. Water will pass more slowly through a bed of finely ground coffee, more quickly through a bed of coarsely ground coffee. (Think of water running through sand and water running through gravel.) The grind must be matched to the brewing cycle, but the length of brewing cycle is affected by the grind. Paradoxically, a finer grind tends to lengthen the brewing cycle when in fact a shorter cycle is called for. The proper brewing time must be produced mechanically—hence the particular importance of the coffeepot.

You should not use very finely ground coffee to increase the strength of your coffee. Since the fineness of the grind has the effect of increasing the length of the brewing cycle, overextraction will occur, and the soluble solids content of the beverage will be above the acceptable limit.

"Aha!" you say. "How about using less of this very finely ground coffee? That should have the effect of shortening the brewing cycle and of bringing the soluble solids content back down." You would do so at great risk to the quality of your coffee. To get the desired soluble solids content from less coffee, you would have to extract more than 19 percent of the available weight of coffee. Put another way, if the soluble solids content of 1.25 percent results from greater than 19 percent extraction, the brew will be composed of more of the bitter taste elements, from that part of the ground coffee which is better left undissolved. The increased surface area of finely ground coffee increases the solubility of the aromatic component less than that of the taste elements. If you use less coffee, you will get a less aromatic beverage; this too, makes the bitter taste more apparent.

You may note that Turkish or Greek coffee calls for a powder fine grind. This method of preparation yields a very bitter brew, and in fact, most recipes for this type of coffee call for the liberal use of sugar and spice.

Remember that strength (percentage of solids in the brew) may vary widely according to individual preference. Make coffee to suit yourself. If you're looking for stronger coffee, you will get it by increasing the amount of coffee or decreasing the amount of water you use. Demitasse, for instance, is double strength coffee resulting from a ratio of one Approved Coffee Measure of coffee to three ounces of water. While properly prepared double strength coffee draws only upon "the good 19 percent" for extraction, be aware that stronger coffee is not simply a matter of more of a good thing. The flavor of the beverage is in fact changed in many ways. While it will not have the unpleasant bitterness of overextracted coffee, taste components that are bitter will be present in double the "normal" quantity. The aromatic component of the brew will also be doubled, but at this level of concentration the taste component overpowers the aroma. Aroma in such strong coffee has less of a modifying effect on the basically bitter taste of coffee, so that taste is dominant. If the flavor and heavy body of such strong coffee appeals to you, by all means achieve it by using more than the standard amount of coffee. Other means of achieving strong coffee, such as using a finer grind or lengthening brewing time, usually have undesirable side effects.

While it is totally permissible to strengthen your coffee by using less water, it is *not* advisable to use less coffee or more water in brewing if you want a weaker than normal coffee. No matter how you look at it, you would be using extra water, *i.e.*, water which will dissolve some of the less soluble and less desirable components of the coffee. If you want weaker coffee, dilute the regular strength brew with some hot water. You will get a weaker beverage, but it will still have well balanced coffee flavor.

The above advice is intended to help you reach the perfect balance between strength and flavor in your cup of coffee. It presumes that you are basically satisfied with the *flavor* components in your brew. Unfortunately it is just these flavor components that are the common cause for complaint. If you aren't satisfied with your coffee, if the coffee itself has a bad taste or no taste, deviating from the recommended coffee:water ratio will probably not help. If your cup of coffee lacks aroma, the coffee you're using may be at fault, or it might be stale, or the aromatics may have been driven off in brewing. If you find your coffee too strong, perhaps overextraction has taken place. Perhaps the grind is too fine, the water too hot, the extraction time too long. Maybe the coffee has been roasted too dark for your taste.

Weak coffee is often the result of too little coffee used. Misplaced frugality prompts us to skimp where we should not. But weak coffee, a result of underextraction, can have other causes. The grind may be too coarse, the water too cool, the extraction time too short. You might find your cup of coffee too weak when it is actually too bland. Blandness or mildness is a function of the blend or roast, and not of the brewing. If the problem with your coffee is arising from some factors other than strength, altering the coffee:water ratio will not, *cannot* solve it. Changing the amount of coffee you use is the easiest thing to do but it rarely has the desired effect. Find out where the trouble really lies and correct it at its source.

When the water hits the coffee, it should be about 200°–205° F. Between these temperatures, the extraction you get is the extraction you want. You obtain the balanced cup. The caffeine is almost all dissolved; the aromatics are not boiled off and changes that result in bitter or woody tastes are avoided. You don't need a thermometer. Boiling water cools to within the acceptable limits as soon as it's been removed from the heat. We don't recommend that you wait for the water to further cool. When the water isn't really hot, underextraction occurs and the beverage will be particularly lacking in astringency and body.

How strong you like your coffee will determine the coffee:water ratio you use. It's only good sense to make sure that, whatever quantities you use, *all* the water comes in contact with *all* the coffee. Otherwise the result will be the same as if you had actually used less coffee than you had intended. We grind coffee to make it wettable, so in brewing we should take care that all the ground coffee gets wet. In some brewing methods the coffee bed tends to float on top of the water instead of mixing with it. This floating is caused by the carbon dioxide contained in fresh roasted, freshly ground coffee. Another cause of incomplete mixing of coffee and water is channelling, when the water creates a channel or pathway through the grounds and proceeds through the pathway rather than through the coffee. Any instance of incomplete mixing of coffee and water causes underextraction and a weak coffee. Below in the section on the various coffee-brewing devices, we will make specific recommendations on how to insure complete mixing.

The variables of grind and extraction time must be manipulated differently for different brewing devices. Before getting on to descriptions of those devices, we need to say a few things about the finished brew. Once you know how to control all the variables of coffee making to make your perfect cup, you don't want to spoil it. There are a few rules to observe here. Brewed coffee should be isolated from the spent grounds. If it isn't, extraction continues unchecked. Never repour coffee through the spent grounds. This practice is more common in restaurants than in the home, but of course a percolator repours brewed coffee in its normal brewing cycle. Weak coffee cannot be corrected by repouring. In the original brewing process the heavy-bodied, more soluble, and more desirable taste materials are extracted before the lighter, less soluble, more astringent taste materials. Repouring will cause the brew to become darker, but also unpleasantly bitter.

Fresh roasted beans, freshly ground, are essential in preparing truly delicious coffee. Drinking or serving it freshly brewed is at least as important. Coffee is best when it's just been brewed. It may be held at a temperature of between 185°–190° F. for up to an hour without seriously deteriorating. (If you want to keep brewed coffee hot use a vacuum bottle.) If held for a longer time, its aromatic component will be destroyed by oxidation, and the coffee will become flat and then bitter. Never reheat brewed coffee that has been allowed to cool. The violence of the temperature changes wrought by reheating is more than the coffee can stand. What aroma may be left is driven out. If the temperature reaches the boiling point, taste components are hydrolized and break down. Our old enemy, bitterness, is the result of such carelessness.

CHOOSING A COFFEEPOT

To make coffee you need a brewing device, a coffeepot. Some pots are capable of producing either bad coffee or worse coffee. Some will give you great coffee if used correctly, terrible coffee if used improperly. Some devices are unnecessarily difficult to operate, and others come with misleading directions; in either case, the odds are against your getting consistently good coffee. Give yourself a fighting chance. The pot you use determines the brewing method and has a big influence on the coffee you'll end up with. There's no need for you to look for a foolproof gadget; you're not a fool. Your coffeepot should not, however, be a booby trap. Simplicity in coffee making is a virtue—up to a point. The less pitfalls, the less opportunity for error. The simplest methods may not, however, yield the kind of coffee you're looking for. After all, how difficult is it to boil a coffee/water mixture for a few hours?

The pot you use should make it possible for you to easily control the variables of brewing. You must be able to get your pot scrupulously clean. Coffee contains oil which forms an almost invisible film on the inner walls and other parts of the pot. Scrub with a light duty detergent or baking soda and rinse very well. Unless this is done very thoroughly the oil will turn rancid and succeeding pots of coffee will be contaminated.

While paper filters are used only once and discarded, cloth filters are intended to be used repeatedly. A new cloth filter should be washed before using to remove any starch or sizing. Between uses, wash the bag with cool water; hot water cooks in the coffee stains. After rinsing, keep the bag submerged in cool water until you use it again. This treatment protects the cloth from bacteria in the air which cause souring.

A metal pot can cause the coffee beverage to taste bitter, astringent, or just plain metallic. Metals are hardly ever dissolved into the beverage; their action is catalytic. Glass and porcelain have no negative effect on beverage qualities. Stainless steel has the least effect of the metals, then nickel and copper; aluminum and tin plate have the most adverse effect on beverage quality.

Every brewing method requires its own brewing cycle, the time during which extraction takes place. Your pot must be able to produce a finished brew in the correct amount of time for the method used. Brewing in a percolator should take six to eight minutes, a drip pot four to six minutes, a vacuum pot one to four minutes, depending on the amount of coffee you are making; more coffee takes more time. The adverse effects of underextraction and overextraction can be avoided only if the brewing cycle is held within these recommended limits. The proper grind for your pot is the one exactly suited to its brewing cycle. Avoid coffee that's called "all-purpose"; there is no such thing as an all-purpose brewing device. The promotion of all-purpose coffee is purely for the convenience of the packers, who would prefer to avoid marketing a variety of grinds. (Would you buy shoes from a sales person who told you that one size fits everyone?) Generally, use drip grind for drip pots, perc or regular for percolators, vacuum or fine for vacuum and pressure pots. Special devices require special grinds; our recommendations will be found included with our descriptions of those pots.

A really good coffeemaker will produce consistently good coffee at all stated capacities. A two- to four-cup pot should make two cups of coffee as well as it makes four cups. A four- to eight-cup pot should yield equally good coffee whether used to make four, five, six, seven, or eight cups. You should not expect the smaller pot to make one cup or the larger one to make any less than four cups. Each pot is designed for the water to be in contact with the coffee for the proper length of time. If you use a pot below its stated capacity, the water will run too quickly through the insufficient amount of coffee. Underextraction and a weak brew is the result. If your coffee pot is rated only by the upper limit of its brewing capacity (e.g., an eight-cup percolator), count on using it at not less than three-quarters of that capacity. You might experiment with smaller quantities but chances are it won't function properly. If you're buying a pot, get one that is appropriate for the amount of coffee you'll be making most of the time. Don't get an eight-cup pot for the few times you'll have company, if you usually make only two or three cups. A pot that's too large for your needs may tempt you to make extra coffee in advance. Next thing you know, you might be reheating the leftover coffee later in the day, and that's a pitfall you really want to avoid.

Some pots have inaccurate cup markings. Check the markings on your pot against measured amounts of water and/or coffee. If the cup markings are not accurate, figure the adjustment you have to make in measuring the proper amounts of water and ground coffee. For every six ounces of brewing water used, the yield will be about one five-and-a-half-ounce serving of brewed coffee. The remainder of the water is absorbed by the grounds. If you use mugs, which have capacities as great as ten to twelve ounces, keep the ratio of coffee to water the same (1 ACM to 6 oz.) and calculate the extra total amount needed.

As we already mentioned, the most precise measurements in the world will not help if all the water does not mix with all the coffee. With percolators there is no problem of wetability, although channelling may occur. When steeping, dripping, or filtering coffee, make sure that the grounds don't float to the top of the water, or crawl up the sides of the filtering device out of the water's path.

If your preferred brewing method requires a pot that has a filtering device, the effectiveness of that device determines the degree of clarity of the coffee beverage. How clear or free from sediment you want your coffee to be is up to you. Like strength, clarity is largely a matter of personal preference. Most Americans seem to prefer a very clear brew. Turkish coffee fanciers have a very different idea about sediment. Keep in mind that coffee with a lot of sediment breaks down and becomes unpalatable more quickly than clear coffee does. If you intend to keep coffee warm for a while, a heavily sedimented brew will break down much faster yet. A filtering device of woven wire screen, perforated plates, or metal disks with holes in them will let larger particles through, and tend to get clogged with coffee residuals. Clogging impedes the rate of flow. A paper filter separates the coffee grounds, however fine, from the brew, while a cloth filter will hold back all but the finest particles.

METHODS OF COFFEE MAKING

There are two modes of extraction: decoction and infusion. All coffee-brewing methods employ one or the other of these modes. These names are also applied to the beverage which results from the mode employed. A decoction is a liquid produced by boiling a substance until its flavor is extracted. In the year 1000 A.D. coffee, as medicine, was a decoction of unroasted dried fruit, beans and hulls. Boiling was done in stone or clay cauldrons. About 200 years later, the decoction was made of dried hulls alone. During the following centuries whole roasted beans and later ground roasted coffee were boiled to make coffee. Coffee remained strictly a decoction for 400 years.

Infusion is extraction accomplished at any temperature below boiling. It is the only alternative to decoction, but can be broken down into various methods: steeping, percolation (dripping), or filtration. Steeping is the simplest form of infusion: hot water is mixed with ground coffee loose in a pot or in a container resting on the bottom of the pot. (Remember that infusion becomes decoction if the water boils at any time that it's in contact with the coffee.) Percolation really means dripping through fine apertures in china or metal. In this book when we've discussed percolators we've always been talking about the pumping percolator, the one you know. A *true* percolator would be a metal or china coffeemaker where the water dripped through the coffee once, but we call such devices drip pots. Where historical accuracy does not dictate otherwise we will continue to use "percolater" to mean the pumping variety only. Filtration is dripping through a porous substance like cloth or paper.

ibrik

TURKISH OR GREEK COFFEE Turkish coffee is prepared by the oldest surviving brewing method: the decocting of ground roasted coffee. It is made in an *ibrik,* a tall, long-handled copper or brass pot which has no cover and tapers toward the top, designed to keep the mixture from boiling over and to keep some of the grounds in the pot when the coffee is served. Measure three ounces of water for each demitasse cup and warm in the *ibrik.* Add to the water one very heaping teaspoon of darker-roast coffee (we like three-fourths brown-roasted Maracaibo and one-fourth Italian roast), ground like flour, and a heaping teaspoon of sugar (more or less to taste) for each cup. Custom dictates that the sugar is left out at unhappy occasions such as funerals. Weddings call for extra sugar. Stir. Bring to a boil over medium heat. Pour off half of the coffee into demitasse cups. Cylindrical cups are usually used as they keep the grounds well away from the lips. Boil remaining coffee again, and remove from the heat. Spoon some of the creamy foam of coffee into each cup. Another way to get foam into the cups—but it takes practice—is to make your hand tremble while pouring. In Arabic, the foam is called "the face of the coffee"—and you lose face if you serve coffee without it. Fill the cups, but do not stir the coffee once it has been poured. While still on the stove the brew may be spiced with a pinch of crushed cardamom or orange-blossom water. As heavily sugared as it is, and even when heavily spiced, Turkish coffee is very bitter. To assure that it is not made unpalatably so, never continuously boil the coffee/water mixture, and always make it fresh.

If you don't have an *ibrik*, you can make Turkish coffee in a regular saucepan, but make sure it's big enough to contain the violent activity of boiling. You'll get less foam and a less aromatic brew, since much of the aroma will escape into the air. Pouring will be a bit difficult.

STEEPED, POT, OR HOBO COFFEE   Coffee was earliest prepared as an infusion by the steeping method. This method was introduced in France in 1711 and by 1760 was generally employed by the people of that country. (In America, we were still boiling whole roasted beans.) To make pot coffee:

1. Measure cold water into a saucepan and bring to a full boil.
2. Add the proper amount of regular percolator ground coffee, turn the heat off or very low, and cover.
3. Let steep for five minutes. Crucial to making good pot coffee is separating the finished brew from the spent grounds, so . . .
4. Pour the coffee mixture through a strainer, cloth bag or paper filter. (If the grounds have been contained in a cloth bag, simply lift out the bag.)

Two types of brewing methods are used to make coffee by the steeping process. The French Melior and the American made Insta-Brewer pots represent one type. To brew coffee in these pots, measure regular ground coffee into the glass cylinder and add the proper amount of freshly boiled water. Instructions notwithstanding, let the coffee steep for a full five minutes. You cannot get good steeped coffee in an instant, or in a minute or two. Then press down on the plunger/filter mechanism which is inserted in the cylinder above the steeping coffee/water mix. There are a number of problems with this pot. Pushing the plunger does not completely separate the finished brew from the spent grounds; and after five minutes the brewed coffee will not be very hot. (Serve immediately.) This type of device is better suited for French than American style coffee, since in the case of the former a slightly more bitter tasting and heavily sedimented brew is not objectionable. The Melior especially is an attractive device and it's possible with this type of pot to brew your coffee right at the table. Are our mixed feelings showing?

The other method of steeping coffee is an unusual one. A pound of medium ground coffee is permitted to steep in a quart of cold water for twenty-four hours. The extract which results is then filtered off and kept refrigerated. To make coffee beverage you dilute the cold extract with boiling water. People who like this method claim that it gives you an aromatic brew, the "essence" of coffee, with no bitterness. We like coffee's basically bitter taste, and the lack of it in our cup leaves us cold.

Steeped coffee produces a very acceptable cup if the finished brew is isolated from the spent grounds, but a drip pot or filter pot will take that step for you. Read on.

café filtre
or machinetta

melior

DRIP COFFEE Percolation, hot water passing through ground coffee and then through small holes in a china or metal container into the coffee pot below, followed boiling and steeping in the developing sophistication of coffee-making procedures. Jean Baptiste de Belloy, Archbishop of Paris, invented the first percolator, not to be confused with the later pumping percolator, in 1800. De Belloy's pot, in reality a drip device, was the preferred choice of the immortal French gastronomist Brillat-Savarin and served as the model for hundreds of other inventors around the world.

One of the inspired was Benjamin Thompson, better known as Count Rumford. One of the most brilliant and bizarre figures in coffee history, Rumford was born in Woburn, Massachusetts in 1753, left his job as a Salem storekeeper for England in 1776 when he turned against the American Revolution, settled in Paris after marrying two wealthy widows with whom he fared abominably, and died famous for his invention and reviled for his arrogance and selfishness.

In between making himself obnoxious to his acquaintances, Rumford explored gunpowder and light, developed the caloric theory of heat, became a Count of the Holy Roman Empire, and attempted to live on diets of boiled seaweed and soft clay mixed with grass. As for his contributions to coffee history, he was not only a pioneer in adding cream and sugar to coffee, but he invented a better percolator. He improved the De Belloy pot by introducing a device which kept the grounds compressed in the container, preventing them from being agitated by the water. Further refinements on this technique were made in French and English drip pots through the early 1800s.

The basic method for making regular strength drip coffee is as follows:
1. Pre-heat pot by rinsing with hot water.
2. Put one Approved Coffee Measure of drip grind coffee per serving into the coffee basket and replace the upper section.
3. Pour six ounces per serving of boiling water into the upper section. When dripping is complete, stir the brewed coffee, and serve.
4. The finished brew should never be allowed to rise so high that the basket holding the grounds sits in it.

The standard form of this pot is a three-piece aluminum or stainless steel device: a water receiver, a coffee basket, a beverage receiver. The French *café filtre* and the Italian *machinetta* are variations of the theme. This pot will yield consistently acceptable coffee but it does have a few drawbacks. Metal is not good for coffee. It's not an easy pot to clean. The brew will contain quite a bit of sediment, since the proper grind does contain particles which are smaller than the holes in the coffee basket. Heavily sedimented coffee is usually more desirable in French or Italian coffee, since bitterness is a more pronounced flavor characteristic of those coffees.

Some drip pots have porcelain beverage receivers. This variation is good and bad. Porcelain isn't metal, but porcelain can't be put on the heat, and the beverage can get cool during a six-minute brewing cycle. Another variation is the all-porcelain drip pot. These pots control the flow of water into the grounds so that no amount of water is in contact with the coffee for too long. However, their design permits only a little water to be poured at a time. It seems to us that the whole process is unnecessarily long and tedious, but some people swear by these devices.

THE PUMPING PERCOLATOR   The objective of the pumping percolator was to heat the water and brew the coffee all in one operation. The first practical pumping percolator was invented in 1827 by Jacques-Augustin Gandais, a Paris jewelry manufacturer. In his machine the boiling water, raised through a tube in the handle, could only be sprayed over the coffee once. Later the same year Nicholas Felix Durant invented a percolator equipped with an inner tube to raise the boiling water and spray it repeatedly over the ground coffee. That sinister plot, the modern percolator, was hatched.

This poor pot, used in over 60 percent of American coffee-drinking households, has been the butt of our jokes, but don't feel sorry for it. It deserves every bit of criticism we can think of. We hold it largely to blame for the debasement of the American coffee experience. Our kinder self says, "Don't beat a dead brew." Our offended taste buds beg you to stand with us and say proudly, "I picked on a percolator today." Its invention, more than a century after the development of drip pots, was one hell of a step backward in coffee-making history. To make the percolator pump, steam pressure is created in the pot by the boiling of partially brewed coffee. It gives you a brew that is in part a decoction. Get a drip or filter pot for yourself and your friends. If you want to make percolated coffee for your enemies, here's how:

Percolator (Range Type)
1. Remove the basket and stem and fill with the correct amount of regular, percolator grind coffee.
2. In the percolator bring a measured amount of water to a boil and remove from the heat.
3. Insert the coffee basket and stem, cover, and return to low heat. Check that the water level is below the bottom of the basket.
4. Percolate gently for six to eight minutes, then serve after removing the basket and stem.

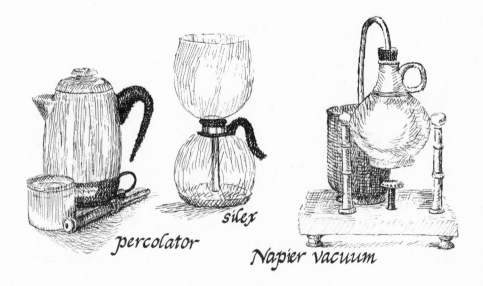

percolator

silex

Napier vacuum

Percolator (Automatic Electric) Who said the sins of the father shall not be visited on the son? Apparently not those responsible for the automatic electric percolator, which we sometimes unaffectionately refer to as the son of the stove-top perc. This wonder boy of a device may automatically extend the brewing cycle up to three times the recommended eight-minute limit. Underextraction will occur in those pots where the water isn't made hot enough. Water that's too hot will cause overextraction. It's not always easy to figure out what the pot is doing. Even if you try your best to manipulate the variables of brewing to your advantage, you may discover that this device has a mind(?) of its own. We recommend that you lose the electric cord and thereby give yourself a reason to throw away the pot.

FILTRATION It can take many fewer words to praise something than to disparage it. Filtration is a great way to make coffee. This method and the devices which it has spawned, enable and even encourage you to make coffee according to the most sound principles of coffee preparation. We have provided you with a fairly detailed description of what those principles are and how you may apply them. If you use the filtration method you can control the brewing process according to those principles. Yes, mistakes are possible, but unlike some other methods, filtration rarely encourages and never forces you to mistreat your coffee. If you like a lot of sediment in your brew, filtration is not for you. If you feel that a filter is robbing your cup of coffee's true nature we may not convince you otherwise. The professional cup tester is making a test and looking for trouble, so he does not make use of a filter. As a coffee drinker you're not looking for trouble but for flavor, body, aroma, stimulation. Filtration will not deprive you of these, the pleasures of good coffee. A filtering medium of good quality will neither add to nor detract from your enjoyment.

Vacuum Type The Napier vacuum machine was the first fully developed filtration system. It was perfected by a Scottish marine engineer named Robert Napier in 1840. The instrument, a gleaming well-made device, consisted of a silver globe, a mixing container, a syphon, and a strainer. Complex, sophisticated, conjuring up images of the alchemist's cell, this brewer was literally centuries removed from the campfires of the Levant. A small amount of water was placed in the globe and heated by a gas burner. At the same time boiling water was added to dry, ground coffee in the mixing container. The steam pressure created in the globe forced steam through the tube into the coffee mixture, causing it to become momentarily agitated.

Then the flame under the globe was lowered, the steam condensed and a vacuum was formed. The vacuum pulled clear coffee back through the filtered tube into the globe and the coffee was ready to serve.

The modern vacuum pot, commonly known as the Silex pot, is a modification of Napier's design. Although this device is no longer very popular, it can be counted on the make good coffee. Directions are as follows:

1. Remove upper bowl, insert filter and add correct amount of fine grind coffee.
2. Bring a measured amount of cold water to a boil in the lower bowl and remove from the heat.
3. Insert the upper bowl tightly and return to reduced heat.
4. Water will rise into the upper bowl. Allow it to mix with the coffee for one minute, stirring slightly.
5. Remove from the heat. Brew will return to the lower bowl, in about two minutes. Serve after removing the upper bowl.

Brazilian Cafèzinho Like the small, steaming cups of coffee called "tinto" in Colombia and demitasse in other Latin American lands, Cafèzinho is made with dark roasted coffee, very finely ground. We like a blend of half French, half Italian. Measure four ounces of cold water per serving into a saucepan and bring to a boil. Meanwhile place one Approved Coffee Measure of coffee per serving into the cloth strainer or cafèzinho bag. Pour the boiled water into the bag, holding it over the coffee pot until all the water has seeped through. Serve, sweetened, in demitasse cups. If you were to use a coarser medium grind coffee and set the bag of coffee in the boiled water so that the grounds were surrounded by it, you would have steeped coffee in five minutes.

Melitta and cone-shaped filter In our home we use the filter paper method. This method is really easy, grounds are thrown away in the filter paper

4cup
Melitta

8-cup
cone-shaped filter

so the pot cleans quickly, and the resulting brew is clear and delicious.

1. Preheat pot by rinsing with hot water.
2. Place filter in the cone and add one Approved Measure of drip grind coffee for each six-ounce coffee cup.
3. Pour about half the amount of boiling water over the coffee in the filter and stir well. Let this drip through and add the rest. Stirring insures wetability, and insures against channelling.
4. Remove the cone, stir the brew, and serve.
5. Most pots of this type are Pyrex and can be kept hot on a tiny flame for a short time. Brew what you need and don't reheat.

The cone-shaped filter pot bears such names as Tricolette, Chemex, and David Douglas.

The Melitta system represents a handy variation on the standard cone-shaped filter method. The flat-bottomed Melitta filter paper requires a grind finer than drip, so that surface area of the coffee is sufficient and extraction time isn't unduly shortened. This system, with its finer grind and shorter brewing cycle, produces flavorsome coffee more quickly and efficiently than the other filter paper methods.

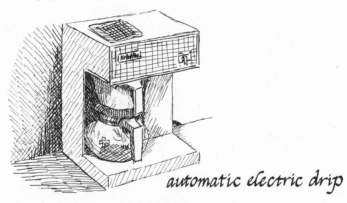

automatic electric drip

Automatic Electric Drip   The automatic electric drip for home use is produced by such companies as Melitta, West Bend, Braun, Mr. Coffee, Bunn, and Norelco. With the exception of the West Bend Quick Drip, which has a permanent plastic filter, all these devices now use a paper filter. Some of them are quite excellent. As we mentioned, their growing popularity seems to augur well for coffee drinking in America. For some years now, sturdier and larger versions have been very widely used in restaurants where urns or vacuum pots were used before. Recently, many offices have equipped themselves with an automatic electric drip machine of some sort, thereby getting more control over the coffee as well as getting coffee more economically.

Because this device is automatic, you must be especially sure that what you don't do yourself, what you don't control, is being done correctly. Is the water being heated to the proper brewing temperature? Is the heated water evenly spread over the grounds? Are all the grounds being completely wetted? Is extraction time within acceptable limits? Is the warming plate maintained at a constant temperature? Is that temperature too high? Too low? While not all the automatic electric drip devices work equally well, they all work pretty much the same way.

1. If filter paper is used, put a fresh one of the proper size and shape in the brewing basket.

2. Put one Approved Coffee Measure of the recommended grind coffee, per serving into the basket.

3. Place the basket in position under the heated water outlet and the beverage receiver under the basket on the warming plate.

4. Pour six ounces of freshly drawn cold water per serving into the water tank.

5. Plug in and turn the switch on. As these devices heat a little bit of water at a time, brewing will begin almost immediately. When the brewing is finished, stir the brew, and serve.

Follow the manufacture's advice concerning their use, care and cleaning. Do *not* follow such directions as "use four ACMs for eight cups of coffee."

Espresso　Espresso is made by a filtration method modified to produce a very special brew. The early espresso machines, with their spigots, handles, and gauges, were designed to provide quickly brewed coffee—hence the

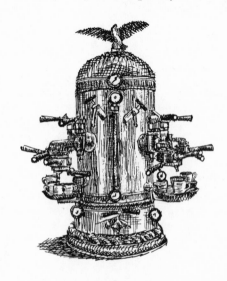

Atomic

Pavoni

Moka-type

Vesuviana

name. Speed was achieved by channelling, under pressure, a mixture of hot water and steam to individual spigots equipped with quickly detachable filters. The early Pavoni machines turned out 150 cups of espresso per hour. The larger "La Victoria Arduino" produced some 1,000 cups per hour.

The modern, streamlined, low-slung espresso machines went into production right after World War II. Their bizarre, multi-spigotted, eagle-bedecked ancestors will be missed, but the newer machines have a form better suited to function. The earlier machines tended to over-extract, to pull too much of the coffee from the grounds, producing a bitter flavor. Live steam, passing through the delicate coffee grounds, scalded the coffee, causing bitterness. In the modern espresso machines, the horizontal water boiler gives steam and water a better chance to mix. Thoroughly blended steam and hot water pushed through the coffee under pressure yields a cup smooth and palatable, with no sacrifice of strength or flavor.

When you make espresso at home, remember that best results may be obtained by using a machine which incorporates the above-mentioned principles. For a truly thick cup, we recommend a steam-pressure machine. These go under names such as Atomic, Vesuviana, Pavoni, and they require a finer than vacuum grind. In Moka-type pots (see illustration) steam is used to force hot water through the ground coffee, but the steam itself does not pass through the ground coffee or extract flavor. A fine vacuum grind should be used for Moka-type pots. Use one Approved Coffee Measure to three ounces of water, and follow the directions that come with the pot. When in Rome, do as the Romans; when making Italian Espresso, listen to the Italian manufacturers. We'll just remind you never to leave the heat on if there's no liquid to be heated. Replace rubber gaskets if they dry out and become ill-fitting. See our recipe section for great espresso drinks.

For a modified espresso you may use the Italian Neapolitan, the machinetta—sometimes called the upside down pot because you turn it over once the water boils to let water flow through the coffee. This device does not make true espresso. The beverage will not be as strong or as heavy-bodied as the brew that's been made by steam and pressure, but it is very widely used to make Italian coffee, and the French *café filtre*.

The machinetta consists of two cylinders, one with a spout and one without, and a two-piece coffee basket which fits between the cylinders. The correct coffee-to-water proportions are three ounces of water to each Approved Coffee Measure of drip grind coffee. Use the full capacity of your coffee-maker. Pour the measured water into the lower cylinder (the one that does not have a spout). Measure coffee into the coffee compartment. Assemble the parts according to directions that come with the machine, placing the spouted cylinder on top. Place on high heat. When steam emerges from the small hole in the lower cylinder, remove from heat and turn the machinetta upside down. When all the brew has dripped through, remove the two upper parts, stir the brew, cover, and serve.

Espresso (or *café filtre*) should be served in demitasse cups or wine glasses with a twist of lemon peel and sugar—never with cream.

INSTANT COFFEE   According to the Pan American Coffee Bureau's 1972 Annual Coffee Statistics, per capita coffee consumption in the U.S.A. in 1953 was 2.57 cups per day. Of that amount, 2.31 cups were prepared from ground roasted coffee; .26 cups were prepared from soluble coffee. In 1972, total per capita coffee consumption was down to 2.35 cups per day. Coffee prepared from ground roasted coffee was down to 1.67 cups per day while coffee prepared from soluble coffee went up to .68 cups per day. This data was compiled on the basis of coffee consumed at home, at work, and in eating places by all persons either ten years old or older.

The processing of soluble coffee has gone through many changes during our more than seventy years as coffee merchants, but none has resulted in an even barely acceptable product. We have refrained from selling it, but major packers of regular coffee, rather than fight this blight on the name coffee, have jumped on the soluble bandwagon. They have committed themselves and millions of their dollars to produce and market a product so poor in quality that it's a wonder they haven't put themselves out of business. The statistics show that soluble coffee currently accounts for more than one-quarter of total consumption, while twenty years ago it accounted for barely one-tenth. (The figures are much higher if we consider only coffee prepared at home.)

The conversion of roast coffee into the instant or soluble form entails extraction of the ground coffee with water to form a concentrated liquid brew, and then removal of water from this brew by some method of dehydration. What's left, the residue, is instant coffee.

Our distaste for instant coffee is not based on any prejudice against newness. (It isn't really new anyway; it was invented at the end of the last century.) Neither do we feel that there's anything inherently wrong with its convenience. Some instant cocoas on the market are no less delicious for being water soluble. Our refusal to have anything to do with soluble coffee is not a case of offended sensibilities but of offended taste buds.

Your taste buds will tell you they're suffering when you drink instant coffee, but you may need a coffee man to explain why. When we hear of instant coffees being promoted as "100 percent pure coffee" we really don't know whether to laugh or cry. That the product is nothing but coffee, we do not dispute. What you aren't told is that the coffee extract from which instant coffee is made usually has a soluble solids content of more than 50 percent. Fifty percent of the beans' weight is extracted! And we've already established that 19 percent extraction is optimum for a well balanced, flavorful brew. If these snake-oil salesmen packaged the spent grounds instead of discarding or burning them, would that also be called "100 percent pure coffee"? An acceptable instant could be produced if extraction were held down to 19 percent, but its cost would have to reflect the use of two-and-a-half to three times the amount of coffee now used. The manufacturers believe that consumers of instant coffee would probably not be willing to pay for convenience *and* quality, so quality is sacrificed entirely.

A brief look at the history and current status of instant coffee processing should convince even the least discerning that they should stay away from this disaster. The quality of instant coffee is better today than it was some thirty-five years ago, but better quality seems never to have been the goal of instant coffee producers. Cup quality has gone up and down over the years as a by-product of changes designed to increase marketability, not because it was pursued in and of itself.

According to Daniel J. Bloch, author of an article entitled "Instants: Quality vs. Cost" in *World Coffee and Tea,* instant coffee in the 1940s "was typically a fine light-colored powder, usually containing as much as fifty percent of added carbohydrates to bulk the product in the jar and in the teaspoon." You can see where not much improvement was needed to beat that. In the early 1950s, the more sophisticated dehydration technique had been developed to the point where larger particles of instant coffee could be produced. Packagers felt this bulkier product was attractive enough to discontinue the addition of carbohydrates. Taste was not a factor.

The processing of instant coffee resulted in a product devoid of coffee aroma. In the early 1960s some processors hit on the idea of adding "aroma" to the instant coffee product in the form of oil removed from the roasted beans prior to extraction, but this "aroma" added as an afterthought did not show up in the cup. Those who put it in the jar knew it wouldn't, but wanted people to be impressed—defrauded—when they opened it and smelled the dry powder. This procedure not only constituted a hoax; it actually made the product worse than it had been. The added oil not only introduced aroma to the jar, it introduced the problem of rancidity. While some processors attempted to overcome the problem by packaging the product under an inert gas, oxidation and eventually rancidity were still inevitable once the jar was opened. The use of larger jars compounded the problem, since the open jar would be around for a longer period of time. Bloch tells us that "once the larger processors had established aromatization as a fact, many of the smaller and medium-sized processors followed suit, although some resisted."

The next great "advance" in soluble processing occurred in the late 1960s, when the process of aglomeration was introduced. Particles of instant coffee were steamed and made sticky so that they would lump together. These lumps were redried by reheating. The result was a product which looked better (*i.e.*, more like ground coffee) because it was chunkier and usually darker. Cup quality was not in any way enhanced; in fact, reheating of the particles may have downgraded the flavor.

Most recently, a new, more complex technique of dehydration called "freeze-drying" was introduced into instant coffee manufacture. Freeze-drying offers manufacturers the spurious advantage of a final product that looks even more like ground roasted coffee than "aglomerated" coffee. It also offers a real advantage in cup quality, because the extract is not exposed to a stream of hot air as in spray drying. Some—though not much—of coffee's aromatic component is retained.

The incredibly high concentration of soluble solids in instant coffee is achieved by extracting under very high pressures. The water doesn't actually boil but the temperatures go well above 212°F. Since the water doesn't boil, the resultant brew is, in the strictest sense, an infusion. Under normal brewing conditions the adverse effects of boiling will only result from actual boiling, but under these artificially high pressures, those effects are produced without boiling. The brew may be called an infusion but it has all the qualities of a decoction. Hydrolysis occurs and the cellulose in the beans is converted to water-soluble carbohydrates. The greater the heat, the greater the degree of hydrolysis, the more soluble solids are extracted. Figure it out. Thirty-one percent of the weight of the instant coffee you buy (yes, even freeze-dried) is not good coffee flavor but bulk; it comes from coffee, but is in no way characteristic of coffee. Manufacturers can call the product pure coffee since they're not "adding" carbohydrates, they're making them out of coffee. The instant coffee of twenty-five years ago was being extracted at about 23 percent. Well folks, that's progress.

6. Recipes

WE PRESENT below the icing on the cake—both literally and figuratively. If you crave the delicious flavor of coffee, there's no reason to limit yourself to coffee as a hot beverage. If anyone has ever lost sleep over coffee it's probably because they were dreaming up recipes that included coffee. We have, with the help of our friends, collected and concocted recipes that are variations on the theme of good coffee flavor. Included are simple instructions on how to make decent iced coffee—well made, it's a delightful refresher, but many people, having tasted the mistakes, have crossed it off their lists. Grandma's honey cake, our own *petite madeleine*, is scrumptious. Mr. Cofacci's Dacquoise is an inspired masterpiece. Once you've tasted really good coffee, the memory haunts you. One taste of Mr. Cofacci's creation will make you redefine dessert.

Our recipes will specify regular strength coffee, extra strength coffee, or double strength coffee:

regular strength coffee:	1 Approved Coffee Measure (ACM) or 2 standard tablespoons to 6 ounces of water.
extra strength coffee:	1 Approved Coffee Measure to 4 ounces of water.
double strength coffee:	2 Approved Coffee Measures to 6 ounces of water.

COFFEE—INTERNATIONAL VARIATIONS

Demitasse

This is the traditional after-dinner coffee, double strong, but not espresso. Use regular brown-roasted coffee but double the amount. For each 3-ounce serving use 1 ACM: 2 ACMs for every 6 ounces of water. Serve in small cups, but make enough for second helpings.

Café Mexicano

4 servings

1½ cups double strength hot coffee
    4 ACM to 12 oz.
4 teaspoons chocolate syrup
¾ teaspoon cinnamon

¼ teaspoon nutmeg
1 tablespoon sugar
½ cup heavy cream

Combine cream, ¼ teaspoon of the cinnamon, nutmeg, and sugar and whip. Using four demitasse cups, put into each 1 teaspoon of chocolate syrup. Stir the remaining ½ teaspoon of cinnamon into the hot coffee. Pour the coffee into the cups and stir to blend with the syrup. Top with spiced whipped cream.

Café au Lait or Café con Leche

This traditional French and Spanish breakfast drink is served in bowls or handleless mugs. It is prepared by simultaneously pouring equal amounts of hot, strong French coffee and hot milk into the cups or bowls. In France it is usually accompanied by flaky croissants or warm French bread and jam.

Viennese Coffee

Use coffee that's been roasted darker than American but not as dark as French *or* coffee that's a blend of the two roasts. We like a blend of half brown-roasted Maracaibo and half French-roasted Mexican. Brew extra strength coffee (1 ACM to each 4 oz. water), and add milk to taste. What makes this Viennese is the *Schlagobers*, a large dollop of sweetened whipped cream as topping.

Spiced Viennese Coffee

6 servings

Brew 3 cups of Viennese coffee, add 4 cloves, 4 allspice berries and 2 cinnamon sticks. Let the brew stand over lowest heat for fifteen minutes and strain. Pour the strained coffee into wine glasses and top with whipped cream. Sprinkle with nutmeg and serve with sugar.

Espresso

The most famous continental coffee drink is espresso, and in our country it has attracted the greatest interest. Authentic espresso should be brewed in an espresso machine, which forces steam and boiling water through finely ground Italian roast coffee. In Chapter 5 we have included a description of the most common espresso makers available and how they are used. An espresso-like coffee can be made in a drip pot using a paper filter. You should use Italian-roast coffee brewed double strength (1 ACM to each 3-ounce demitasse cup of water).

Cappuccino

Cappuccino is espresso served with steamed frothy milk in a regular 6-ounce cup. The best way to make Cappuccino is to use an espresso machine with a milk steaming attachment, but these are expensive. An alternative is to froth up the hot milk for this recipe in a blender; about one minute will do it. Combine equal quantities of Italian coffee and of frothed milk. Dust with cinnamon or nutmeg, and serve with sugar.

Chocolaccino

This is a really delightful variation of Cappuccino. Brew the Cappuccino and serve it in a tall cup or glass, topped with whipped cream and a mound of shaved semi-sweet chocolate.

Caffè Dante

We discovered this delicious concoction at Caffè Dante on MacDougal Street in New York City. There it's called Caffè Fantasia, a most appropriate name. Place a thin slice of orange in each cup. Over the orange pour equal quantities of hot chocolate and steaming Italian coffee. Top with sweetened whipped cream; then sprinkle with grated orange peel or cinnamon.

Cinnamon Coffee *About 6 servings*

Pour 4 cups of hot extra strength coffee (8 ACM to 32 oz. water) over 3 sticks of cinnamon and let stand one hour. Remove the cinnamon sticks, add heavy cream and sweeten to taste. To serve, pour over ice and place a cinnamon stick in each glass as a stirrer.

Coffee for a Crowd   *25 servings*

Use ½ pound of drip grind coffee (2 cups plus 6 tablespoons) and 4¼ quarts of boiling water. Place the coffee in a bag of muslin or fine cheese cloth. The bag should be tied tightly so that the grounds can't escape, but the coffee in the bag should be loosely packed to permit the water to circulate through it. Drop the bag into the boiling water in a large pot. Turn the heat very low, cover, and let the brew steep for five minutes, moving the bag in the pot several times. Then remove the bag and stir the brew. Serve it as it's needed, keeping the coffee over low heat, but not boiling.

COFFEE WITH SPIRITS

Irish Coffee

This most famous combination of coffee and spirits is a sure cure for a cold winter day. It is served in pre-warmed Irish Coffee or wine glasses. Place 2 teaspoons of sugar and 1 jigger of Irish whiskey into each glass and fill with extra strength, freshly brewed coffee. To finish it off, top each glass with whipped cream.

Café Brûlot   *4 demitasse servings*

8 cloves
2 small cinnamon sticks
10 pieces of lump sugar
2 tablespoons chocolate syrup

2 strips each lemon and orange peel
4 ounces cognac
2 measuring cups hot extra strength
  coffee (4 ACM to 16 oz. water)

Cafè Brûlot should be prepared at the table so that all can share its marvelous aroma and colorful blaze. Place all of the ingredients *except* the coffee into a chafing dish. Heat, stirring gently for about two minutes. Ignite this mixture, and when the flame burns out, pour in the 2 measuring cups of extra strength coffee and continue to stir. Strain and serve.

Coffee Grog   *6 servings*

Sit in front of the fire on a cold winter's evening and sip this:

1 tablespoon butter
⅓ cup firmly packed brown sugar
⅛ teaspoon each cinnamon,

4½ cups of fresh extra strength
  coffee (9 ACM to 36 oz. water)
¾ cup rum

nutmeg, allspice, cloves

¾ cup light cream
6 twists each lemon and orange
   peel

Cream the butter and the brown sugar. Blend in the spices. Add the hot coffee followed by the rum and the cream. Serve the grog in mugs and garnish with the lemon and orange twists.

Coffee with Liqueurs

Start with demitasse cups three-fourths full of hot espresso. Fill with anisette, kummel, white creme de menthe, cognac, or Cointreau. Coffee mixes sociably with many liqueurs and liquors; these are just some suggestions to get you started.

Bob Morse's Coffee Wine

We haven't tried this, but our friend tells us it makes a gallon of delicious wine. There is certain specialized equipment for wine-making which can be purchased at wine supply stores. Says Bob: "It sounds complicated but actually the wine making process just flows when you have the right equipment."

7 teaspoons freshly ground Java
   coffee beans
1 gallon hot tap water
3 pounds sugar

1 teaspoon yeast nutrient
1 teaspoon acid blend (mixture of
   citric, tartaric, and malic acid)
1 package wine yeast

Combine all the ingredients except the yeast in a plastic container or crock. Cover with a cloth. Using a hydrometer, adjust the sugar content to yield 1100 specific gravity. Allow the mixture to cool to room temperature; add yeast. Let it set for twelve hours. Stir daily. Taste and enjoy the changing flavor. At the end of one week, siphon the mixture into a gallon jug or glass carboy and attach the fermentation lock. Rack it in three weeks and again in three months. Bottle when the wine is clear. Age for one year.

Sambuka

Serve this liquour with an odd number of Italian roasted coffee beans floating in it and you're showing that you like your guest. An even number of beans is a curse.

COFFEE COOLERS

Iced Coffee

Iced coffee should be made with freshly brewed extra strength coffee (1 ACM to each 4 oz. water) and poured over ice cubes. The extra strength coffee is important so that the melting ice doesn't dilute the brew.

or

Brew a pot of regular strength coffee and freeze it in the ice cube tray. Fill the glasses with the "coffee cubes" and pour regular strength coffee over them. Add sugar to taste and for a special treat, top with whipped cream.

This excellent summer refresher has unfortunately lost some popularity because of careless preparation, especially in restaurants. Yesterday's leftover coffee is often used, and it is usually poured over a tall glass filled with ice cubes. When coffee is left to stand and cool down slowly, its aromatics are lost and it becomes flat and bitter. Since most restaurants brew coffee regular rather than extra strength, the melting ice cubes dilute it, resulting in a weak and watery beverage. The trick is to take the same care with iced coffee as you would with hot. Don't think of it as a way to use up leftover coffee, but as a delicious drink in its own right.

Mocha Frost
4 servings

If you like milk shakes, try this refreshing coffee-based variation on a hot day:

2½ measuring cups (20 ounces) iced coffee
5 tablespoons chocolate syrup
1 pint coffee ice cream

Put all of the ingredients in a bowl and blend with a rotary beater until smooth. Serve in tall glasses.

Mocha Punch
16 servings

1 cup heavy cream
½ teaspoon almond extract
⅓ teaspoon salt

1 quart chilled regular strength coffee
1 quart chocolate ice cream
¼ teaspoon nutmeg

Whip the cream with the almond extract and salt. In a cold punch bowl, blend the coffee and half the ice cream until smooth. Fold in the whipped cream and the rest of the ice cream. Each punch cup should be topped with nutmeg.

Brandied Coffee Punch

About 48 ounces

6 eggs
grated peel of 1 lemon
½ cup sugar

3 measuring cups cold extra
  strength coffee
⅔ cup brandy or cognac

In Denmark this punch is served as part of the Christmas festivities. Beat the eggs and the grated lemon peel until the mixture is light and fluffy. Add the sugar a little at a time, beating continuously, and continue to beat until thick. Slowly stir in the coffee and then add brandy or cognac. Serve in chilled glasses.

DESSERTS

Mocha Sauce for sundaes

Melt 6 ounces of semi-sweet chocolate bits in ¼ cup of extra strength coffee (to get ¼ cup (2 oz.) of extra strength coffee brew 4 ounces of coffee with 1 ACM, or brew ¼ cup with 1 tablespoon of coffee). You can try spiking your sauce with a little cognac to add some zest.

Coffee Syrup

Coffee syrup may be used as a coffee flavoring in milk drinks and ice cream drinks such as coffee sodas. To make coffee syrup, combine 1 cup of sugar and 1 measuring cup of extra strength coffee (2 ACM to 8 oz. water) and simmer for three minutes.

Coffee Concentrate

Grind 3 ACMs of fresh coffee beans powder fine, as for Turkish coffee. Add ½ cup boiling water, and let steep for five minutes. Filter the coffee through a "cafèzinho" bag or filter paper. This should make about 2 tablespoons of very strong coffee. Coffee concentrate can be used to turn chocolate desserts into mocha desserts. For an even stronger coffee flavor in mocha desserts you can add 1 tablespoon of the fine moist coffee grounds in addition to the liquid concentrate.

Mocha Mousse   *4 servings*

4 oz. German sweet chocolate	2 egg yolks
2 teaspoons butter	2 egg whites
2 tablespoons coffee concentrate	2 tablespoons sugar

1. Heat the chocolate and butter in a double boiler or small saucepan over low heat, stirring occasionally until the mixture is creamy.
2. Add the coffee concentrate. Remove from the heat and blend the coffee thoroughly into the chocolate and butter. Let the mixture cool.
3. While the chocolate-coffee mixture is cooling, beat the egg whites and sugar until stiff.
4. Blend the egg yolks into the cooled chocolate-coffee mixture.
5. Fold the chocolate-coffee-egg yolk mixture into the egg whites. Pour the mousse into individual custard dishes.
6. Refrigerate at least two hours. The mousse can be served plain or garnished with strawberries or finely chopped nuts.
   These servings are small but *very* rich.

Granita di Caffè

This Italian "snow cone" is an easy-to-make dessert.
brewed espresso
shaved ice
sugar to taste

Add the sugar to the espresso while hot and let the espresso cool to room temperature. Pour the sweetened espresso over the shaved ice and place in the freezer in a bowl or ice-cube tray. Freeze to a semi-slush consistency. You can eat the *Granita* just as it is, or you can pour a little heavy cream over it just before serving or top with a dollop of whipped cream.

Dacquoise   *10-12 servings*
(Almond Meringue Layers with Mocha Butter Cream)

This recipe was developed by Gino Cofacci especially for the Trattoria Da Alfredo in Greenwich Village.

MERINGUE LAYERS:

1¼ cups nuts, toasted and ground
1 cup granulated sugar
1½ tablespoons cornstarch
6 egg whites

¼ teaspoon cream of tartar
pinch of salt
3½ tablespoons sugar
⅛ teaspoon almond extract
⅛ teaspoon vanilla extract

On parchment paper draw 3 circles, each 10 inches in diameter. Set them on cookie sheet. Set aside.

Preheat oven to 275 degrees. In a bowl mix nuts and 1 cup of sugar. Sieve cornstarch over them. Mix and set aside.

In a mixing bowl whip egg whites until foamy. Beat in cream of tartar and salt. Increase beating until soft peaks form. Beat the sugar and the vanilla and almond extracts into mixture. Fold in nuts-and-sugar mixture.

Scoop mixture into a pastry bag and fill in circles. Smooth with metal spatula before baking. Bake for one hour or until meringue is firm to touch. Allow to cool for a few minutes and peel off parchment paper.

MOCHA BUTTER CREAM:

⅔ cup sugar
⅛ teaspoon cream of tartar
⅓ cup espresso

6 egg yolks
2 sticks butter, softened

In a small heavy saucepan combine sugar, cream of tartar, and coffee. Over moderate heat stir mixture until sugar at bottom of pan has dissolved. Cover pan and bring mixture to boil. Remove cover and allow mixture to reach 236 degrees on a candy thermometer.

In a bowl beat egg yolks and add the syrup in a thin stream, while constantly beating. Continue beating until completely cool. Beat in butter a tablespoon at a time. Cover bowl and refrigerate for half an hour before using.

Spread butter cream between meringue layers. Cover sides with more butter cream. Sieve ⅓ cup confectioners' sugar over the top. Refrigerate.

Mocha Drop Cookies

½ cup butter, softened
1 cup sugar
1 cup beaten egg
1 teaspoon vanilla

1¼ cups flour
¼ teaspoon salt
1½ teaspoons double-acting baking
  powder

½ teaspoon grated lemon or
orange rind

½ teaspoon cinnamon

2 tablespoons coffee concentrate

2 ounces unsweetened chocolate,
melted and slightly cooled

1. Cream butter and sugar together.
2. Add beaten egg, vanilla, lemon or orange rind, and cinnamon and stir until thoroughly mixed.
3. Stir together flour, salt, and baking powder.
4. Mix the dry ingredients thoroughly with butter mixture.
5. Add the coffee concentrate and the melted and cooled chocolate. Mix thoroughly.
6. Drop by spoonfuls on greased cookie sheet. Bake at 350 degrees about fifteen minutes or until the cookies are firm on top. Makes about three dozen cookies.

Lena Brenner's Honey Cake

1 pound honey

1 cup hot extra strength coffee
(2 ACM to 8 oz. water)

2 tablespoons shortening

4 cups unsifted all-purpose flour

3½ teaspoons baking powder

¼ teaspoon salt

4 eggs, separated

2 cups sugar

2 teaspoons baking soda dissolved
in 1 tablespoon cold water

2 teaspoons vanilla

1 large orange, grated rind and
pulp

1 cup shelled walnuts, crushed

Grease two 9-inch square cake pans.

1. Heat the honey to boiling and set aside to cool.
2. Melt the 2 tablespoons shortening in the hot coffee.
3. Sift together the flour, baking powder, and salt.
4. Beat the yolks until thick, adding the sugar gradually. Add honey.
5. Add the sifted flour mixture and coffee alternately to the egg yolk mixture.
6. Dissolve baking soda in cold water and add to the mixture. Add vanilla, grated orange, and ½ cup of crushed walnuts.
7. Beat egg whites until stiff, but not dry, and fold into the mixture.
8. Pour the batter into the two pans and sprinkle each top with half of the remaining walnuts. Bake forty minutes at 350 degrees. Test for dryness with a toothpick or cake tester.
9. Turn out of pan onto cake rack and immediately turn topside up. Cool.

Return to pan and cover with aluminum foil until ready to serve. This recipe makes two 9-inch square cakes. Wrapped in foil, they will keep for about a week, and freeze very well.

Diane's Pumpernickel Bread

This delicious peasant bread isn't really dessert, but it's as good as cake:

3 tablespoons cornmeal

¾ cup cold water

½ ounce unsweetened chocolate, melted

1 tablespoon butter, softened

1 egg

3 tablespoons molasses

1 tablespoon salt

3 teaspoons caraway seeds

1 cup hot, fresh extra strength coffee (2 ACM to 8 oz. water)

2 packages active dry yeast (2 tablespoons)

2 cups rye flour

2 cups whole wheat flour

about 1 cup unbleached white flour

1 egg white beaten with 2 tablespoons cold water

1. In a large bowl, mix the cornmeal into the cold water and stir well.
2. Add the butter, egg, molasses, salt, 2 teaspoons of the caraway seeds, and melted chocolate. Combine these ingredients.
3. Add the hot coffee and blend well.
4. Add the yeast and blend again thoroughly.
5. Add the flours a little at a time, reserving the white flour for last. Stir as you add the flour.
6. When it is no longer possible to stir, turn the dough out on a lightly floured board and knead, working in the remainder of the flour.
7. Knead thoroughly to make a firm, dense, elastic dough.
8. Grease a large bowl with oil or butter. Form the dough into a ball and turn it in the bowl to coat it entirely with oil.
9. Cover with a damp cloth and place in a warm spot to rise until double in size (about 1½-2 hours).
10. Punch down and knead for a few minutes. Divide the dough in half. Sprinkle the bottom of a greased pan with corn meal. Shape the dough into loaves, place in pans and let rise till double in size (about ½-1 hour).
11. Brush the tops of the loaves with the egg white and cold water mixture and sprinkle with 1 teaspoon caraway seeds.
12. Bake at 375 degrees for about fifty minutes or until the bread sounds hollow when tapped on the bottom.

TEA

1. The Story of Tea

THE ORIGINS OF TEA

THE BEGINNINGS of tea are shrouded by the mists of antiquity and intertwined with myth and legend. An ancient Chinese oral tradition places tea within a complex, stylized version of the creation. When Heaven and Earth were split asunder, giving birth to the world, the universe was ruled by the twelve effulgent Emperors of Heaven who each reigned for 18,000 years. They were followed by the eleven Emperors of Earth, who were also each in power for 18,000 years; the nine Emperors of Mankind, who altogether reigned for 45,000 years; the sixteen sovereigns, and finally, the Three Sovereigns: Fu Hsi, Shên Nung, Huang Ti. Fu Hsi and Huang Ti lived in Honan, south of the Yellow River, and invented all the arts and crafts which they presented to men. Shên Nung, the Divine Cultivator, was the first to till the earth and so gave the gift of tea to man. He is supposed to have written in the *Pen ts'ao*, a medical book composed by him in 2737 B.C., that tea "grows in winter in the valleys by the streams and on the hills of Ichow, and does not perish in severe winter. It is gathered on the third day of the third month and then dried." After describing its beneficial medicinal properties he asserts, "It quenches thirst. It lessens the desire for sleep. It gladdens and cheers the heart." So tea, like coffee, was from its earliest appearance imbued with the aura of the gods and extolled as a combination medicine and elixir.

Another legend concerning the origin of tea tells of Bodhidharma, or Daruma, an Indian saint who founded the Ch'an (Japanese, Zen) school of Buddhism. In 520 A.D. Daruma traveled from India, the land where Buddhism originated, to China, where he was called Ta-Mo or the "White Buddha" by the Chinese. When he reached Canton carrying the sacred bowl of the patriarchs the Emperor, Liang Wu Ti, offered him as sanctuary a cave-temple in the mountains surrounding his capital, Nanking. Here

Daruma demonstrated the particular emphasis of the Zen sect by sitting before a wall in meditation for nine years. One day he fell asleep during his contemplation and when he awoke he was so vexed at this sign of weakness that he cut off his eyelids on the spot. Where the bloody lids touched the earth a strange and holy plant appeared which served as a reminder of the sage's momentary weakness and a memorial to his sacrifice: From the leaves of this holy tea plant a drink could be made which would diminish the desire for sleep.

Daruma's lesson that spiritual awakening was more important than the righteous acts or deeds of the mighty so offended the Emperor that Daruma left Nanking by crossing the wave-tossed Yangtze River on a reed. Fat, swarthy, often pictured with a gaping yawn and stretched out with an expression of angelic *satori*, Daruma died in Japan on Kata-oka Mountain in 528 A.D. His legend was spread by reverent Zen priests. It is said that his ascent to paradise was so rapid and ecstatic that he left one shoe behind in his coffin; he often appears in scrolls barefoot, holding a shoe in his hand. Three years after his death and burial he was seen hurrying across the western mountains of China home to India, shoe in hand. When the Emperor ordered an inspection of Daruma's tomb it was empty—except for one old shoe.

Numerous other stories passed down orally by the ancient Chinese connected tea with central themes in philosophy, religion, and literature. These legends began to incorporate tea as the symbol of a higher good that was as near as a freshly brewed cup and as evanescent as the vanishing steam. Tea was to become the spiritual touchstone of a way of life. It would play an integral part in the great religions of Taoism and Buddhism. Taoist alchemists named tea, "froth of the liquid jade," as an indispensable ingredient of the elixir of immortality. Adventurers and priests searched for the fabled drink on expeditions to the elusive, paradisiacal islands in the Eastern sea. Strange tales handed down by Buddhist priests told of a cult who trained monkeys to gather wild tea leaves from luxurious plants growing among high, dangerous rocks. Confucius is said to have mentioned tea in a poem called "The Lament of a Discarded Wife." Gan Lu, a Chinese scholar studying Buddhism in India, returned, as legend has it, with seven tea plants which he planted on Meng Mountain in Szechwan. And Taoist holy men related the story of how the custom of offering tea to a guest originated. Lao Tzu, the founder of Taoism, had become aged and disillusioned. Seeing the imminent collapse of his homeland, the kingdom of Chou, and acknowledging that his teachings were ignored, he mounted a buffalo and rode westward out of China. Yin Hsi, warder of the gate at Han Pass on the border, was himself a famed sage who had grown old beside his grass hut waiting for an Immortal to go through the pass. He stopped Lao Tzu, offered him a cup of tea, and persuaded him to write down his teachings. The result was the renowned book of the Taoists, the *Tao Te Ching*.

Another Chinese creation myth embodies a central idea in Oriental philosophy which would be expressed in future tea lore: the importance of the asymmetrical and the incomplete. Out of the Chaos at the beginning of Eternity, Spirit and Matter joined in a battle to the death. Finally the son of Heaven, the Yellow Emperor, prevailed over Chu Yung, the demon of earth and night. In his cosmic anguish the dying god struck the blue jade roof of heaven with his mighty head and shattered it into countless fragments. Planets and stars faltered in their orbits; huge solar winds threatened galactic existence. The Yellow Emperor searched desperately for someone to repair the Heavens. From the waves of the Eastern sea rose the Goddess Nü Wa, sister, consort, and successor to the first of the Three Sovereigns, Fu Hsi. Horn-crowned and dragon-tailed, she brought the power of the coiled green dragon who, writhing through the skies, eased the troubled planets with its aura of serene potency. Dressed in fiery robes, Nü Wa created the rainbow and used it to rebuild the damaged sky. But she overlooked two tiny cracks, and so began the drama of love—two spirits careening through time and space, never resting until by their union they complete the universe.

A key concept in this myth would be reflected later in tea room architecture, where frailty of the structure was a matter of spiritual emphasis, and in Taoist and Zen Buddhist art and decoration, where symmetry was avoided. Worship of the imperfect allows the imagination to complete the incomplete. It is the process through which perfection is sought, not perfection itself, that is important in Zen and Taoist thought. Tea, the salt of the East, imparting savor and fullness to ordinary life while retaining its inner essence of simplicity, was a symbol around which Taoist and Buddhist thoughts could coalesce. The extent to which tea would come to symbolize personal and spiritual qualities is indicated in the Oriental epithet for the insensitive individual as the man with "no tea" in him, or the admonition to the decadent or over-emotional that they had "too much tea."

As written records began to replace the older oral traditions the history of tea entered a new phase. Mythic imagination gave way to scholarship, though the transition from folklore to fact was not always clear-cut. There are a number of problems awaiting the tea historian. First, it is difficult to trace Chinese written references to tea. The Chinese language is composed of ideograms—symbols representing ideas or objects—rather than words as we know them. The modern ideogram for tea, *ch'a*, did not come into use until the seventh century A.D. Before this the symbol *t'u* was used for tea as well as another plant, the sow thistle, making it hard to tell which plant the writers were referring to.

A second stumbling block to pinpointing tea's origins stems from the Chinese custom of manipulating history. Chinese dynasties flowered and faded, rising from a morass of warring feudal states only to eventually sink back into chaos. As each group took control, they set about changing or destroying the history of the previous rulers. A ruling emperor would employ every technique at hand, from historical distortion and deletion to book-burning, in order to impress upon the people the idea that the new empire was the only workable form of state. If an emperor thought it in his interests to say he invented tea, he would tell his scribes to change all the history books, perhaps awing the populace and strengthening his rule, but creating problems for twentieth-century scholars.

Venturing across the hazy, evanescent boundary between myth and fact, we may say that aboriginal tribesmen living in the hills southwest of the China border, in the area that is now Southeast Asia, made a drink by boiling the green leaves of wild tea trees in ancient kettles over crude, smoky campfires; from them the Chinese learned the use of tea. Wild tea leaves were also prepared as a food before tea was widely cultivated for use as a beverage. In northern Siam (now Thailand), steamed tea leaves were fashioned into balls to be eaten with salt, oil, garlic, pig fat, and dried fish—similar to African tribesmen's use of wild coffee as an energy plant. The Koreans sucked raw eggs from the shell in between sips of tea. In Kashmir tea was served with red potash, anise seed, and salt. The Burmese were famous for their *letpet* or pickled tea salad. Boiled and kneaded jungle tea leaves were wrapped in paper or stored in hollow bamboo and buried. Months later they would be dug up to be enjoyed as a delicacy at some great feast. In Tibet enormous quantities of breakfast tea were prepared by combining barley meal, tea, salt, and goat's-milk butter and churning it to the consistency of chocolate.

Most historians agree upon 350 A.D. as the earliest credible record of tea cultivation. The *Erh Ya* is an ancient dictionary, attributed to the Duke of Chou, eighteenth century B.C. When it was annotated by Kuo P'o in 350 A.D., he added this definition of tea: "a beverage is made from the leaves by boiling." This drink was a bitter medicinal decoction taken to cure a variety of digestive and nervous disorders. Its healing qualities were so respected that it was often applied as an external paste to cure rheumatic pains. By 500 A.D. tea was described in another dictionary, the *Kuang Ya*, as a pleasing beverage. The leaves were formed into cakes which were roasted until reddish brown in color. The cakes were then pounded into bits and combined with boiling water to which was added onion, ginger, and orange.

Tea has been a food, medicine, beverage, and part of a religious ritual— Zen Buddhists drank tea before an image of Daruma—but almost from its first appearance, tea was also used as money. China developed banking before the West was civilized, but the tribes of the interior, farmers and herdsmen who had little use for either paper or coin money, prized crude compressed bricks of tea, made by primitive ox-presses, which they both consumed and traded. While minted money often decreased in value the farther it travelled from the center of imperial might and authority, tea cakes had the virtue of gaining in value as distance increased from the gardens of their origin.

THE RISE OF TEA IN CHINA

When demand for tea leaves increased in southwestern China, around 350 A.D., farmers and woodsmen realized that they could not continue to supply the growing tea market by simply cutting down the thirty-ft. wild tea trees and stripping the branches bare—this technique threatened to destroy the tea source. Instead, they began to develop a primitive form of tea cultivation in the soil deemed best suited to the new plant—that composed of crushed stone around the hill districts of Szechwan.

By the middle of the fifth century tea was listed in a contemporaneous history as an article of trade along with vinegar, noodles, and cabbage. At the same time special groves were set aside to provide the emperor with high quality leaves. Although tea is taken to this day to settle the stomach, its role started shifting from that of a purely medicinal drink to that of a pleasing beverage at the beginning of the sixth century. Chang Meng-yan, a Ch'in dynasty poet, wrote, "Fragrant tea superimposes the six passions: the taste for it spreads over the nine districts." This use of tea as both medicine and refreshment caused demand to soar even higher and most farmers down the Yangtze valley and along the seaboard began utilizing portions of their land and surrounding hillsides for the cultivation of the leaves. Tea received its official credentials as an integral part of Chinese civilization in 780 A.D., when the government imposed the first tea tax.

At this time tea had yet to undergo its metamorphosis from a beverage slowly gaining popularity to a full-fledged cultural symbol. Methods of cultivation, manufacture, and preparation were still primitive, and were spread almost entirely by word of mouth. Tea merchants began to search for someone who could write a book which would bring together practical information with a refined aesthetic sense of tea and its lore—a work that would be a true expression of the Chinese sensibility.

The tea merchants succeeded beyond their wildest dreams when they found Lu Yu—poet, visionary, buffoon, mystic, scholar, patron saint of tea and author of the *Ch'a Ching* or Classic of Tea. Lu Yu's origins are mysterious; he was a foundling discovered and adopted by a Buddhist priest. When Lu Yu refused to become a monk, he was assigned the dullest drudgery to break his spirit and induce him to follow the ways of his foster father. Instead he ran away, joined the circus, and became a clown. Though immersed in the world, pleasing crowds throughout the cities of China, Lu Yu retained from his rejected Buddhist background a strong thirst for knowledge. He was able to fulfill this passion with the help of a wealthy admirer who made available to him the learning and wisdom of ancient China in the books from his immense library. It was at this point in his career that Lu Yu undertook the writing of the *Ch'a Ching*. Calling on experiences derived from the three phases of his life—as orphan, earthy vagabond, and serious scholar—he invested the *Ch'a Ching* with the concept that dominated the religious thought of his age, whether Buddhist, Taoist, or Confucian: to see in the particular an expression of the universal. Lu Yu saw in the simplicity and beauty of the tea service the same harmony and flow that ordered the entire universe. The *Ch'a Ching* caused a sensation; Lu Yu was befriended by the Emperor Te Tsung and idolized by countless admirers. In the midst of his fame, his life took a sudden twist backward toward the meditative atmosphere of his early life. He withdrew to the mountains, where he became a hermit, and died in 804 A.D.

The *Ch'a Ching* is a three-volume work consisting of ten parts. The entire known world of tea is described: the nature and origin of the tea plant, the pleasures and benefits of tea drinking, the method of preparation, the varieties of tea, and a description of the twenty-four utensils which is the basis of Lu Yu's tea code, later to evolve into the Japanese Tea Ceremony. The poetic force of Lu Yu's writing can be seen in this famous description of different types of tea leaves:

Tea has a myriad of shapes. If I may speak vulgarly and rashly, tea may shrink and crinkle like a Mongol's boots. Or it may look like the dewlap of a wild ox, some sharp, some curling as the eaves of a house. It can look like a mushroom in whirling flight just as clouds do when they float out from behind a mountain peak. Its leaves can swell and leap as if they were being lightly tossed on wind-disturbed water. Others will look like clay, soft and malleable, prepared for the hand of the potter and will be as clear and pure as if filtered through wood. Still others will twist and turn like the rivulets carved out by a violent rain on newly tilled fields.

Those are the very finest of teas.

But there are also teas like the husk of bamboo, hard of stem and too firm to steam or beat. They assume the shape of a sieve. Then there are those that are like the lotus after frost. Their stem and leaves become sere and limp, their appearance so altered that they look like piled-up rubble. Such teas are old and barren of worth.

> —from the *Classic of Tea*
> translated by Francis Ross Carpenter

The beauty of the comparisons are threefold. They are pleasing. They are practical, in that every Chinese farmer would understand them—even the reference to the Mongol's boots, a reminder of invasions from the north that all Lu Yu's contemporaries were familiar with. And they are philosophical; the drifting clouds, mist-shrouded mountains, and breeze-stippled water described by Lu Yu represent the universal harmony of Taoism, just as it might be expressed in a T'ang dynasty landscape painting.

The T'ang dynasty (618–906 A.D.) was the classic period in Chinese art as well as in the history of tea. Just as later art would be measured against the greatness of this age, all future methods of preparing and drinking tea would have as a model Lu Yu's tea code. At this time cakes of compressed tea leaves were roasted over a fire until they were "soft as a baby's arm" and were added to boiling water that had passed through three stages: bubbles "like the eye of fishes; like crystal beads falling in a fountain; when the billows surge wildly in the kettle." Sometimes flavorings like salt, dates, or peppermint were used. The reddish brown color of cake tea had an important influence on T'ang dynasty ceramics. An exquisite blue glaze was developed in the south which Lu Yu considered ideal for the teacup because of the green jadelike quality it added to the beverage.

The spirit of Taoism ruled over the age. Wise men with hearts as "warm as jade" like Lieh Tzu, who rode the wind and so became the wind; and the Aged One who lived between Heaven and Hell because he was subject to neither, float through Taoist legend. Taoism, the religion of proportion and relativity, has been called the "art of living in the world" and it has empha-

Lu Yu

sized making the most of an often imperfect present. Confucius, Buddha, and Lao Tzu each dipped a finger into one jar of vinegar—the symbol of life—and tasted it. Confucius called it sour, Buddha found it bitter, and Lao Tzu said it was sweet. Lu Yu's sublime ordering of the world of tea into an artistic blend of taste, the manipulation of delicately beautiful implements, and tradition become poetry, captured the Taoist ideal forever.

The Sung dynasty (960–1280 A.D.) was the romantic age of tea. Tea called The Pure Delight, The Pearl, or Precious Thunder was served, at first flavored with onions, pickle broth, ginger, and orange. Later these other ingredients were eliminated so that the pure beverage could be enjoyed for itself. Whipped tea was the fashion in the Sung period. The dried tea leaves were ground to a fine powder in a small stone mill and whipped in hot water with a delicate bamboo whisk. Tea epicures held tournaments to judge new and rare varieties. The Emperor Hui Tsung, who had an extremely artistic sensibility, dipped heavily into the royal treasury to finance the search for ever more exotic species. His personal favorite, as described in his dissertation on the twenty kinds of tea, was the obscure but fine "white tea."

The Sung era began as one of consolidation and introspection following internal strife and sorties by the nomads on China's borders. Artistically this led to a rejection of the cosmopolitan T'ang period and an emphasis on the development of a purely Chinese style. In ceramics this philosophy combined with the delicate coloring of whipped tea to produce the heavy, strangely beautiful monochromatic teacups of blue-black, dark brown and dark purple, characteristic of the Sung. Another artistic concept of the time was the blending of several art genres in one work. A landscape painting would include a finely lettered original poem. In the Sung the world of tea was treated similarly. The leaves themselves were praised for their rarity, the contests were a refined social event, and the cups and equipment were also collector's items.

In the T'ang dynasty, colored as it was by Taoism, tea was a symbol of divine mystery. In the Sung dynasty tea and art were appreciated for themselves. Tea became a method of self-realization. Wang Yüan-ch'i described tea as "flooding his soul like a direct appeal, that its delicate bitterness reminded him of the after-taste of a good counsel." An important contribution of Zen Buddhism is the concept of the mundane and the spiritual as having equal weight. If the small incidents of life are also full of grace, serving a cup of tea to a fellow monk becomes as significant an act as Buddha reaching Nirvana. Cosmic mystery was not *reflected* in the actual world; the real world *was itself* a cosmic mystery.

The Mongol invaders who conquered the Sung and established an empire under Kublai Khan were themselves driven out by the Ming dynasty (1368–1644). A hundred years of barbarian domination had wrought great changes in art and tea. During this period of recovery an attempt was made to revive them, but the arts no longer were supported by the court. Kublai Khan and his hordes had been incapable of understanding the beauty and subtlety of T'ang and Sung poetry, calligraphy, painting, sculpture, and tea. The Ming court, composed of peasants, former outlaws, and political opportunists, had little sympathy for the elite artists and connoisseurs who were versed in the ancient traditions. So the artisans and scholars took their skills to the increasingly interested but less refined and sophisticated populace. If the T'ang dynasty represented the classic and the Sung dynasty the romantic, the Ming might be called the naturalistic period of Chinese tea.

The results for tea were varied. The method of preparation changed again and powdered, whipped tea disappeared from common use. The more easily made steeped tea came into fashion. The color of the teacup evolved once more to the characteristic Ming white and gaily patterned light porcelain. These shades enhanced the clear honey-colored beverage, and the simpler style was pleasing to the Chinese middle class and the growing number of European traders. A golden age was over. The exotic, ceremonial world of the T'ang and Sung periods, the poetry and polished tea utensils, had vanished.

TEA IN JAPAN

During her early history Japan remained overshadowed by her giant neighbor, China. Mainland culture, government, civil service, art, and the use of tea were all copied by the Japanese, who were overwhelmed by the magnificence of the early T'ang court. Yet it would be in the Island Empire that the tea ideal was to reach its apotheosis.

Historians write that in 729 A.D. the Emperor Shomu gave powdered tea as a gift to 100 priests who attended a four-day reading of Buddhist scriptures at the palace. This event inspired many of the monks to return to their districts and plant the new shrubs. The first record of tea cultivation in Japan comes to us as a result of this historic meeting: Gyoki, 658–749 A.D., spent his life building forty-nine temples, each with its garden of tea plants. For over a century after Shomu's inspired gesture, enthusiastic Japanese monks and emperors worked hand in hand spreading tea throughout Japan. In 794 A.D. the Emperor Kammu moved the capital from Nara to Kyoto and built his new imperial palace in the Chinese manner, with an enclosed tea garden. He created a new government post, Supervisor of the Tea Gardens, so that the new plants would be tended properly. Since the position was part of the government's medical bureau, it is apparent that the early Japanese tea drinkers respected the beverage, as did the first Chinese users, for its curative powers.

This period of harmony and civilization came to an abrupt end. The imperial mode of government, borrowed from China, could not withstand the powerful feudal thrust of Japanese society. By the beginning of the tenth century the emperor, symbol of centralized government, had become a puppet; Japan was ruled by regents of the Fujiwara clan, who married their daughters into the imperial family to help maintain their power. Later other clans gained supreme power. In 1185 Minamoto Yoritomo came to power as a military dictator, and had himself declared Shogun (approximately equivalent to "generalissimo") by the emperor. The title became hereditary within the ruling clan, and the nobles fought for control of the emperor, forgetting about tea gardens as one of the bloodiest periods in Japan's history ran its course.

Although a form of government and a cultural style based exclusively on that of China disappeared forever during this period, actual communications with China improved greatly during the twelfth and thirteenth centuries. In 1191 the monk Eisai returned from China, where he had been studying Zen, the school of Buddhism founded by Bodhidharma. Eisai was not only the first to introduce Zen Buddhism into Japan; he also started a tea renaissance. He brought new seeds from China which he planted near the castle of Fukuoka on Seburi Mountain and in the temple grounds of Shokokuji. He also wrote the first Japanese work on tea, *Kitcha-Yojoki* or the Book of Tea Sanitation, in which he describes tea as a divine elixir of the gods. A seemingly miraculous occurrence made Eisai's book seem like prophecy and dramatically increased the already growing popularity of the beverage: A Minamoto official, at the brink of death after a period of excess and gluttony, called for Eisai to pray for his recovery. The shrewd monk did not rely on a purely spiritual remedy. He sent to his temple for some of his personally cultivated tea leaves and between prayers plied the ailing warrior with his own blend of the heaven-sent balm. The mighty potentate miraculously recovered and asked about the holy beverage. Eisai gave him a copy of his book and the official became a passionate tea enthusiast. The story spread like wildfire, and to keep up with the incredible demand tea cultivation spread virtually throughout the entire island empire.

Zen Buddhism also spread rapidly among Japan's new military class; it offered a means of attaining the ultimate truths of Buddhism without book learning—which it rejected as useless—and in a way well suited to soldiers. It stressed discipline and self-reliance, and did not rely on salvation by a compassionate Buddha or Bodhisattva; each individual was to attempt to relive the mystical experiences by which Buddha had achieved enlightenment. The focal point of Zen is the intense meditation on one or more of the *koans* or cosmic riddles given a neophyte by the master. Perhaps the most famous of these in the West is "What is the sound of one hand clapping?" By applying himself rigorously to a *koan* many hours a day for periods of up to ten years or more the monk, under the guidance of a Zen master, hopes to eventually achieve *satori*, or a state of awakening to perfect clarity, an enlightenment in which the true nature of things—people, actions, flowers, tea—is perceived.

Keizan, 1268–1325, Great Patriarch of the Soto sect, took holy orders at twelve years of age. When he was twenty-one he thought he achieved *satori* while reading the Saddharma Pundrika Sutra but his master, Tettsu, rejected it. After seven more years of intense meditation he reached a genuine awakening which he expressed as "A pitch-black ball flies through the night." When Tettsu asked him to rephrase it Keizan exclaimed, "I drink tea at teatime, eat rice at mealtime," and the master beamed in approval.

What is the link between these two statements? It can be seen that the intellect is not a useful tool here. Rather, the Zen monk struggles his entire life for an intuitive grasp of absolute nothingness. Once he achieves this realization dualities drop away, and even the simplest things are transformed by the experience. To see into the nature of one's own being, to cease the battle between the finite and the infinite, is the goal of Zen. A master once said, "When I began to study Zen, mountains were mountains; when I thought I understood Zen mountains were not mountains; but when I came to full knowledge of Zen, mountains were again mountains." *Satori* also unlocks the meaning in tea—the meaning that was always there—the meaning embodied in the Japanese tea ceremony.

Forerunner of the ceremony was the rite of *Cha-no-yu*, "hot water tea," held in temple groves by Buddhist monks; the altar of the monastery was the prototype of the *tokonoma*, or place of honor in later tea rooms. When the ceremony moved to the towns and expanded to include the laity, a simple room in the middle of a garden was used, in an effort to recapture the natural harmony of the earlier ritual.

In 1477 the shogun Yoshimasa retired to his Silver Pavilion Palace on the outskirts of Kyoto. Here the priest Shuko, under Yoshimasa's patronage, set forth the first rules of the tea ceremony, made up of word-of-mouth remembrances of the old rite. The first nine-by-nine tea room was built and *matsu-cha* (powdered tea) was served. Yoshimasa gave many tea parties and was an avid collector of tea artifacts, with which he rewarded his soldiers instead of arms.

Rikyu, Tea Master under Hideyoshi in 1588, personified the tea ideal in Japan. His innovative examples and seven rules for the tea ceremony set an exquisite philosophic tone for tea gatherings that has never been equalled before or since. He did away with the ostentation and superfluity that had encroached upon the ritual since Shuko's time. He emphasized simplicity, purity, harmony, love of nature, proper frame of mind, politeness, and the esthetic aspects of the experience. Also, by keeping the ceremony simple, Rikyu brought it within financial reach of the middle-classes.

At first the tea room was a screened-off portion of the drawing room of a Japanese house known as the *kakoi*, or enclosure. The separate tea room or *cha-seki* came next. The final step, created by Rikyu, was the *sukiya* or tea house. This consisted of the tea room; the *mizu-ya*, or anteroom where the tea utensils were kept; the *machi-ai*, a waiting room some distance away from the tea chamber where the guests waited until summoned by the host; and the *roji*, or garden path which connected the tea room and the *machi-ai*.

Kinship with nature and the evanescence of earthly life have been main-stays of oriental thought for centuries. Tea-house architecture symbolizes these concepts. The lightweight natural materials that went into the con-struction of a tea house—thatched grass roof, pillars of unplaned wood, bamboo supports—recall the frailty of the incomplete sky in the ancient Chinese creation myth recounted earlier. The humble hut, fugitive and light, could be returned with a few strokes to the forest from which it was cre-ated. The size of the tea room, ten feet by ten feet, was suggested by a passage in the Sutra of Vikramaditya. In this Indian holy book 84,000 disciples of Buddha meet together in a room with these dimensions; to the truly spiritually aware, space does not exist. The doorway to the tea room was never more than three feet in height. Samurai had to remove both long and short swords to pass through, and all guests had to crawl as they entered—symbolic of humility.

The *roji*, the path from the waiting room to the tea room, consisted of irregular flagstones that meandered through shrubs, rocks, plants and small lakes of a little garden. Evergreens overhead and a few moss-covered stone lanterns were common features. The *roji*, with its aura of calm detachment and melancholy serenity, represented the first stage in Zen Buddhist medi-tation—the passage into self-illumination. One day Rikyu's son Sho-an had finished sweeping and watering the garden path. His father said "Not clean enough." After another hour of toil Sho-an complained that all was spot-lessly clean and that not a twig remained on the ground. Rikyu, calling him a fool, shook the branch of a tree and leaves of autumnal red and gold floated onto the path, transforming it from a clean but sterile walk to a way adorned with the casual beauty of nature.

The inside of the tea room was of utter simplicity. The sole decorations were arranged about the *tokonoma* or place of honor. These usually con-sisted of a *kakemono* (a subtle, monochrome painting), and a flower arrangement hanging from the side of the *tokonoma*. Ever since Buddhist saints gathered storm-ravaged blossoms and placed them in water, floral displays have been important in oriental life. The T'ang and Sung dynasties created magnificent ceramic containers for plants. Elaborate rituals were developed for cleaning the leaves of flowers with rabbit-fur brushes. Each plant had its sympathetic attendant; a beautiful virgin in complete costume bathed the peony, a thin, ascetic monk watered the winter-plum. To protect his garden from birds, Emperor Hsüan Tsung of the T'ang dynasty hung little golden bells on the branches of his flowers. This monarch, showing an intuitive knowledge of flowers that science is just beginning to explore, treated his flowers to concerts by court musicians.

Subtle flower rules were developed by the tea masters. White flowers were not shown when there was snow on the ground. Red flowers were avoided as too "noisy." Heavily perfumed blossoms were frowned upon as too distracting to the ceremony as a whole. In the sixteenth century, when morning glories were as costly as orchids are to us, Rikyu miraculously cultivated a whole garden of them. Their fame had spread to the Imperial Palace and the Emperor sent word that he would like to see them. Rikyu invited him to morning tea. The ruler walked through a garden of sand and pebbles in anxious anticipation, but not a blossom was in sight. A dangerous rage began to mount within him. But when he entered the low doorway of the tea room he saw on the *tokonoma* a rare Sung bronze containing a magnificent single morning glory, the pick of the entire garden.

The Japanese tea ceremony is still cultivated by Japanese Buddhist monks, the Imperial Family, and middle-class housewives. It began centuries ago in the courts, palaces, and monasteries, when a few men—never more than six—would gather together for several hours to drink tea. The experience was and is unique. The delicate scent of incense wafts through the small, plain room. The murmured conversation is inspired by the fine workmanship of the tea utensils, the scroll on the *tokonoma,* or a single dew-covered lily. After an interval water in the heavy iron tea kettle begins to boil. The pieces of iron in the bottom of the kettle are arranged so as to produce a sound like the wind sweeping through trees or surf moaning against the rocks. In the subdued light the guests, in carefully selected neutral costumes, the art objects, the flowers, the tea, the atmosphere, all blend together into an experience designed to challenge relativity, to lift the mind from finite to infinite realms.

THE SPREAD OF TEA TO THE WEST

Missionaries, explorers, and travelers who returned from the Orient in the sixteenth century brought back tales of a strange people and their customs —pigtails, silk, and the laquer, bronze, and porcelain of the magnificent Chinese court. The staple food was rice; and peasants and nobles alike drank an unknown, slightly bitter beverage—tea.

Venice was then the geographic and commercial center between East and West. The combination caravan and boat routes to China and India were controlled by Arab traders. Silks, dyes, spices, and other Oriental treasures came from them into Venice, where they were exchanged for Europe's goods. Venetian merchants and scholars were always interested in any new, exotic product that the Orient had to offer. Travellers from the East were treated with the best of hospitality, food and drink in the hopes that their tales of fantastic wonders could be turned to a profit.

And so Giambattista Ramusio, secretary to the Venetian Council of Ten and author, heard of *chai catai* (tea of China) from Hajji Mahommed, a Persian merchant, while entertaining him in his official capacity. The information, in which tea is praised for its curative powers, appeared in Ramusio's *Voyages and Travels,* published in 1559—the first mention of tea in a European book.

It is no wonder that Venetians heard of tea through a Persian merchant. Persia was one of a number of Asian countries where Chinese tea had attracted a considerable following. But although tea drinking had spread to other Asian countries, it was still only in the Far East that it was cultivated and manufactured. Western countries were forced to turn to China and Japan to obtain tea—and other Oriental luxury goods.

But to reach the Far East by the overland route was a long, complex, and treacherous journey. Spain and Portugal had perfected long-range sailing ships by the middle of the sixteenth century, and the Portuguese, following the route discovered by Vasco da Gama, sent their fleets to the Malay Peninsula, China, and eventually Japan, becoming the first Europeans to reach the Orient by sea. Portugal stole the East Indies trade from Venice because the sea route allowed her to sell goods more cheaply than her competitor. The Dutch served as bankers for the Portuguese as they had for Venetian traders. Dutch gold went to Lisbon, where it was traded for Oriental goods. Dutch ships then carried the goods to the ports of France, Holland, and the Baltic.

The Chinese were suspicious of the Portuguese, but their desire to take part in the lucrative European trade outweighed their fears of invasion. In 1557 they permitted Portugal to establish a trading center on the island of Macao in the Canton River—European traders, seamen, and adventurers were considered too dangerous to be allowed on the mainland.

Tea was not yet among commodities traded—silks and spices were more in demand—but curiosity grew in the West as reports proliferated. Knowledge of Chinese customs and tea fell first to the only group tolerated by the wary Chinese—the missionaries. The Portuguese Jesuit, Father Gasper da Cruz, was the first to preach Catholicism in mainland China. When he returned to his homeland in 1560, he described the "bitter, red and medicinal" drink he encountered in his travels. Another Jesuit from Portugal, Father Matteo Ricci, arrived in China in 1598. Although he had to wait two years for an audience with the Emperor, his patience was rewarded, for he was made scientific advisor to the Chinese court and was allowed to remain until his death in 1610. He wrote home about the new drink and, after describing its cost and method of preparation, maintained that it was the cause of Chinese longevity and vigor. A third Portuguese cleric, Father Alvaro Samedo, spent twenty-two years at the Chinese court and so had a chance to observe in detail the social refinements of tea drinking there. He wrote that presenting tea to a guest was an honor to him, but serving the visitor with a third cup was a hint for him to leave. Missionaries and travellers from France and Italy also reported on the new drink, but it wasn't until the beginning of the seventeenth century, when Holland supplanted Portugal in the Indies, that tea began to make an appearance as an article of trade in the countries of Europe.

In 1595 Jan Hugo van Lin-Schooten, a Dutch navigator who had acquired his experience of the East while sailing to India for the Portuguese, published a journal of his travels in which he described Japanese tea customs and the high esteem in which the Japanese held their rare tea artifacts, and also mentioned a host of other marvelous Oriental treasures. Excited by this news, the Dutch sent four ships to Java, where they set up a trading depot for Oriental goods on their way back to Holland. The cargoes were so rich that by 1602 over sixty ships had made the round trip. Competition was fierce. Holland was flooded with luxury products and bankrupt merchants were common. In that year the Lords 17, the most powerful merchants in Holland, chartered the Dutch East India Company to bring order to the Indies trade, act as the government in the East, and aid in the war against Spain and Portugal. In 1610 the first Japanese and Chinese teas were shipped from Java to Europe. And by 1637 a letter from the Lords 17 in Holland to the Governor General of the Netherlands East Indies at Batavia, Java instructed, "As tea begins to come into use by some of the people, we expect some jars of Chinese as well as Japanese tea with each ship."

Still, tea remained a relative rarity in the West before 1700. It was found in England and Europe only at court, in the homes of the wealthy, or as an exotic, expensive drink in coffee houses. Another novelty from the East—like silk and porcelain—tea was served as much for its strangeness as its taste. Drinking tea was one way aristocrats of the West could participate in the exciting voyages of discovery being made in their age.

In Holland, in the latter half of the seventeenth century, before tea was shipped in enough volume to sell at a reasonable price, outlandish tea gatherings were held that resembled bizarre parodies of the Japanese tea ceremony. Tea that cost the equivalent of $100 per pound was served from silver and porcelain containers with much pomp and ceremony. Sugar and saffron were added to the beverage, which was sipped noisily from a saucer. Conversation was monopolized by the tea and rich cakes served with it. When as many as fifty cups had been drunk by each guest, brandy, sugar, raisins, and pipes—smoked by the women as well as the men—ended the party.

Tea has been a symbol of England for centuries and is so today. Seldom has a foreign beverage been so intimately associated with the history of a nation; for three centuries the pursuit of this commodity mirrored the rise and fall of one of the wealthiest and most powerful empires the world has known. The drink from China gave the English their most characteristic social custom, dictated government policy, influenced commercial patterns, caused wars, and contributed to the loss of the valuable American colonies. In 1598 the first printed reference to tea appeared in an English translation of Lin-Schooten's *Travels*. Like the earlier Italian and Dutch travel accounts and later original works in English, this translation was not meant only to entertain; it was the serious reading of merchants who were looking for profitable ventures in the East.

A sharp rise in the price of pepper from Dutch merchants furnished the impetus for chartering the British East India Company in 1600, but it would be as the world's largest tea monopoly that John Company, as it came to be known, would exercise its remarkable powers. These included the right to annex territory, coin money, export goods duty free, command troops, make war, try court cases, and inflict punishment. In short, the Company would be the voice of England in the East, bringing the laws, might, and trading patterns of Britain to the natives while making the pound sterling the strongest currency in the world for centuries.

In 1601 Captain James Lancaster made the first voyage in the Company's behalf and established a factory at Bantam in Java. (A "factory" during the age of imperialism was a center for foreign trade, not necessarily a place of manufacture.) By 1615 the Company agents were interested in tea and drinking it themselves, as is shown in the earliest known reference to tea by an Englishman—a letter from the agent in Hirado, Japan, requesting "a pot of the best sort of chaw" from the agent in Macao. It seems curious that the man in Hirado could not find some tea from the countless tea-drinking Japanese at his own post. But this blindness to the natives around him was typical of the British trader; the same attitude was to eventually lead to a monumental blunder in India.

The Dutch wanted no competition for the Indies trade. In 1623, when British agents attempted to encroach upon Dutch territory on the island of Amboyna in the Indonesian Archipelago, the Dutch seized the factory, executed its occupants, and put an end to British hopes for extensive East Indies trade. They retreated to India, where they erected fortified trading factories, provoked the hostility of native rules, and established trading monopolies by paying off the Mughal Emperor. The English were too obsessed with reaching mainland China to see that the tea plant was indigenous to India. Englishmen would not drink tea grown in India for two centuries—and then only after the British East India Company, deprived of its monopoly in the China trade, was forced to look elsewhere for tea supplies.

The English finally reached China in 1637, when three ships entered the mouth of the Canton River, successfully challenged the Portuguese at Macao, and began direct trading with Chinese merchants. The Chinese remained suspicious of all Europeans, however—and a number of incidents of pillage of coastal towns or piracy of Chinese trading junks on the high seas by Portuguese, Dutch, and English traders confirmed their suspicions. They attempted to restrict and delay English trade. Violence broke out when the English captain attempted to move his ships upriver from Macao to Canton, and he and his men were eventually forced to leave. Although the British transformed the Fukien word for tea (*t'e*) into the word we use now, trading in the Chinese beverage still remained elusive to them.

The first public sale of tea in England was in London at Garway's Coffee House in 1657—and it was Dutch tea. In the first Tea Broadside Garway claimed that the Chinese often valued it at "twice its weight in silver," and then went on to enumerate all the real and fantastic claims made for tea since Chinese antiquity. Besides the usual benefits to the spleen, kidneys, eyes, stomach, and most other parts of the body, Garway assured his customers that their mental and spiritual state would also improve with a few sips of the wonder drink from the East: "It vanquisheth heavy dreams, easeth the Brain, and strengtheneth the Memory." Tea became quite popular, and the other London coffee houses added it to their menus of tobacco, coffee, sherbet, and chocolate.

On September 20, 1660, Samual Pepys wrote in his famous diary: "I did send for a cup of tee (a China drink) of which I never had drank before." And two years later when Charles II married Catherine of Braganza, a Portuguese princess, her devotion to the beverage made tea a fashionable drink among the English aristocracy and further legitimatized it in a way the coffee houses could not. Two years later the British East India Company secured a factory at Macao and, perhaps in deference to Catherine, sent a handsome gift of tea and cinnamon oil in a silver case to Charles. From 1668 to 1689 the Company imported from Bantam tea which agents bought from trading Chinese junks, and from Surat, tea obtained from the Portuguese trading out of Macao. In 1684 a riverside factory at Canton was built. But it was not until 1689, when the Company's ship *Princess* sailed from Amoy to London, that tea was imported directly from China to England. Toward the close of the seventeenth century tea grocers, as distinguished from those who did not carry the leaves, began selling tea to wealthier London families, and the new drink started making its first appearance in Scotland and Ireland.

By 1700, after a century of operation, the British East India Company had survived attacks by Malay pirates and competition from the Dutch and Portuguese. The Company had its headquarters in Bombay—which had been given by the Portuguese to Charles II as part of Catherine of Braganza's dowry—and had factories in Bengal and in the south Indian city of Madras. With its ships also importing direct from China, it was poised to exploit for the next two centuries the absolute trading monopoly it had achieved.

Tea reached Germany via Holland about the middle of the seventeenth century. After the first flurry of excitement, which included several reports pro and con by various doctors, the Germans largely ignored the new drink and continued to imbibe tremendous quantities of their old and true favorite—beer. Tea arrived in France shortly thereafter. Doctor Gui Patin, a famous French conservative physician, welcomed it in a letter by calling tea "the impertinent novelty of the century." This set off the kind of raging debate the French are celebrated for, including wildly varying opinions from medical, religious, and governmental circles. When the furor died down the French too gave up on tea and returned to the beverages that had become intimately connected with their life style—excellent and cheap wines, and dark-roasted coffee. While tea was conquering the countries of western Europe via the ocean route, it was moving overland from China to Russia by way of the famous caravan trade. Two Cossacks, Ivan Petroff and Boornash Yalysheff, brought word of the new drink to Russia in 1567, but no tea entered Russia until several chests were presented to Czar Alexis in Moscow as a gift of the Chinese embassy in 1618. Regular caravans did not start until 1689, when Russia and China signed the Treaty of Nerchinsk which established a boundary between them, and designated Kyakhta as a border trading town. The caravans of 300 camels, each carrying 600 pounds of tea, struggled to complete an almost impossibly arduous task. The entire trip from China to Russia via Mongolia was 11,000 miles and took 16 months.

Tea was shipped from the producing regions to the northern part of Tientsin. Horses and mules struggled to bring the tea 200 miles over the mountains to Kalgan, northwest of Peking. Then the tea traveled by camel 800 nightmare miles across the Gobi desert to Kyakhta, and from there to Russia. After the Trans-Siberian Railway was completed in 1905, tea took only seven weeks to reach Russia, and the mighty caravans faded into history. Genteel Russian ladies could no longer say with pride that they were sipping "caravan tea."

When greater volume of trade brought prices down in the beginning of the eighteenth century, everyone in Russia began drinking tea. To accommodate the new habit a samovar—a combination hot water heater and teapot—was invented with a capacity of forty glasses. The Russians drank a mixture of one-quarter tea and three-quarters hot water with lemon or jam, sipping it from glasses through a sugar cube held between the teeth. Since by tradition and for economic reasons the Russians were accustomed to eating only one large meal a day, the giant samovar was a pleasant and inexpensive way of seeing them through the rest of the day.

The precise date of tea's arrival in America is unknown, but it is likely that Dutch settlers in the colony of New Amsterdam first drank tea around the middle of the seventeenth century. Old records show lists of silver and porcelain tea utensils similar to the ones used back home in Holland; the social importance of tea was the same in the New World. Saffron, peach leaves, and sugar were used for flavoring, and powdered sugar and cinnamon were sprinkled on the hot buns and waffles that were served with tea. Tea moved north to Massachusetts around 1670 and was licensed for sale in 1690. It took a while for the New England colonists to get the hang of the new drink. In Salem tea leaves were boiled for hours, producing a brew so bitter as to make one wonder about those rumors of witchcraft. Then the leaves were sprinkled with salt and butter and eaten.

After New Amsterdam became New York in 1674, tea gardens were built around the town in emulation of the London pleasure gardens. Tea, coffee, and hot rolls were served at all hours. Entertainment consisted of fireworks, band concerts, dancing, and evening strolls down walks lit by lanterns. For domestic tea making New Yorkers purchased special water from vendors who obtained it from well-known springs or tea-water pumps; their cries of "Tea-water!" brought housewives running.

The catalytic role of tea in the War for Independence cut short the growing influence tea was having on colonial furniture and china. Beautiful silver, porcelain, and earthenware pots, cups, and saucers along with richly-grained wooden tea trays and tables, had evolved around the new beverage. After the Revolution tea reappeared for a time as an accompaniment to American meals. George Washington breakfasted on tea and Indian cakes with butter and honey. In the evenings he dined lightly on tea, toast, and wine.

By around 1700 the spread of tea in the West was complete. Every country had had a taste. Italy, Portugal, and Holland had taken turns dominating the tea trade. Most of the West didn't think too much of tea and after the novelty wore off they lost interest in it. Tea caught on in Russia, though, because of the common border with China, and was consumed in great quantities. And in England it was becoming a way of life.

THE TEA TRADE AND "THE COMPANY"

At the beginning of the eighteenth century an emerging West began to show strengths that would make it a dominant force in the world, politically and economically, in the centuries to come. Using tools that would one day epitomize the West—power, technology, drive, and organization—the British East India Company began to create a vast mercantile empire for England. Company ships carried with them proponents of a vigorous new culture that would sorely try the ways of old China. The end product—a cheerful pot of tea on the table—belied the desperate struggle between East and West that was taking place.

Until well into the latter half of the nineteenth century, for a complicated series of geographic, cultural, agricultural, and economic reasons, the Western demand for tea was met solely by China. Before detailing the curious history of the Company in China, perhaps it would be a good idea to explain some of the causes and effects of China's monopoly on tea production. After all, the Arabs tried to maintain a monopoly on the cultivation of coffee—why then were the Chinese successful where the Arabs were not?

Until the sixteenth century coffee and tea developed along similar lines. Although tea had an older history, both played an important role as ceremonial and social beverages, and both were discovered by Western adventurers in the 1500s. Coffee took hold throughout the West and the Americas and, with the help of Gabriel de Clieu in the early eighteenth century, its cultivation quickly spread from the point of origin in Arabia to the West Indies and Latin America. Tea, however, continued to be cultivated only in Japan and China.

In the mid-sixteenth century Japan was weakened by warring feudal lords and political disunity. In this climate of confusion, adventure, and piracy the least powerful warriors encouraged trade with the West, since it allowed them to accumulate wealth, power, and prestige out of proportion to their small land holdings. Since the Christian missionaries were the forerunners of the merchants, they were encouraged at first for this reason as well as for their religious faith and strong characters in a dissolute time. Toward the middle of the seventeenth century, after Japan had achieved political unity, increasingly harsh restrictions were placed on Western trade and religious activities. After a conflict with Portuguese missionaries in 1637–38, Japan closed her ports to all but a few Dutch and Chinese traders for over two centuries. (Even the trade they did have with Holland was very limited, consisting mainly of copper and camphor.) All missionaries were expelled; travel abroad by Japanese was forbidden. No ships large enough to engage in foreign trade could be built. Only in 1853, with Commodore Matthew Perry's famous visit to Japan, did the first tentative moves toward re-opening trade with the West begin.

China was almost twice as far by land from Europe as Yemen in Arabia, and the sailing voyage around the Cape of Good Hope to China was enormous. Centuries of traffic in the Mediterranean and the religious crusades of the eleventh and twelfth centuries had familiarized Europe with the culture of the Near East. The geographical proximity of Arabia to Europe and the mingling of the two cultures made the spread of coffee and coffee cultivation simpler than the spread of tea.

By contrast, Chinese culture has always been somewhat of a mystery to the West, and the puzzlement has been mutual; the first Western travelers were regarded as little more than barbarians by the Chinese. Subsequent encounters have been equally confused and complicated. The Chinese, authors of some of humankind's most important inventions—paper and gunpowder to name two—as well as some of the most profound philosophic concepts, have always been slow to share their secrets. Tea was no exception.

Chinese cultural isolation and China's great distance from the West are only two of the reasons why tea remained in China until the late 1800s. The botanical difference between coffee and tea reinforced Chinese secrecy. The method of preparing tea for market was inherently more complex than that of coffee. Coffee had to be shipped green and unground, otherwise it would lose its freshness. Green coffee beans needed only to be stripped of their outer hulls before being shipped. The processes which turned the beans into a usable substance—roasting and grinding—took place only after exportation, requiring the purchasing nations to have some knowledge of coffee processing. By contrast tea had to be withered, rolled and fired before leaving China; otherwise it would spoil. All the consumer had to do was add boiling water to it. Since the purchasers didn't *need* to know about tea processing, why tell them?

Lack of a great Western demand was a final reason for China's long monopoly in tea. To this day almost all Chinese tea is consumed by China itself. Only Russia, with its common border and history of trade with China, and with the blending of cultures in Mongolia, imported all its tea from China. England, like the rest of Europe, chose coffee as its favorite non-alcoholic beverage in the seventeenth century. The British East India Company, backed by a Government that viewed the coffee houses as a hotbed of political dissent, changed the drinking habits of a nation almost overnight. Armed with a government-granted monopoly in China trade the Company, composed of the most privileged and powerful people in Britain, saw no reason for tea to be grown outside China. Indeed, they founded the greatest mercantile empire of the age upon the perfect base—a constantly depleted commodity.

The early John Company ships were generally 499 tons in size. (This was to get around the law that vessels of 500 tons or more had to carry a chaplain. Company directors were quick to get their relatives on the payroll, but paying money to a strange cleric was another matter entirely.) It was not unusual for the captain of an East India ship, a position which became practically hereditary, to make a profit of £10,000 on a single voyage, made up of freight money, generous pay, and the permission to trade privately in certain commodities.

China, like Japan, might have eventually forbidden all foreign trade, had not the badly weakened Ming dynasty, in the years before its last adherents were overthrown, succumbed to the prospect of European trade. The Manchu conquerors remained suspicious of the foreigners, whom they regarded as barbarians, but they could not resist the favorable balance of trade: For Chinese porcelain, silk, and tea the Europeans had nothing to offer but silver; the Chinese were not interested in buying European products. They made strict commercial rules which limited their contact with the West while assuring the highest possible profits.

Canton was singled out as the only port where European trade was permitted. Foreign factories, including the house of the British East India Company, were clustered together at the edge of the city. The Western merchants were forbidden to venture outside the walls of their compounds, and so were like prisoners as long as they remained in Canton. On the first floor of the three-story buildings were counting houses, tea-tasting rooms, massive vaults, and rooms for the assistants and laborers. The second floor consisted of dining rooms and lounges. Sleeping quarters for Europeans were on the third floor. Since white women were forbidden to enter Canton, a desperate trader would occasionally smuggle in his wife, wearing men's clothing. The Chinese officials would in time discover the ruse and the woman would be forced to leave. Barbarism, it would seem, was practiced by both sides.

The hoppo, or Emperor's merchant, as the sole agent for Western purchases of Oriental goods, was the primary buffer in the Chinese-European commercial system. The hoppo had received his post through the patronage of a court noble, and was expected to keep that dignitary's pockets well lined. Government taxes and duties were not fixed, but negotiated between foreign traders, the hoppo, and the Chinese merchants. Out of the vast sums the hoppo was able to extort from the flourishing tea trade he paid tribute to his benefactor, bribed his enemies at court, accumulated his personal fortune, and placed friends and relatives on the payroll.

As the volume of Western trade increased, the hoppo admitted to the monopoly thirteen hong merchants, so called for their hongs or warehouses which adjoined those of the Europeans. These men in time controlled all the foreign trade in China. They bought silks, tea, and other goods from the interior, re-packed, weighed, matted, and marked them, and then squeezed whatever they could out of the Europeans. Famous among the Cantonese hong merchants was Howqua, sometimes known as the Chinese Croesus. He rose from humble beginnings to become senior hong merchant, and in an ambience of deceit and extortion his word was respected by both Europeans and Chinese. When one of his subordinates embezzled $50,000 from a trading company, Howqua immediately paid back the entire sum. His residence was renowned as the most splendid in Canton, and his personal wealth was estimated at $26,000,000.

As the John Company's monopoly over tea coming into England strengthened, imports increased, prices dropped somewhat, and tea became more available to the masses. At the beginning of Queen Anne's reign, in 1702, she introduced several innovations which became part of the gradually developing body of English tea manners. She substituted tea for ale at breakfast (much the same way New Yorkers gave up beer in favor of coffee for breakfast). Anne also was fond of using a large, bell-shaped silver teapot rather than the tiny China pots in fashion at the time. "Tea" at first was any occasion where the beverage was served and "teatime" marked the corresponding hour. Gradually, in the eighteenth century, two distinct customs evolved. "Low tea" was aristocratic in origin and consisted of a snack of pastries and sandwiches followed by tea, at around six in the evening. It was a prelude to the really serious eating, which would begin about nine o'clock. "High tea" or "meat tea" was bourgeois in background, and was made up largely of the leftovers of the huge middle-class lunch: cold meats, relishes, bread, and cheese. These were served with tea to form the evening meal. By the middle of the eighteenth century Samuel Johnson was able to answer the medical and social detractors of the popular beverage and sum up a nation's future taste when he called himself a "hardened and shameless tea-drinker, who has for many years diluted his meals with only the infusion of this fascinating plant; whose kettle has scarcely had time to cool; who with tea amuses the evening, with tea solaces the midnight, and with tea welcomes the morning."

Since the government duty on tea between 1711 and 1810 ranged from 12½ to 200 percent, it was almost inevitable that a lively smuggling industry would flourish. In fact, it has been estimated that during this time over half the tea drunk in Britain was contraband, spirited ashore along the rugged coasts of Cornwall, Dorset, Kent, and Hampshire, whose numerous lonely coves and inlets were ideal for the illicit trade. Most Englishmen did not regard smuggling as a crime, and customs officers were rather reluctant to board a ship full of pirates. When a ship loaded with contraband tea anchored off the coast, small fishing boats went out to meet it and bring the tea back to shore, where it was stored in caves before moving out through tunnels to be carried by pony trains to the retailers. Only when Parliament lowered the import duty enough to wipe out the smugglers' profits, did smuggling disappear.

Another problem caused by the artificially high tea prices generated by the British East India Company monopoly was that of adulteration. Entire forests were decimated for sawdust to be added to the tea. Willow, sloe, elder, and ash leaves were mixed with tea, along with gunpowder and used tea leaves. In this way the supply of extremely expensive Company tea was artificially expanded to meet the needs of a growing populace. Strict government controls plus increasing consumer awareness of what good tea should taste like finally put an end to this obnoxious practice.

In the third quarter of the eighteenth century the privileged anachronistic position of the British East India Company began to be challenged by dual winds of change blowing through the West: free trade and free government. The unfolding political drama had tea as its fulcrum and pitted an English Parliament dominated by conservative aristocrats—most of whom had substantial financial interests in the British East India Company— against the revolutionary politicians and angry merchants and farmers of the American colonies.

After the French and Indian Wars ended in 1763, the British government under George III felt the colonies should help pay the costs of the war, since it was fought for their benefit. The ill-conceived vehicle for this dubious concept was the Stamp Act of 1765, which taxed tea and numerous other commodities. A fury of protest arose on both sides of the Atlantic. Both the colonists, led by Patrick Henry of Virginia, and the Opposition in England, represented by William Pitt, challenged the right of the British Parliament to tax the American colonies without the consent of their assemblies.

The Government retreated and repealed the Act the following year. But in 1767 Parliament pased Townshend's Act, levying duties on paints, oils, lead, glass, and tea. The furious colonists responded with a complete boycott of British goods. To satisfy English merchants Parliament was forced in 1770 to repeal every tax but one—the threepenny tax on tea. The colonists countered by using tea smuggled from Holland. The stage was set for the final catastrophe.

The British East India Company was on the verge of financial disaster. Decades of fiscal mismanagement, inefficient business practices, and employee pilfering were taking their toll, and the flourishing smuggling was making inroads on Company profits. With 17,000,000 pounds of tea in British warehouses and more piling up every day, the desperate Company convinced Parliament to approve a package deal for their salvation which included a loan of £1,400,000 and passage of the Tea Act. This Act, which led to the Company's ultimate downfall, smacked so blatantly of favoritism and privilege that it enraged British merchants as well as the colonists. The British East India Company was to be allowed to ship tea duty-free directly to its own agents in America, who would pay the token tax themselves and sell the tea at a very cheap price to supposedly grateful colonists.

The colonists decided to fight against this violation of the principles of free trade and free government. The Sons of Liberty were formed and arms were cached against the inevitable day. On the evening of December 16th, 1773, at a meeting called to decide what to do about three ships loaded with the hated tea then anchored in Boston harbor, John Rowe asked, "Who knows how tea will mix with salt water?" This remark sparked the Boston Tea Party. Other tea parties followed, the British retaliated—and suddenly, the War of Independence had begun.

The British East India Company was staggered by the American Revolution, but it survived, buoyed up by favorable legislation and sheer size. But the close of the eighteenth century brought it another blow. Thirty thousand independent London tea dealers, led by Richard Twining, organized a campaign to expose the evils of the Company to the consuming public. The prospect of better tea for less money made them put pressure on Parliament and in 1813 the Company's India monopoly was ended. To redress the unfavorable balance of trade, the Company forced opium cultivated in India on an increasingly dismayed and weakened China, in return for silk and tea. Athough John Company's last remaining government-granted monopoly, the China trade, was finally abolished in 1834, the pernicious hold of the drug gave it continued power there, and the fact that they maintained the largest private army in history in India made the Company a strong force in India as well. The Indian Mutiny broke out in 1857–58 and in 1858 the British East India Company gave up its rule in India to the Crown.

The end of the British East India Company monopoly and repeal of the

Navigation Acts, which had required that all foreign goods bound for the colonies be shipped from English ports, meant that American ships could carry tea straight from China to England. This gave rise to the clipper ship era, one of the most exciting periods in the history of tea transportation. These ships, inspired by the speedy American privateers developed during the War of 1812, made the slow, bulky East Indiamen obsolete. Since the first tea shipment landed on the London docks commanded premium prices, shipowners awarded substantial cash prizes to the earliest ship in. Keen competition between American and British vessels led to the development by America's Donald McKay around 1850 of the extreme clipper and the memorable tea races of the 1850s and 1860s. In these clippers safety and stability were sacrificed to speed; the hulls, though built extremely slim and streamlined, were nevertheless expected to carry three masts and an enormous spread of canvas. These beautiful ships were true aristocrats of the ocean; they were, and still are, the fastest sailing ships known to man. It took the *Flying Cloud,* a Donald McKay ship, 89½ days to complete a run around the Horn to San Francisco. This record has never been equaled. Another McKay ship, *Lightning*, did 436 sea miles in 24 hours. This averages out to over 18 miles an hour, the record for a sailing vessel for all time and a speed matched by only a few modern steamships. The opening of the Suez Canal in 1869 gave the steamships an economic edge over the tea clippers and meant the gradual decline of these majestic vessels.

China was undergoing severe political trauma and becoming increasingly hostile to a West she felt was trampling her sovereignty in the greedy pursuit of trade. The Opium War between Britain and China (1839–42) in which the Chinese attempted to struggle free from the stranglehold of Western trade domination, climaxed a long dispute over the importation of opium, which China had declared illegal, but which Britain continued to ship. Chinese defeat resulted in the humiliating Treaty of Nanking in 1842. The opium trade was legalized, four new ports were opened to the British, Hong Kong was ceded to them, and China was forced to pay Britain a gigantic sum for confiscated opium, and grant Britain other concessions. The floodgates opened. America, France, and Russia joined Britain in carving up the Chinese empire, a bloody era that ended with popular uprisings, civil wars, and eventual establishment of a Communist regime on the mainland. It took China three and a half centuries to end the tyranny begun in 1600 by the British East India Company and other foreign merchants. China became completely alienated from the West and has only recently shown signs of friendliness that may one day result in a renewal of the enormous tea trade that once was. Since 1972 small amounts of tea have been imported from China to the United States.

By around 1850 tea was almost a part of the British character. Although John Company was responsible for the spread of tea in England, it was also the cause of most of the evils connected with the industry during this period. But tea had survived smuggling, adulteration, and excessive taxation. The British East India Company had lost its monopoly in China and the question was, "Where would the West get its tea next?"

THE DEMOCRATIZATION OF TEA CULTIVATION

The demise of the British East India Company around 1850 and the unreliability of China as a tea source moved tea from a restricted commodity manipulated by aristocrats for their private fortunes to a freely grown crop This democratization of tea cultivation was a triumph of the free enterprise system and the law of supply and demand over the anachronistic practices of the hong merchants and John Company. Adventurers, botanists, and businessmen opened up the jungles of Java, Sumatra, India, and Ceylon to create new tea sources for the West.

Two notable experiments in tea growing were conducted by European nations in roughly the first half of the nineteenth century: by the Dutch in Indonesia—the first country after China and Japan where tea was successfully cultivated—and by the English in India and Ceylon.

Tea was first grown in Java in 1684 by the German physician Andreas Cleyer. Having made a fortune in the smuggling trade he planted Japanese tea seeds in the gardens of his magnificent estate on the Tiger Canal at Batavia (now Djakarta). Cleyer was only interested in the ornamental effect, but he proved that tea could indeed be grown in Java. In 1728 the Lords 17, the Board of Directors of the Dutch East India Company, became interested in importing Chinese seeds and laborers to Java and starting a new colonial industry. This plan failed to bear tea because, instead of seriously implementing it, the Dutch dissipated their energy in trying to keep abreast of the British in the China trade. Essentially merchants and adventurers, not farmers, they preferred to sail rather than plant. Little happened in the way of tea cultivation for a century, except for some experimental growing of Japanese plants in Netherlands botanical gardens. Then in the 1820s the same liberal political climate that was to cause the demise of the British East India Company precipitated an extraordinary shake-up in its Dutch counterpart. A progressive group who favored opening up the colonies to private enterprise gained the upper hand in Parliament and the King and his Government, seeking to revitalize the failing colonial economy, decided to back the development of a privately operated tea industry in Java.

Jacobus Isidorus Lodewijk Levien Jacobson, the father of tea culture in Java, was appointed in 1827 to start the infant industry. Expert tea-taster, adventurer, writer of two pioneer technical books on tea (*Handbook for the Cultivation and Manufacture of Tea* and *About Sorting and Packing of Tea*), holder of the Cross of the Dutch Lion, this man, the Gabriel de Clieu of tea, almost singlehandedly founded the Java tea industry. In a trip to China in 1832, the culmination of six voyages, Jacobson brought back to Java, 7,000,000 seeds, fifteen workmen who knew the planting techniques, and a large amount of the necessary implements and materials. The Chinese government, increasingly disillusioned by their contacts with Europeans, watching their empire begin to disintegrate in part because of trade with the West, were infuriated that Jacobson should defy their order forbidding Europeans outside Canton and dare to flee the country with men and seeds. They put a price on his head and the mandarins, aided by Cantonese spies, attempted to capture and kill him. But he escaped, and by the middle of the century plantations started with Jacobson's seeds were spreading throughout Java.

Still, tea did not flourish in Java until after 1860, for two major reasons. The first was the reactionary system of government culture. The Dutch government, as owner of all the land, parceled it out in contracts to European planters, who employed native workers under feudal conditions. The workers were unhappy and tea, which thrives only under expert care, suffered in quality. The second reason was that the China seeds did not take to the Java soil and produced tea with a characteristic sharp "Java taste" that was unable to compete in world markets. The government, which had lost 6,000,000 florins on tea, turned its efforts to the booming coffee industry and let tea go completely to private ownership.

In the 1870s tea planters were at their wits' end. Faced with competition from the coffee growers on Java and the teas of China, Ceylon, and India, they teetered on the brink of commercial disaster. Then a combination of events saved them and launched Java into its golden age of tea. In 1878 John Peet introduced Assam tea seeds from India. These produced sturdy plants in tune with Java's soil, and grew first-rate leaves which made excellent tea. At the same time lands planted in coffee were ravaged by *Hemileia vastatrix*. Tea gardens that would produce tea as famous as Java coffee replaced the coffee plantations, and extended over the entire land. Success on Java enticed tea prospectors to try their luck on the nearby island of Sumatra, and soon the forest lands and *lalang*, or tall, wild grass fields of the larger island, were dotted with tea plantations.

John Albrecht von Mandelslo, in his *Travels Into the East Indies,* published in 1662, discussed tea as the beverage "used all over the Indies, not only among those of the country, but also among the Dutch and the English, who take it as a drug." Officers of the Dutch and British East India Companies cultivated shrubs grown from Chinese seeds ornamentally, and English naturalists grew experimental plants at the Botanical Gardens at Calcutta and Saharanpur. As early as 1788 Sir Joseph Banks, commissioned by the Court of Directors of the East India Company, recommended tea cultivation in India, but reactionary forces in the British East India Company, intent on preserving their monopoly, quashed the move. In 1823 Major Robert Bruce discovered wild tea plants growing all around the hills at Assam and arranged for a collection of plants and seeds to be delivered to his brother, C. A. Bruce, who planted these in his garden at Sadiya in 1825.

In spite of these indubitable proofs that tea could be cultivated in India, the John Company was strong enough to block the natural outcome of these experiments in order to protect what it believed to be its best interests. It turned out that Indian tea was to dominate the world's markets, replace China as the major supplier, and become one of the greatest sources of private wealth and government taxes in the British Empire. But by that time the John Company would be out of the picture. As things turned out, it was only in 1834, when the Company lost its China monopoly, that it gave serious consideration to growing tea in India. Even tea not under its strict control was better than no tea at all, and indeed, they lost control.

After 1834 the English tea mechants gained increasing power with the Crown because of the growing demand for tea at reasonable prices—a demand which the British East India Company could not or would not meet; the Company wanted to keep prices artificially high. John Company was in administrative control of India until 1858, and therefore governed India during the forming of the new tea industry in the mid-1830s, but private merchants, backed by a sympathetic Government, were taking control of the infant industry. The Bentinck Commission of 1834 was formed because Mr. Walker, a London tea man, echoed the sentiments of the industry when he expressed concern "that some better guarantee should be provided for the supply of tea than that already furnished by the toleration of the Chinese Government."

Lord William Charles Cavendish Bentinck, Governor-General of India from 1828–35, appointed a Tea Committee to survey the situation thoroughly. His reputation—he was a hero of many campaigns against the French and Italians, he had abolished *suttee* (the custom where Hindu widows threw themselves on their husbands' blazing funeral pyre), and put down *thugee,* or ritual murder—lent a special importance to the new tea venture. The scientists, explorers, and merchants on the Committee voted overwhelmingly in favor of starting a tea industry in India, but they made the same blunder that planters in Java and Ceylon made. Instead of working with shrubs growing wild in the area, they went thousands of miles away to China, for seeds ill-suited to the Indian climate.

Tea had been intimately connected with the religion, art, and culture of China for thousands of years; the Chinese regarded it as a gift of the gods. Whether or not it was simple botany that caused the failure of Chinese seeds outside the country of their birth will always be a mystery. A strange and supernatural force seemed to be at work destroying the Europeans' attempts to duplicate the sacred beverage. Some say the Chinese boiled the seeds before selling them to foreigners. Yet seeds and plants shipped in good condition often arrived moldy, diseased, or dead, and even if the seeds were good and did survive, the tea grown from them was never the same as in China.

While some tea from the China plants was produced, it was not until the pioneer work of C. A. Bruce, who worked for the Crown as Superintendent of Government Tea Forests, toward the middle of the nineteenth century, that Indian tea cultivation received the thrust that was to make India the strongest tea nation in the world. Bruce was an adventurer whose life was punctuated with military and naval campaigns against the French, a term as their prisoner, and a series of actions against native uprisings. After the Burma War Bruce found himself stationed in Assam. Essentially an explorer rather than a scientist or bontanist, Bruce possessed a formidable knowledge of hundreds of miles of trackless jungles, the climate, and often hostile tribesmen. He knew where hundreds of wild tea trees grew and, through the force of his personality, actually persuaded native chieftans to help him find others. He reclaimed wild tea colonies from the jungle and pruned them to bear rich growths of tea. He grew cuttings in the shade, withered the leaf in the sun, had his native laborers roll it by hand, and dried it over charcoal fires.

When C. A. Bruce proved high-quality tea could successfully be cultivated in India, the Government stopped its support of experimental tea estates and allowed private merchants to step in. Tea capitalists in Calcutta formed the Bengal Tea Company in 1839 and their counterparts in London formed a joint stock company. The motive of the two companies was identical; they wanted to purchase the British East India Company's estates and cultivate tea in Assam. By 1846 John Company had been taken over by the Assam Company, the new organization formed when the London and Calcutta tea men merged.

The first shipments of native Indian tea from Bruce arrived in London in 1838 and caused a sensation. Established merchants like W. J. & H. Thompson, Joseph Travers & Sons, and the Messrs. Twining were amazed at its quality and predicted a bright future for the infant industry. The British Government stepped out of the picture and private growers formed the Assam Company. This prototype survived labor problems, cholera, and fiscal mismanagement to become, once its original Chinese plants were replaced by the native variety, the finest example of a tea-growing company in India. Its success and enormous profits soon led to the formation of other companies, and—after the speculative excesses of the tea mania of the 1860s, which saw worthless jungle tracts bought up at outrageously inflated prices by an ignorant public—Indian tea finally came into its own, almost a century after its serious cultivation was recommended by Sir Joseph Banks.

After the 1860s many British families and individuals opened up tea estates; these were followed by limited-liability companies. The industry was given impetus by the invention in the 1880s of William Jackson's rolling machines and Sir Samuel C. Davidson's tea driers. The Indian Tea Association was formed in Calcutta in 1881 to further the interests of all persons involved in Indian tea cultivation. The current counterpart for Indian-owned estates is the Indian Tea Planters Association in Jalpaiguri. Now 60 percent of tea estates are owned by Indians and 40 percent by foreigners, mainly British. These agencies act to control labor recruitment, promote home and foreign markets, encourage scientific research, and regulate tea exports so that supply and demand are balanced.

In 1903 the Indian Tea Association requested that the Tea Cess Act be passed. This act, and subsequent renewals in 1923 and 1933, set aside a small percentage of tea profits to be used to develop foreign markets for Indian tea. As a partial result of this propaganda campaign, sales to America, Europe, and Africa have increased more than tenfold since 1915, and tea drinking in India itself has increased. As of around 1960 per capita consumption of tea in India was three-quarters of a pound per annum, or the same as the United States. By comparison the United Kingdom had a per capita consumption of ten pounds per annum. Today 440,000,000 pounds of Indian tea is consumed each year by 575,000,000 Indians. Internal tea consumption is increasing by 6 percent, or 30 million pounds, per year.

The International Tea Regulation Scheme was entered into by the three major exporting countries—India, Ceylon and the Netherlands East Indies—when a serious slump in tea prices occurred in 1933. The newer tea-producing countries in Africa eventually joined the scheme, and the agreements were extended until 1955.

Since World War II tea yields in India have increased from around 480 pounds of tea per worker to close to 700 pounds, due to improved health of the labor force, scientific planting procedures, and improved fertilizing techniques. Estate yields have reached from 1,200 to 1,600 pounds of tea per acre.

Tea history in Ceylon is connected, like tea in Java, to a declining coffee industry. The first European coffee estate was established in 1824 by Governor Sir Edward Barnes. Others followed, and for the next half-century huge tracts were carved out of the jungles and transformed into cultivated forests of young coffee trees. Then disaster struck in 1877. On the undersides of the leaves appeared the orange-red blots of the dread coffee disease *Hemileia vastatrix:* fast-spreading and incurable. Planters stood by helplessly as the blight spread over their plantations; most of them left for the nearby Malay States, which were just opening up to Westerners. In a strangely surreal yet prophetic gesture, dead coffee trees were stripped and exported to England to make legs for tea tables.

The ruined planters who remained, some of them too poor to buy seeds, settled down with that pluck characteristic of British colonists, determined to turn the shambles around to their advantage. They scraped up enough money to buy tea seeds and planted them in the dead coffee rows. By the end of the 1870s tea in Ceylon was an established commercial success, producing some of the finest teas in the world.

The success of these pioneer tea growers outside China assured the Western tea-drinking world of today—mainly England, Ireland, Scotland, Canada, Australia, and the United States—of a plentiful supply of top-grade, relatively inexpensive, fine-tasting teas.

2. How Tea Is Grown

WE CALL a civilized man cultured and a cultured one cultivated. To transform what is primitive in us through the artifacts of culture is the great human task. The hunt becomes the novel, emotion becomes music, joy poetry, terror faith, chaos order. Shaping things is man's destiny. As character ripens in the slow pastures of time, man reinforces this process of the soul by turning his hand to the physical world around him.

Cultivation of domestic crops was the literal and figurative beginning of civilization. The controlled food supply which replaced wild animals and plants ended nomadic wandering, and the eventual surplus created by improved husbandry gave man the. leisure to think, instead of spending his life ceaselessly hunting for food. He thought of religion, art, science, and politics. He even thought of domesticating wild tea.

The cultivation of tea plays a special role as a metaphor for civilization. A contemporary of grain and cabbage at the beginning of written history, tea was cultivated for pleasure, not nourishment. Impractical as fuel for the body, tea was grown on precious bits of land diverted from life-giving crops, as a sign that man would no longer be driven by necessity alone. He would flower, as the plants he cared for, by transforming the world to match his elegant dreams, by refusing to accept the brutal reality of the savage.

THE CULTIVATION OF TEA

When boiling water is poured over tea leaves in a cup, the end of the long, complex process of tea growth and manufacture has finally been reached. The leaves unfold and their flavor, tannins, and caffeine are released. Tea men call this "the agony of the leaves." But in truth the agony begins long before the leaves undergo their last chemical transformation from dried plant to delicious beverage. Every step in the growth of tea is laden with difficulty. The tea plant is most prolific only in a jungle atmosphere of continual heat and humidity; but in any given region the finest tea is grown at over 5,000 ft. above sea level, where extremity of climate is traded for extremity of altitude. The coolness of the heights causes the plant to grow more slowly, producing a richer, more complex leaf—but an excess of cold will turn the leaves black on the bush. Severe pruning is another necessary agony. Left to itself tea would grow thirty feet high, but to channel the vital forces of the plant into creating flavorful leaves the bush is kept at one-tenth its natural height.

The tea plant, originally designated *Thea sinensis* in 1753 but now called *Camellia sinensis,* is a flowering evergreen shrub. The mature leaves are elliptical with serrated edges, dark green, smooth, of a leathery texture, and from one to twelve inches in length. The best tea comes from the tiny young shoots and their thin, unopened buds. The round blossoms, not used in the beverage, are white and fragrant, about one inch in diameter with from five to seven petals. The seeds are smooth dark brown spheres, about one-half inch in diameter.

All tea comes from local variants of this plant caused by differing conditions in the tea-growing countries. The differences in types of tea arise not from any diversity in species but from where it is grown, when and how it is plucked, and what is done to the leaf after it is plucked—in other words, the process of tea manufacture. By exposing the leaves to varying degrees of evaporation, twisting, oxidation, and heat the three great tea classifications—black, or fermented tea, green, or unfermented tea, and oolong, or semi-fermented tea—are created.

Tea can grow nearly everywhere, but it is produced commercially only in the tropical and subtropical regions of the world. The leading countries of production are China, Japan, Taiwan, Indonesia, India, and Sri Lanka (Ceylon). Tea is also grown in other parts of Asia, Africa, the U.S.S.R., and South America.

Here in the United States several attempts have been made to establish tea-growing as a commercial enterprise. The first effort was started in 1775 by a French botanist, André Michaux, near Charleston, South Carolina. Because it was necessary for him to return to France, this experiment was discontinued, and not until 1848, when a Dr. Julius Smith started a plantation in the same area, was there a second attempt, also a failure because of his death in 1852. In 1858 the U.S. government became interested in tea growing, and sent horticulturist Robert Fortune to China for seeds, which were distributed free among planters of the southern states. A number of bushes were raised in the Carolinas, Georgia, Florida, Louisiana, and Tennessee, but no commercial production was attained. From 1890 on several unsuccessful attempts were made, the last about 1920. It is our belief that the comparatively high cost of labor and land will preclude additional experiments.

For luxuriant leaf growth an average annual rainfall of at least 100 inches is required. Long dry spells or insufficient rain will sap the strength of the bush, making it prey to disease. A hot temperature (around 85° F.) is necessary for heavy growth. Rich loamy soil is generally best for growing tea. However, tea can and does thrive in almost any type of soil. Tea can be found growing on plains and on hillsides, in sandy soil or clay. The optimum earth for tea is a light, deep loam, well drained and with an abundance of plant nutrients. An acid soil well supplied with nitrogen meets the ideal mineral requirements of the tea plant.

Methods of preparing the land to grow tea vary according to the topography and customs of the producing country. In the jungles of Sri Lanka, Java, and Sumatra, undergrowth is hacked and burnt out first; then heavy trees are felled and either burned or removed, often with the aid of elephants. Grassland is merely burned off. When the land has been surveyed for drainage, roads, and building and nursery sites, the actual planting layout is considered. Tea may be planted most efficiently in hot, moist plains areas, usually in squares or equilateral triangles containing from 3,000 to 4,000 bushes per acre. The leaf yield is higher on this type of estate, but the tea is generally not distinguished in flavor. Tea grown on the slopes and hillsides of higher altitudes must be terraced or contour-planted to conform to the terrain. This land is more difficult to pick, and the yield is less because the growing season is usually shorter due to a cooler climate. Consequently high-grown teas generally cost more, but are renowned for having the finest flavors.

A contrast to the large estates of India, Sri Lanka, Java, and Sumatra are the tea gardens of China and Japan. Most tea in these countries is grown on small holdings, bits of waste land unsuitable for more important crops like rice. The bulk of Chinese and Japanese tea is produced for consumption within the country itself; large-scale operations necessary for a profitable export trade are not as important. If tea prices fall too low, the Chinese farmer picks what he needs for himself and ignores his bushes until prices rise again.

While the land is being prepared, nurseries are started so that the young tea plants can be planted when they are about fifteen months old. Seeds are dropped in water to test their germination potential. The dried or partly empty ones float and are discarded; the heavy "sinkers" are used. They are carefully nurtured in well fertilized, shaded nursery beds until ready for transplanting to pre-dug holes in the garden or estate. Only the Japanese do not follow this procedure, but plant seed directly in the field. In recent years interest has grown in vegetative propagation, or growing bushes from cuttings or grafting. High-yield, disease-resistant strains may be more exactly duplicated using this method. In Taiwan planters use the grafting method extensively, to prevent hybridization.

Low-grown tea bushes in the plains start producing in about two and a half years, and are fully developed in another few years. High-grown hill bushes sometimes take ten years to mature because of the seasonal changes and cooler climate. Once a bush matures, though, it may produce for as many as sixty years.

Any tea plant, and especially a young tea plant, must be carefully tended to give good tea. After planting machines keep the soil between the rows free of weeds and men with hoes clear the area at the base of the bush. After several years the wide, flat-topped shape of the bush itself is enough to prevent weeds from growing directly underneath it. Where weeding threatens the loss of top soil, leguminous ground covers are used.

Tea grown in a shaded area is always better than unshaded tea, and shade trees are planted among tea bushes for this reason. Despite the fact that they compete with the tea for food and water in the soil, their advantages far outweigh these disadvantages. The trees curtail high-growing grasses, aerate the soil, and protect the tea from scorching by the sun. In addition the falling twigs and foliage of the trees deliberately selected for shade enrich the soil with nitrogen, essential to the production of leaf crops. Extensive organic and chemical manuring supplies additional nitrogen plus two other essentials for tea cultivation: potash and phosphoric acid.

A variety of insect pests may attack the tea bush through the sap in the young leaves, by webbing clumps of leaves together, or by boring holes in the branches. Vegetable parasites or blights can attack the plant through its leaves, stems, or roots. Fortunately none of these is too serious. Since it is usually weak and flimsy bushes that are attacked, disease can be cured or prevented by rigorous, careful cultivation and manuring.

Pruning, the single most important aspect of cultivation, is what distinguishes domestic from wild tea. Unpruned, or uncut, the tea plant would become a sizable tree with many large, tough leaves quite unsuitable for making the beverage. Cutting the shrub back with a specially designed, sharply curved knife every few years, depending on climate and country, is essential for two reasons. By maintaining the bush at a height of around three feet it is more easily picked. And, more important, pruning stimulates the growth of "flush," or the tender young leaves from which tea is made.

Without intervention by man the tea plant would follow a natural and, for the purposes of tea drinking, unproductive pattern. As the plant grew older it would stop yielding flush, or new leaves, the sap passages would become partially blocked, the wood would harden, the leaves would grow, and the bush would produce seed. In short, it would become a tree. Removing the excess foliage and overmatured wood by pruning signals the plant to produce more young leaves. Constant plucking has the same effect to a lesser degree: that of maintaining the tea shrub in the artificial state of a perpetual leaf-producer.

PLUCKING THE LEAVES

All crop cultivation has one aim: the harvest. For tea this process, known as plucking, comes when the mature bush sends forth its fresh, green and tender new leaves and unopened buds. Plucking is a skilled and intricate task that has traditionally been done by women. In recent years some attempts have been made at mechanical plucking but it remains to be seen whether machines can take over this operation.

An even pluck is of prime importance in the making of high quality tea. The leaves must be the same size so that when they are withered, an evaporating process in tea manufacture, they dry uniformly. When the pluck is uneven the finer shoots wither faster than the coarser ones and poor tea is the result.

When the flush is ready to be plucked the tea grower must make an economic decision which will directly affect the quality of the tea. He must decide whether he wants a large quantity of ordinary tea or a small amount of good to fine tea. Since the best tea is produced from the youngest, most delicate leaves of the flush his judgment will be one of pluck.

The three types of pluck are "normal," "fine," and "coarse," depending on how many leaves are taken from the bush and how long the flush is permitted to grow between rounds of plucking. Normal plucking consists of two leaves and the bud and produces average to good tea. In fine plucking fewer leaves than normal are plucked, producing superior quality tea. Coarse plucking includes an extra leaf or leaves and produces poor to average tea. "Young leaf" is the result of finer pluckings, "old leaf," left longer on the bush, is harvested in the coarser pluckings. All plucked leaf is called "natural" or "fresh" leaf.

Plucking time varies from country to country according to periods of flushing, which in turn depends upon climate and altitude. Tea grown near the equator in southern India, Sri Lanka, Java, and Sumatra, where there is no cold season, flushes all year and may be plucked every seven or eight days. South India produces its highest grade tea in December and January. The finest Sri Lanka (Ceylon) tea comes from the February, March, August, and September pluckings. In Java the best tea is generally plucked from June through September. In Sumatra the tea is of uniform quality throughout the year. In north India, China, Japan, and Taiwan the growing season lasts roughly from April to late autumn and there are only four or five flushes. The first and second flushes produce exceptional tea in these countries, but the quality decreases with each successive flush and the coarse, old leaves of the final crops are rarely exported.

It is important for the consumer to remember those aspects of cultivation that are usually most directly associated with superior quality tea: good soil and water supply, high elevation, young leaves or fine pluck, and a favorable plucking season. The name of a tea will identify the country it comes from and the tea district within that country. Regions famous for producing tea with any or all of the above desirable qualities should be high on the list of those seeking the finest teas.

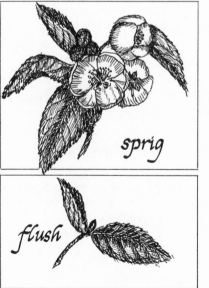

sprig

flush

3. Making the Leaf:
The Manufacture Process

TEA IS BORN on the bush but must be made in the factory. While most herbals need only be dried, the tea of commerce must be transformed. Newly plucked leaves, called "natural leaf" or "fresh leaf," are transported to factory by oxen, donkey, or truck, by aerial ropeway, or on the heads of laborers. In the places where tea is grown there is an aphorism which says, "manufacture starts in the field." Fresh leaf is the raw material of tea manufacture and finished tea the raw material of tea brewing. The quality of our cup depends on the quality and condition of the fresh leaf as it reaches the factory. Only if the right leaves have been plucked, if the extraneous matter has been removed from them, if they were transported quickly and if they were not bruised, can manufacture have the best results. The processes of tea manufacture, by inducing physical and/or chemical changes in the leaf, produce the three major types of "finished tea": Green tea which is unfermented, oolong tea which is semi-fermented, and black tea which is fully fermented.

An infusion of fresh leaf would be harsh, raw, and thin, its flavor as different from that of green tea as the flavor of maple sap is different from that of maple sugar. An infusion of fresh leaf would resemble not at all the brew we get from steeping any of the fermented teas. It is the primary aim of all tea manufacture to establish the character of the finished tea, the dry leaf, by controlling the degree to which the leaves undergo fermentation. Fermentation oxidizes the leaves and changes their chemistry. In green tea manufacture, fermentation is prevented, the constituents of the natural leaf are mostly conserved, and the character of the finished tea largely reflects that of the leaf from which it is made. In oolong manufacture, partial fermentation results in the development of some essential oil, while some of the naturally occurring oils and tannins remain unchanged. Fully fermented black tea has the highest concentration of essential oil and least resembles the natural leaf.

Tea manufacture must not only change the leaf but also stabilize those changes so that the finished leaf will not spoil. To preserve the character of finished tea until brewing releases into the cup that balance of flavor, aroma, and stimulation created in manufacture, the leaves are thoroughly dried. Drying is accomplished by "withering," and/or "rolling" and "firing," depending whether fermented or unfermented tea is being made. Rolling not only facilitates the drying of the leaves but imparts to them their characteristic twist. The twist of the finished leaf determines the rate at which it will infuse when brewed. So manufacture not only establishes the character of finished tea, but shapes the finished leaf and provides the code by which the delightful attributes of tea are released into the brew in pleasing proportions.

For the spirit of tea we look East, where tea has long been not only a beverage, but a philosophy and an art. The tea leaves that we brew are the embodiment of eternal change. Experience tea and experience the ever-changing universe. In the manufacture of tea, we see changes both passive and active, positive and negative. In the finished leaf, change is in equilibrium.

Lu Yu provided this ancient prescription for manipulating tea: It is: steamed, pounded, patted, baked, packed, and re-packed. Centuries later and centuries ago, the first commercial manufacture of tea was begun in China. A look at the old ways evokes in us a feeling of respect for the time, patience, and skill that traditional tea manufacture required.

The leaves were spread about five or six inches thick on bamboo trays in a well ventilated place. They were attended by a workman or *ching fu* from noon until six o'clock, when they began to exhibit an apple-like fragrance. They were then poured into large bamboo trays and hand tossed 300–400 times. Called *to ching*, this operation resulted in oxidation of the leaves and turned their edges red. This slightly fermented leaf was then carried to the *Kuo*, a shallow iron pan let into the top of a brick stove. The leaf was roasted there and afterward poured onto flat trays to be rolled. The workman manipulated the leaves into twisted shapes by rolling them with his hands against the tray. Thoroughly rolled leaf required that he work his way around the tray at least 300–400 times. Again the leaves were carried to the *Kuo* and again they were roasted and rolled. This process of rolling and roasting was repeated a third time. With each rolling fermentation proceeded a little bit more; with each roasting fermentation was checked. The leaves were then conveyed to the *poey long* (the fire fierce), and turned continually until they were 80 percent dried. Old yellow leaves and stalks were picked out. The leaves were "poeyed" again over a slow fire, turned once, and packed in chests.

Tea manufacture has since been much mechanized and streamlined. Not all the procedures have direct parallels in modern methods, but if the process is less painstaking, it does not require less care and skill.

BLACK TEA

The steps in black or fully fermented tea manufacture are as follows: withering, rolling, roll breaking, fermentation, and firing. During the withering or drying process much of the moisture content of the tea leaves evaporates, causing them to become flaccid and pliable and ready to be rolled. Leaf not made flaccid would be torn rather than crushed in rolling. Also, the loss of water means a higher concentration of cell sap and a more controllable fermentation. Withering is accomplished by spreading the leaves thinly and evenly on racks made of stretched cloth or wire mesh where they remain for from eighteen to twenty-four hours. In India the relatively dry climate makes a natural wither, the free passage of fresh air over the racks, possible. In the more humid atmosphere of Sri Lanka, Java, and Sumatra, controlled withering, or the blowing of heated air over the racks, is practiced. The natural wither is preferred because it never results in local overheating of the leaf. Black, well twisted leaf indicates a good wither.

Rolling is bruising and crushing the tea leaves in order to break up the plant's cells and release the juices and enzymes locked inside, which produce tea's flavor. The rolling process takes from one to three hours. The tea is fed into a circular brass table from an open-bottomed round box which rotates under pressure, crushing the tea against the top of the box and the sides and surface of the table. Oxidation starts, heat is generated, and the juices remaining on the leaves start the development of the essential oil of tea, important in taste and aroma. During rolling the leaves receive their characteristic twist. When you brew tea some components of the leaf will infuse more quickly than others. Well twisted leaf affects the rates of infusion so that a balanced cup is obtained and flavor and pungency complement one another. Flat, open leaf produces a brew with less flavor and more pungency.

Tea that is being rolled forms twisted lumps or balls which must be broken up afterward to allow for even fermentation. This is done on the roll-breakers, vibrating wire sieves that separate the clumps back into individual leaves.

Fermentation is the process during which the crushed and bruised leaves develop the chemistry of finished tea. Fermentation is begun in the rolling machines and will continue until the tea is fired. The leaves are spread thinly on a cement, glass, or tile floor for several hours until they turn a bright copper color. The oxidation that takes place during fermentation is largely responsible for the flavor, strength, body, and color of black tea. These characteristics are in turn determined by chemical changes in the tea tannin and the development of the essential oil. Tannin in its natural state is colorless and pungent to the taste, but the longer it ferments the more color it develops and the less pungent it becomes. A more pungent tea liquor will result from a shorter fermentation, and a more flavorful liquor with deeper color is produced by a longer fermentation. Black tea is generally manufactured so as to bring out either its pungency (astringency) or its flavor, so it is usual that only one of these characteristics will predominate in a particular tea. A tea with some marked quality, *i.e.*, flavor or pungency, has a better market value than one that is a compromise between the two.

When fermentation is considered sufficient, the tea is fired—exposed to a blast of hot, dry air. Firing stops further oxidation by destroying the enzymes and bacteria which take part in the fermenting process. The hot air passes through an enclosed iron chamber through which the tea travels in trays. Careful regulation of temperature and the rate at which the tea goes through the dryer insures that all the leaves are evenly and thoroughly dried. If tea is fired too quickly it becomes case-hardened and the center of the leaf remains moist. This tea will lose quality or even go moldy. If the firing temperature is too high, the tea will produce flat rather than sparkling brews. Under-firing produces a stewed or over-fermented leaf which in turn will yield a flat liquor. Black tea is packed with a residual moisture content of 7 percent which results in post-fermentation and insures that the "finished" tea will mature. If more than 7 percent moisture remains after the final firing, the tea will spoil. If less, the tea will not mature.

When the fired tea leaves come from the drier, large and small, broken and unbroken leaves are mixed together. Since there is no market for ungraded (unsized) tea—tea that is a mixture of different sized leaves—the leaves are sifted through a succession of sieves with gradually smaller holes to determine their grade. Unsized tea cannot be sold because it is unreliable.

The smaller leaves would sift out in packets or consumers' caddies and the different sized leaves would infuse at different rates. Measurements of ungraded tea would also be inconsistent, since a given volume of smaller leaf will be heavier than the same volume of large leaf tea; measured packages of differently sized leaves would weigh different amounts even though the packages were the same size. A tea blender attempting to use unsized tea would have to constantly deal with possible separations, inconsistencies, unpredictable behavior and constant variation from batch to batch.

It is important to remember that black tea is graded by size alone, and that no grade is indicative of any particular flavor or quality. But it is true that the larger grades are susceptible to more complete scrutiny. It is easier to identify qualities such as wither, fermentation, and firing in large-leaf tea and more difficult in small-leaf tea.

Black tea is divided into leaf grades and broken grades. The leaf grades consist of the larger leaves left at the top of the sifting process. Flavor and color generally come out more slowly in leaf grades than in broken grades. The broken grades, which make up approximately 80 percent of the crop, are made up of broken and smaller leaves. They generally make a darker, stronger tea and are essential in the production of tea bags.

The leaf grades are as follows: Orange Pekoe is long, thin, well defined, closely twisted wiry leaves which sometimes contain yellow tip or bud leaf. The liquors are light or pale in color. Pekoe consists of small, tightly rolled leaf and some more open leaf. It is not so wiry as orange pekoe, but the liquors generally have more color. Souchong is the largest and coarsest leaf picked, with pale liquors.

The broken grades are: Broken Orange Pekoe, much smaller than any of the leaf grades and usually containing yellow tip. The liquors have good color and strength in the cup and are often used as the mainstay of a blend. Broken Pekoe is slightly larger than Broken Orange Pekoe, with rather less color in the cup; useful as a filler in a blend. Broken Pekoe Souchong is a little larger or bolder than Broken Pekoe and in consequence lighter in the cup; also used as a filler. Fannings are much smaller than Broken Orange Pekoe. Their main virtues are quick brewing with good color in the cup. Dust is the name for the smallest grade produced. Very useful for a quick brewing, strong cup of tea; used only in blends of similar sized leaf, generally for catering purposes.

The above classifications are for the black teas of India and Sri Lanka. In China, Java, and Sumatra the gradings for black tea are the same but with these additions: China has a grade called Flowery Pekoe, and Java and Sumatra one called Flowery Orange Pekoe. These indicate the presence of tips, very young tea leaves which turn light-colored when fermented and fired. Tips may or may not signify superior quality tea. In Java and Sumatra there is also a grade called Bohea, which consists of stalks and is not generally exported.

GREEN TEA

Green tea is produced mainly in China, Japan and Taiwan and in lesser amounts in India. The goal of green tea manufacture is to produce unfermented tea; therefore the leaves are not withered, since withering would contribute to fermentation. Instead, the leaves undergo three principal manufacturing processes: steaming, rolling, and firing. These processes work together to preserve, concentrate, and make accessible to the brew the naturally present oils and tannins of the tea. Physical changes are induced while chemical change is prevented. Steaming the leaves immediately after they have been picked softens them for rolling and, more importantly, the heat (over 160° F.) inactivates the enzymes and prevents fermentation. Steaming insures against the oxidation of leaf juices that in black tea manufacture produces the essential oil. The leaves are then both rolled and dried (fired) again and again until they are crisp. The repeated rollings liberate the juices which will be held within the finished leaf and which give tea its flavor. Rolling imparts to the leaves their characteristic twist.

Because the leaves are not withered in green tea manufacture they contain all their moisture until fired. As the leaves are alternately rolled and fired, water is expressed and evaporated. Only gradual drying achieved by repeated firings can produce a stable, thoroughly dried product, tea that is not case-hardened and will not spoil. (If the tea were permitted to dry out slowly, as are many herbals, unwanted fermentation would occur, and the result would not be green tea.) After firing, the tea leaves remain green in color. Green tea is packed with only 3 percent residual moisture so that the finished tea will not undergo any further change.

Green teas are usually graded according to the age and style of the leaf. Unlike black tea, there will be a connection between grade and quality. Green tea from China is classified in the following manner: Gunpowder is tiny balls made from rolled young or medium-aged leaves. Young Hyson is long, thinly rolled and twisted young or medium-aged leaves. Imperial is the loosely balled remains of Gunpowder made from older leaves. Hyson is old leaves formed in a style that is a mixture of Young Hyson and Imperial. Twankay is an old, open leaf of poor quality. Hyson Skin is even poorer. Dust is whatever is left.

Green tea from Japan is classified according to methods of manufacture and leaf style in the following ways: Pan-fired or straight leaf; Guri, or curled leaf; Basket-fired; and natural leaf. The quality gradings are: Extra Choicest, Choicest, Choice, Finest, Fine, Good Medium, Good Common, Nibs, Fannings, and Dust.

Green Indian tea is graded as follows: Fine Young Hyson, Young Hyson, Hyson No. 1, Twankay, Sowmee, Fannings, and Dust.

OOLONG TEA

Oolong tea may be said to represent a marriage of the qualities of black and green tea as it is only partially or semi-fermented. It is coaxed to perfection by being slightly withered, fermented, fired, rolled, briefly fermented again, fired again, and finally re-fired before packaging. Almost all oolong tea comes from Taiwan (Formosa). Pouchong is oolong tea mixed with highly perfumed blossoms of the gardenia or jasmine flower. Formosa Oolong is graded on a straight quality basis: Choice, Finest to Choice, Finest, Fine to Finest, Fine up, Fine, On Fine, Superior to Fine, Superior Up, Fully Superior, Superior, On Superior, Good to Superior, Good Up, Fully Good, Good, On Good, and Standard.

BY-PRODUCTS

There are several "exotic" by-products of the tea-manufacturing process. Brick tea is made in China for use in Tibet and Russia. Leftovers from high-grade tea—old leaves, stems, and twigs—are steamed and forced under hydraulic pressure into flat bricks weighing from two to four pounds. Black and green tea is used, and to brew it a small amount is shaved from the slab, ground up and combined with boiling water.

Tablet tea is pill-sized wafers of fine quality tea pulverized and formed into small tablets under pressure. Sold in handy tin boxes, these tablets are popular with backpackers and travelers.

Cake tea is made in China from bitter leaves which are steamed and formed into circular cakes eight inches in diameter. It has a reputation for easing digestion while stimulating the nervous system. Cake tea is the oldest form of tea manufacture and was mentioned by Lu Yu in 780 A.D.

Tea fluff is the residue of fiber, dust, and leaf hair that collects on the sorting machines in tea factories. Collected and sold, it is a source of commercial caffeine.

PACKING AND SHIPPING

We now come to the last lap of tea's journey from bush to cup. After grading, tea is packed for shipment in chests. holding from 80 to 130 pounds, and half chests holding from 50 to 90 pounds, depending on leaf size. The chests are made of plywood and lined with aluminum foil to keep moisture out. Tea in chests moves by rail or truck to port.

World tea production totals about 2,130,000,000 pounds annually. India and Sri Lanka produce about half of this in equal amounts. The balance comes out of China, Indonesia, East Africa, Taiwan (Formosa), Japan; small amounts come from Argentina, Turkey, Brazil, and other countries.

The most important tea-shipping centers in the producing countries are Calcutta and Cochin in India; Colombo and Trincomalee in Sri Lanka, Djakarta (formerly called Batavia) in Java, Medan in Sumatra; Shimizu and Shizuoka in Japan; Shanghai, Foochow, and Canton in China; Keelung and Taihoko in Taiwan, and Nairobi in Kenya.

These tea centers conduct public auctions where astute buyers must be familiar with the districts each tea comes from, manufacturing techniques used, characteristics of each tea, how they will fit into various blends, and the exact price they are willing to pay. In order to bid intelligently on the teas, buyers test for purity and quality.

Amsterdam, Hamburg, and London are the only European cities that conduct public auctions; London, because of the great variety of teas that it handles and the high rate of tea consumption in Great Britain, virtually sets the world price of tea. Tea coming into consuming countries such as the United States, Canada, South Africa, New Zealand, and Australia is purchased directly from the producing country, at Amsterdam or London at auction, or by direct arrangement with an agent.

4. Varieties of Tea

GOOD TEA IS A BARGAIN

FOR MOST Americans, tea drinking means using tea bags. To what extent is our experience of tea limited by the tea bag and by the scarcity of alternatives? Is it true, as many advertisers claim or imply, that what is most widely used is also most desirable? Or would tea drinking be more satisfying if the tea were let out of the bag?

Lu Tung, a Chinese poet of the eighth century, wrote these words about tea:

> The first cup moistens my lips and throat, the second cup breaks my loneliness, the third cup searches my barren entrails but to find therein some five thousand volumes of odd ideographs. The fourth cup raises a slight perspiration—all the wrong of life passes through my pores. At the fifth cup I am purified; the sixth calls me up to the realm of immortals . . . Let me ride on this sweet breeze and waft away thither.

More than a thousand years later, the American consumer finds himself hard pressed to find a tea that could inspire such feelings. The supermarket shopper, in selecting his box of tea bags, is forced to choose between the mediocre and the vile. Perhaps he's picked the brand on sale or the store's own brand, which always sells for a few cents less than those of the major packers. Perhaps the choice has been based on a clever and heavily financed advertising campaign. The decision is very likely based not at all on the quality of the tea since, "tea is after all . . . tea." Isn't it?

The offerings of almost all major tea packers are blends of perhaps fifteen to twenty teas. This fact is not evidence of exotica (advertisers have tried to get some mileage out of it) but rather is dictated by the exigencies of mass production and mass marketing. The large packer is selling a particular "flavor" and, for the sake of consistency, that "flavor" must be composed of many flavors; he covers his bets. If certain components of his blend should become unavailable due to changes in climate (or price!), he can make substitutions without detection. The customer may not have been won by the excellence of the blend, but he would probably be lost by a marked deviation from it. Already denied the ecstacies of Lu Tung, the consumer might revolt at being denied the particular brand of mediocrity to which he's accustomed. Or so, at any rate, think the people who mass market tea.

The shopper is told that a special blend of Pekoe and Orange Pekoe teas has been created especially for his tea-drinking pleasure. That sounds pretty good, doesn't it? Well, it's just about completely meaningless, if not viciously misleading. Pekoe and Orange Pekoe refer only to the size or cut of the leaf. They in no way describe a tea's point of origin or its degree of fermentation, the two most imporatnt indices of flavor. Marketing teas this way is like marketing cheeses as sliced, unsliced, and thin sliced, without any reference to whether they are cheddars or bries, sharps or milds, domestics or imports. Thousands of years ago, the term Pekoe (white-haired) was applied by the Chinese to those teas which showed a bit of white on the leaves. To these, they sometimes added orange blossoms for scent, hence Orange Pekoe. It deserves repetition that while these rather lovely terms have survived the journey of a few thousand years, their original meanings have been lost along the way, and these terms have been used to perpetrate a rather unlovely hoax.

Major tea packers are highly competitive. Tweedledee can't allow his price to differ more than a few cents from Tweedledum's if he wants to hold his share of a very large market. Tea is a staple consumed in the U.S.A. to the tune of 150,000,000 lbs. (.75 lbs. per capita) per year; 66,000,000 lbs. are sold in the form of tea bags. To keep his price down, he buys cheap teas. Cheap teas are generally those that grow in lowland areas, where climate and soil conditions create such luxuriant growth that the flushes (clusters of freshly formed leaves) may be harvested every ten days. The teas growing in the cooler, higher altitudes take longer to mature and may permit only five pluckings in seven months. These teas bring higher prices, but not simply because they are available in smaller quantities. The slower maturation of these high-grown teas allows them to develop more character. They are deservedly prized, but not by Tweedledee and not by Tweedledum. The mass marketers cater to people who, at least when it comes to tea, are penny wise and pound foolish.

After water, tea is the world's most economical beverage. From one pound of leaves, loose or in bags, we get 200 cups of tea. A box of 100 tea bags, selling for about a dollar, yields tea at the cost of about a penny per cup. At triple that price, at three cents a cup, tea would still be inexpensive. Truly superb teas, in tea bags, are available at that price and, indeed, at lower prices in bulk form. The real bargain, we think, would be to get close to what Lu Tung was talking about for just a couple of pennies. And it is possible.

Did we just say that one can get truly superb tea by using a tea bag? We did. It's true. If fine tea is put in the bag in sufficient quantity, and proper brewing procedure is followed, fine tea will result. The bag itself is an odorless and tasteless filter paper. It offers the convenience of an individual pre-measured portion; it is easily disposable; there are no "messy leaves" to clean up. Each tea drinker can brew his cup to the strength he himself enjoys. In fact, people sitting down to tea together may suit themselves with different teas; it is no more difficult than to select from the cupboard a Darjeeling tea bag or a Formosa Oolong one. Why do people who fancy themselves tea connoisseurs screw up their faces in disgust at even the mention of using a tea bag? Why does the person who's just looking for a better cup of tea look a bit skeptical when told he can indeed get an excellent cup without sacrificing the convenience of tea bags? In both cases, experience has been the teacher—the unpleasant experience of the generally available tea bag, improperly brewed. The common pitfall of dunking the bag in tepid water two or three times must be avoided. The result, no matter how good the tea, would be underbrewed and insipid. Restaurateurs often serve the tea bag on the saucer alongside a cup of water that may have boiled long ago. Such practice reveals a total lack of understanding of what tea needs, and could only yield an unsatisfying cup.

While high quality tea bags should not be shunned, no one should underestimate the pleasures that may come from a close acquaintance with loose tea.

The carefully cultivated and well made tea leaf is the raw stuff that makes a sacred beverage. Precluded from growing or manufacturing tea yourself, you must become a participant in the commercial process. The key link in bringing you the tea you want is the professional tea taster.

THE TEA TASTER

The tea you purchase will have been pre-selected by the importer and the tea tasters in his employ. The job of the tea taster is one of crucial interest and importance to you, the consumer. A discerning tea taster, whose only criterion is the quality of the cup, can teach the interested consumer a great deal about how to find and appreciate an excellent tea. A tea taster who is only concerned with maintaining the same level of blandness in his company's blend is no model at all.

The task a tea taster sets for himself will depend on the kind of product he wants to end up with, and that depends mostly on whom he is working for. Most teas on the market are commercial blends, so most individual tea growths are tested for what they might potentially contribute to a blend. Most of these tea blends are slated for use only in tea bags. Competition among major packers has made the cost factor so crucial that tea tasters are often prevented from even considering the better, more expensive teas.

But let us put aside the exigencies of commerce and consider what the tea taster does as he or she examines tea only for the quality of beverage it will produce. An experienced tea taster has not only his palate to guide him, but a long and distinguished body of tea literature, perhaps foremost among which is Lu Yu's *Classic of Tea*. A tea taster must first note the appearance of the dry leaf: its color, size, twist, and smell.

The tea taster will next judge the color, brightness, and odor of the infusion, and pay close attention to the development in the infused leaf. Lu Yu judged the judges of tea when he wrote:

> Among would-be connoisseurs there are those who praise the excellence of a tea by noting its smoothness and commenting upon the glossy jet shades of the liquor. They are the least capable of judges. Others will tell you it is good because it is yellow, wrinkled and has depressions and mounds. They are better judges. But the really superior taster will judge tea in all its characteristics and comment upon both the good and the bad.

The tea taster further follows Lu Yu's good counsel when he finally and loudly slurps the infusion. "Its goodness is a decision for the mouth to make," the old master said of tea. The slurp creates a finely atomized spray of liquor, draws it against the taster's palate, and sends its aroma into his nasal passages. A taster lets the liquor slosh around in his mouth so that while it makes repeated contact with his palate, he can note its characteristics and place it among his vast repertoire of tea-tasting experiences. The sampled mouthful is never swallowed, as this would soon bloat the taster and dull his senses. The taster is judging the flavor (taste and aroma), pungency, and thickness or strength of the brewed tea.

In judging the appearance of both dry and infused leaf, a taster is looking

for a well made tea. He will discover a good deal about how much care was taken in manufacture. In examining black or oolong tea, the taster will see the effects of the plucking, withering, rolling, fermenting, firing, and sorting. Green teas are neither withered nor fermented but should have been properly steamed, rolled, and fired. The dry leaf of good tea will be free from stalks and twigs, and uniform in size. The former contribute worthless weight and sometimes off-flavors to the tea. If the leaf is not uniform in size, it will not behave consistently from one brewing to the next.

Well made black tea will generally appear small, hard, well rolled, and uniform. Well twisted leaf denotes a good wither, flaky leaf a poor wither. Although the wither is only a preliminary to rolling, which in turn paves the way for fermentation, this preliminary procedure has an effect on the quality of tea produced. Not only is the leaf made flaccid so that rolling can break the leaf cells and expose the juices and enzymes to the air. Also, the evaporation of water during withering makes the cell sap more concentrated. For the subsequent manufacturing processes to work, the wither must have occurred fully and evenly. If the leaf retained too much water, fermentation could not have the desired effect on the leaf, nor could firing eliminate the excess moisture without adversely affecting flavor. Very black leaf does not usually liquor up as well as leaf which shows a slightly brownish-black shade. Very black leaf may be an indication of over-fired tea. The dry leaf is sometimes subjected to a touch test: A quantity of the leaf is gently squeezed in the hand. The tea should be hard but not brittle. Young tea will give under gentle compression. Old tea will break or crumble in the hand and show dust.

Some teas are "tippy"; others are not. Tips, sometimes called Pekoe Tips, are the buds or very young shoots of the tea plant which turn white or golden in the firing. The firing of unfermented tea doesn't produce tip so green tea never shows any. The presence of tip, while it makes a tea pretty to look at, does not necessarily indicate quality. Some teas, for example Keemun, do not show tip. The choicest tea of Darjeeling does not show tip, but some very fine Darjeelings do. The presence of a lot of tip does indicate that the plucking included mostly young shoots and, while the young shoots of a particular growth make finer tea than the older shoots of that tea, the young shoots of one growth are not necessarily finer than the older shoots of another. When tip is present it should be golden, long, and well twisted. The presence of such tip does at least indicate that the manufacture of the tea was carefully enough carried out to preserve it. The manufacturer of the tea might not have been so careful with a tea that he knew to be of low quality. The tippiness of a tea should only be given consideration in conjunction with many other, more important criteria.

Black tea is graded according to size, and while leaf size does affect brewing procedure, it is *not* an indication of quality. A given quantity of tea must be uniform in size if it is to be properly brewed, which is why size grading is useful. (A listing of leaf grades and broken grades is given in Chapter 3 pages 191–92.) Broken grades, made up of smaller and broken leaves, now represent roughly 80 percent of the total crop. These grades, used in the manufacture of tea bags, are so prevalent in the market that it has become difficult to obtain leaf-grade teas.

It is worth noting that though leaf size as such is not indicative of quality, teas having larger leaf sizes can be more easily judged by other criteria. It is generally accepted that defects which may be suggested by examination of the dry leaf cannot be detected in very small grades. Fannings have no leaf style. It is possible that more care is taken in the manufacture of larger grades.

Dry leaf may be smelled. In evaluating the "nose," the tea taster will of course look for a pleasant aroma, but more important, he will establish whether or not the tea possesses its characteristic fragrance.

Remember that none of these criteria should be applied indiscriminately, without being given proper weight. Since tea is ultimately not something to look at, the more important parts of the tea *taster's* job remain. What are the characteristics of the tea infusion? What is the experience of taste? A tea taster prepares an infusion by pouring boiling water into a five-ounce cup containing 35 grains (about 2¼ grams or 1/14 ounce) of tea. This weight of tea was set, in accordance with trade custom, by the Tea Act of 1883, and at the time it equalled the weight of a silver half dime. The coin has since passed into oblivion but the specification survives in the language of FDA regulations. A tea taster witnesses the "agony of the leaves." As they unfold, he examines by sight and smell the infusion itself and the infused leaf.

The taster inhales the steam as it rises out of the cup and so determines the tea's "nose." He gauges the rates of infusion. As he spoons the leaves around in the cup, he notes the changing color of the brew. Next, a spoonful of drained leaves is removed from the cup. The color of the infused leaf is important. It should always be even. In the case of black tea, rich golden leaf invariably denotes quality; a reddish hue, a rich full liquor. Yellowish leaf denotes pungency. If the infused leaf remains black or even dark, this is a sure indication of low quality. Greenish leaf is a sign of underfermentation, and if only slightly present, a "brisk" tea can be expected—a tea that's alive, almost effervescent. Too much green and the beverage will be over-brisk or "raw." Rawness describes a bitter taste, reminiscent of the flavor obtained from infusion of unmanufactured leaf. In the case of green teas, the infused leaf should very simply be green, indicating that no fermentation has occurred. Oolong should show green with reddish-brown edges. This type of tea-leaf reading won't tell the taster much about his future, but it will help him to determine the future of the tea he is tasting.

Before the definitive slurp, the taster examines the finished infusion. The liquor of a good tea will invariably have a bright sparkling appearance, the color varying with type of tea. If the infusion of a black tea is at all greenish, this indicates an under-withered and over-fermented tea. Green teas should produce liquors of a greenish-golden color, bright and lustrous to the bottom of the cup; a dull brownish-yellow color indicates old or low-grade leaf. The lighter the liquor, the younger the leaf, and probably the better the tea. The pale-colored liquor of green teas certainly does not indicate a lack of strength or flavor.

Now the tea is tasted. Is this a "standout" tea, one possessing character and body? Or is it "common" tea, possessing only a plain light liquor and no particularly desirable flavor? Tea that's "gone off" must be rejected—this is tea that's become moldy or tainted. Tainted tea is also known as "sweetish." If the tea is "brisk" it will be lively. If the tea is neither brisk nor pungent, it is considered "flat." A "strong" tea is pungent, brisk, and full without being bitter. A full-liquoring tea, one with body, is "sappy." Coarse flavor is said to be "rasping" while a "soft" cup is smooth and gentle. "Roughness" is associated with a harsh flavor. A tea has "point" if the taste reveals a certain intensity. If no such highlights are present, the tea is said to lack point or be "stewy."

While most of the world's tea originates in a relatively few countries, a tea taster chooses from literally thousands of distinct types. In the United States, all the tea we import must come under the scrutiny of and be passed on by one of three FDA Tea Examiners. In the U.K. tea is tested by H. M. Customs. Our FDA examiners derive their authority from the Tea Act of 1897 and work to protect importers from having substandard teas foisted upon them. The United States Tea Standards are established annually by the United States Board of Tea Experts, a seven-member group. Six are appointed by the commissioner of Food and Drugs from among United States tea importers, packers, and brokers. The seventh member is the FDA's supervisory tea examiner. The consumer as well as the importer is protected by this screening process, but we would stop short of calling the procedure a consumerist one. The industry is, after all, setting its own standards, so while the consumer is protected against really bad tea, he is hardly insured of getting excellent tea. Very little tea is rejected, but this is not an indication that standards are low, since exporters are aware of the standards and avoid arranging shipment of teas that won't pass muster. Our message is that the useful service provided by the diligent Tea Examiners must be complemented by your own carefulness in selecting your tea. While the Tea Board and the Examiners now guard against the importation of dyed teas, the practice of dying teas was instituted only at the insistence of the nineteenth century American consumer. As Pogo said, "We have met the enemy and they are us."

An importer of course does his own taste testing and sets his standards to suit his customers. He receives samples from his own agents or brokers in the exporting countries and makes his decision on the basis of quality and cost. Since most truly "standout" teas do not fall within the mainstream of the American tea trade, they are not easily obtained. While mass packers look for useful enough, cheap enough teas to be used in a blend, we as specialty merchants seek the truly superior self-drinker. When we blend teas, we don't resort to alternate just-get-by varieties. We use the teas that stand up on their own. Again, when it comes to making tea bags, we use the same top quality tea, even if it means cutting the leaf. The specialty merchant's struggle to maintain quality, to pluck the best from the rest, can be seen in the events following the reopening of trade between this country and China. We were naturally excited at the prospect of receiving samples from China, our first in over thirty years. However, in the cup they simply didn't measure up. China Keemuns were being offered at considerably higher prices than the Keemuns of Taiwan, but they were not even as good. The disappointment was great. Our tea customers, especially those who remembered the fine teas of China, were of course anxious to get their hands on these newly available teas. Certainly we were no less anxious to offer them, but we had to reject these first offerings, and counsel patience. We knew that in the excitement of the reopening of trade, there would be much jumping on the mainland China tea wagon, but we stayed off, even at the risk of appearing somewhat unenterprising.

Were the great teas of China no more? We knew that tea production was down from pre-Revolutionary days. The People's Republic did indeed have more pressing needs to attend to, such as adequately feeding 800,000,000 people. Still, if not flourishing, the China tea trade had been going on with other countries. Perhaps (we hoped) the first hook had not had the best bait on it. About six months later it came, a sample of an absolutely exquisite Keemun. We were very glad to see it, to smell it, to taste it, to know it again. Having the sample did not mean we could have the tea, because we could not alone import the twenty chests that was considered a minimum order. Fortunately there were enough merchants around who recognized the merit of this very special tea. It was brought in and by now has a steady following.

Following is our guide to the world's teas. Use it to find your way out of the sea of mediocre ones.

ASIA

SRI LANKA (CEYLON) Sri Lanka produces about 500,000,000 lbs. of black tea annually, on more than 500,000 acres. Over 400,000,000 lbs. are exported, accounting for approximately 25–30 percent of the world's supply. The United States takes about 10 percent of this country's annual exported crop. The teas, known as Ceylons, are grown in the central and south central regions; the better known district names are Dimbula, Badulla, Dikoya, Haputale, Nuwara Eliya, Uva, Pussellawa, Maturata, and Maskeliya.

Ceylon teas are known by their marks, which are stenciled on the tea chests and which denote the particular garden from which the teas originate. There are more than 2,000 such garden marks.

Except among brokers, little attention is paid to the district from which a tea comes. The buyer looks for good tea, tea which satisfies his requirements, and is guided by past experience with a number of particular estates. Buyers of Ceylon teas may go after a particular mark if past experience has proved it satisfactory. The growing district is an unreliable indicator of quality, since one district may produce tea at altitudes differing as much as 3,000 ft. As with most rules, this one has exceptions. The districts of Nuwara Eliya (6,000–7,000 ft.), Uva and Pussellawa (3,500–5,500 ft.), and Dimbula (3,500–6,000 ft.) can be depended upon for very fine tea. Tea grown in such districts as Alagala (700–2,700 ft.), Kegalla (400–1,500 ft.), Kalutara (100–500 ft.), and Kurunegala (500–1,500 ft.) will be plain.

In the trade, Ceylons are classified, but not marked, as High-Grown (over 4,000 ft.), Medium-Grown (2,000–4,000 ft.), and Low-Grown (below 2,000 ft.). Generally, the higher-grown Ceylons show very good strength in the cup, a wonderful delicate flavor and pronounced, almost perfume-like aroma. A good high-grown Ceylon (*e.g.*, Dimbula) is hard to beat. Lower-grown Ceylons do possess strength and, as good liquoring teas, are useful in blending. But they lack the brightness or point of their loftier cousins, and should not be considered good self-drinkers.

The liquors of Ceylons are generally of a softer character than those of any other black tea. As they are fully withered, fully fermented teas, Ceylons do not produce liquors as strong or pungent as those characteristic of Indian teas. The flavorsome Ceylons produce a reddish-brown infusion.

In Sri Lanka, tea is produced throughout the year, but the finest pluckings are in February and March and again in August and September. Ceylon teas are generally very well made, the leaf being even, black, and carefully graded. Tip is often in evidence, but is not indicative of quality. In fact, the leaf style of the strong, finely-flavored high-grown Ceylons is entirely unremarkable. Leaf style may be a useful guide in judging teas from other countries, but is of very little use in selecting a good Ceylon. The tea is graded according to leaf size into such categories as Flowery Orange Pekoe, Orange Pekoe, Pekoe, Pekoe Souchong, Souchong, Fannings, and Dust. We stress that these "grades" are much more alike in quality than not, as they are subdivisions of a single plucking. As a consumer you should not be misled by advertising which would have you equate Orange Pekoe with high quality. The Orange Pekoe grade of a particular plucking is composed of relatively younger and juicier leaves, and so it will represent better tea than the Souchong *of that plucking*. However, what makes the label practically meaningless is that the Souchong grade of this plucking may in fact be superior to the Orange Pekoes and even Flowery Orange Pekoe grades of a hundred other pluckings of tea from different areas, grown in different seasons, at different altitudes.

The very small broken grades, especially Fannings and Dust, are not well suited for sale or use as loose or bulk tea. Used without a filtering medium (*e.g.*, tea bag), they infuse very quickly, measurement is difficult, and straining almost impossible. However, being poorly suited to certain brewing methods is not the same as being bad tea.

The growing popularity of tea bags and instant tea in this country has meant that the proportion of smaller grade teas being imported from Sri Lanka is steadily increasing. Bulk teas are not very much in demand here, and good Ceylons, suitable for sale and use as bulk tea, are harder to obtain.

INDIA Incredible India produces, on close to 900,000 acres, nearly 1,000,-000,000 lbs. of tea annually. A staggeringly large population coupled with a per capita consumption of 0.95 lbs. annually has meant that only half that amount is available for export. Of the total annual exportable crop, which has recently been about 450,000,000 lbs., the United States has imported on average 17,000,000 lbs. or less than 4 percent. The United Kingdom takes about 150,000,000 lbs. or about one-third of India's export. The Republic of Ireland imports about 12,000,000 lbs. of Indian tea. India exports very nearly the same amount of tea as Sri Lanka, and together they account for about 50 percent of all exported tea. However, while the United States imports almost three times the amount of Ceylon tea as it does Indian, the United Kingdom gets considerably more from India.

India is a large country, and one finds a great variation in soil and climate from district to district. The characteristics and quality of Indian teas differ markedly depending on where they are grown, much as do the coffees of Brazil. In a district that produces fine tea the higher-grown teas will be the finest, but the high-grown tea from other districts may be of poor quality. Ceylon teas are judged primarily by the altitude at which they are grown. India teas may not be judged by how high-grown they are without regard to the region from which they come. There are over 4,000 garden marks in India,

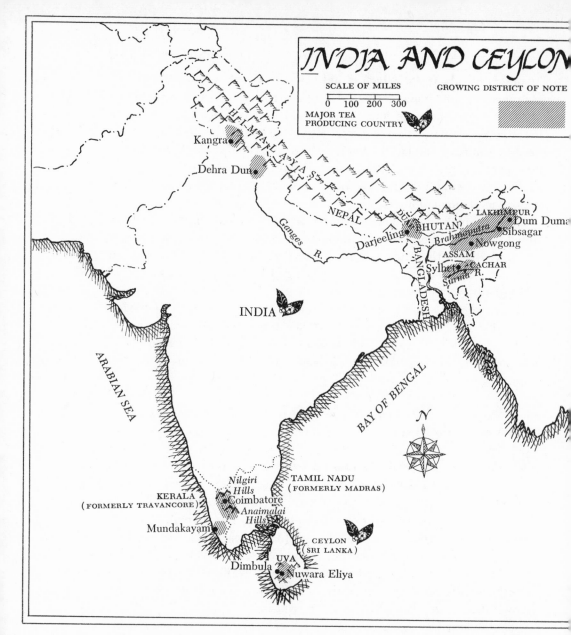

SCALE OF MILES

0   100   200   300

MAJOR TEA
PRODUCING COUNTRY

GROWING DISTRICT OF NOTE

HIMALAYAS

Kangra

Dehra Dun

Ganges R.

NEPAL

Darjeeling

BHUTAN

Brahmaputra

ASSAM

LAKHIMPUR

Dum Duma

Sibsagar

Nowgong

Sylhet

CACHAR

Surma R.

BANGLADESH

INDIA

ARABIAN SEA

BAY OF BENGAL

N

Nilgiri
Hills

TAMIL NADU
(FORMERLY MADRAS)

KERALA
(FORMERLY TRAVANCORE)

Coimbatore

Anaimalai
Hills

Mundakayam

CEYLON
(SRI LANKA)

UVA

Dimbula

Nuwara Eliya

and teas are graded by size into the standard grades of black tea.

The two great tea divisions are north India, which produces three-quarters of India's teas, and south India. Almost all of India's crop is manufactured into black tea. (The northwestern districts of Kangra and Dehra Dun produce some of the small amount of green tea made in India. Kangra tea is quite fine, with a peculiarly delicate character and somewhat spicy flavor. Dehra Dun is a poor grade of green tea, largely reserved for the local market.) All north Indian tea is seasonal, produced from April through November and marketed from June through the end of January. The second flush (plucked in the summer), and the autumnals are the best of the crop of northeast India. At these times, slow growth makes for fuller flavor. South Indian tea is grown throughout the year, but the finest quality is produced in December and January. The poorest south India tea is made in early autumn. (You can see that in India not all autumnals are the same.) South Indian teas are more like Ceylons in character than they are like the teas of north India.

In northeastern India, where most of India's tea originates, Assam is the most important growing region. From the Brahmaputra Valley, a subdivision of the Assam Valley, come teas which are generally referred to as Assams. Among the Assams, the major growths are from Lakhimpur and Sibsagar (the two heaviest producers), Darrang, and Nowgong. Assams are full, thick, rich, heavy teas possessing rough pungency and a grabbing strength. The better Assams, which show a handsome tippy leaf, have a wonderful malty flavor along with strength. They are excellent self-drinkers. From Lakhimpur, especially in the area of Dum Duma, come most of the finer Assams. Very much sought after for blending are the Medium grade Assams, whose strength and pungency make them well-suited for mixing with plainer, lighter teas. These are the mainstay of British tea blenders. The high-fired Assams are quite black throughout most of the season, but autumnals do show a more reddish-brown tint in the dry leaf. Autumnals also have a characteristic flavor. Assams liquor up red and sappy.

The Surma Valley, the other subdivision of the Assam Valley, produces teas which are known chiefly by the subdistrict names of Cachar and Sylhet (Sylhet is in Bangladesh). The best of the teas produced in this area are of medium quality. Here the climate is not as good for tea as it is in the Brahmaputra Valley. Rainfall is heavier and not so well distributed. Spring droughts are not uncommon. Lacking the brightness of the Assams, they are used in blends not because they are wonderful, but because they are useful.

From Darjeeling, a northeastern district along the slopes of the Himalayas, comes one of the world's most prized teas. Darjeeling tea is cultivated at elevations of from 1,000–6,500 ft., the higher-grown the finer. The famous "Darjeeling mist," so beneficial to the tea, envelops the gardens above 4,000 ft. The soil is loamy, highly porous, and rich in mineral nutrients. The dry leaf, generally off-black in color, varies greatly in style from small to bold, plain to tippy. Although well-made tea should always be looked for, when it comes to Darjeeling the style of the leaf and the amount of tip

should never be given much weight. The incredible, hardly describable flavor that often emerges from a coarse, unsightly Darjeeling is more than good reason to recall Lu Yu's dictum: "goodness is a decision for the mouth to make."

The rich golden-red liquor of a fine Darjeeling and its exquisite, penetrating aroma foreshadow a truly unique tea-drinking experience. The second flush, picked in June, and the autumnal, made in October, yield Darjeeling's best. Teas grown and picked during Darjeeling's very wet rainy season do not develop the greatness that devotees of this tea have come to expect. Darjeeling puts its unmistakable stamp on any blend. As a self-drinker, it shines.

The Duars, which come from a region just southeast of Darjeeling, bear a family resemblance to the Assams. They cup dark and full-bodied but the liquor is softer and mellower, the flavor less pungent than their cousins to the northwest. The infusion of Duars is very bright, and brightest from the sought-after autumnals. These teas are much used for blending.

The south Indian teas behave like and are similar in character to the Ceylons of Sri Lanka. From the Nilgiri Hills, a district with altitudes ranging from 4,000–6,000 ft. come fine, flavory teas that are both brisk and pungent, though somewhat thin in liquor. As we would expect, teas coming from lower down on the slopes of this region are plain, but still good. In the southern part of the state of Kerala, in the region once called Travancore, the district of Kanan Devan (High Range) produces a not stylish but fine, flavory tea. A good useful tea is also produced in Mundakayam. The teas from central Travancore are medium grade teas, but south Travancore produces only low-grown plain teas. In the state of Tamil Nadu (formerly Madras), the Coimbatore district produces the tea known as Anaimalai. This tea possesses good body and strength as do the teas from Kerala, but Anaimalai is stronger than they, and is preferred.

The consumer is unlikely to find any unblended Indian teas other than Assam or Darjeeling. The other growths are likely to be those included in "Indian" blends.

INDONESIA Indonesia, the world's fourth largest tea country, produces about 170,000,000 lbs. annually. Three-quarters of the crop grows in Java, one-quarter in Sumatra. Of the nearly 100,000,000 lbs. annually available for export, the United States takes a little over 10,000,000, a tremendous increase in recent years. The United Kingdom imports about 14,000,000 lbs. and Australia is a good customer for Indonesian tea, but this country's best tea customer has traditionally been The Netherlands. In 1971 Holland's ex-colony sent her 27,000,000 lbs. of tea. (But The Netherlands re-export about three-quarters of their annual imports.)

At first glance, it may seem strange that the commercially important teas of Indonesia are unavailable in the unblended form. A tea merchant may offer as many as four or five Ceylon teas, but nary a single Java. In this respect they are quite like the coffees of Angola, which constitute the world's fourth largest exported coffee crop but are virtually unknown out-

INDONESIA

SCALE OF MILES
0 100 200 400

GROWING DISTRICT OF NOTE

MAJOR TEA PRODUCING ISLAND

side the trade. The world of tea is, especially for Americans, a world of blends. Just as the more than 150,000,000 lbs. of Angola Robustas find their way into America's coffee blends, so are teas of Java and Sumatra employed by our tea blenders. Like the relatively innocuous coffees of Angola, the serviceable, attractively priced teas from Indonesia are useful to the mass packers. To be sure, a very few standout teas are produced in certain selected regions, but one would have to wade through a lot of medium grade stuff to find it. Even were such a search to prove fruitful, the tea would be comparable to, but not better than, a more readily available good grade of Ceylon. We suspect that The Netherlands, Indonesia's best and oldest customer, gets much of the latter's finer tea.

While you won't find it as such, Indonesian tea may be a component of the tea you're drinking, so we'll briefly survey this country's output. Only black tea is manufactured. Teas are known as Javas or Sumatras and by their garden marks, which are often accompanied by the name of the districts in which they are grown. Quality and flavor vary greatly with altitude, which in the case of Indonesian tea is determined by the district. Tea is chiefly grown in the western part of the island; the best comes from the Pengalengan Plateau, where weather is dry and altitudes range from 400–6,000 ft. Tea grows all year round in Java, but the best comes from pluckings made during the dry season, from June through September. The dry leaf is ordinarily attractively black, but these better pluckings exhibit a brownish hue. The liquor of a useful Java is soft and of medium strength; the lower-grown teas are heavy, without flavor or point.

Sumatran teas are not so much affected by seasonal changes as are the Javas. The best of the lot comes from the district Pematangsiantar, from estates whose elevations are from 800–2,400 ft. The attractive black leaf yields a consistent if uninspiring cup.

TAIWAN On the island of Taiwan, nearly 60,000,000 lbs. of tea are produced annually. About 85 percent of this crop is exported, the United States taking an average 7,500,000 lbs. each year. The U.K. takes as much and sometimes more. Black, green, and oolong teas are produced. Assam-like teas known as Formosa Blacks are cultivated primarily for the United States market, as they are popular with blenders here. Keemun type and the smoky Lapsang type are among the other important black teas grown. Production of these teas, originally grown in China, was stimulated by the stoppage of trade between China and the United States. Green tea is available as Special Chun Mee, Chun Mee, Sow Mee, and Gunpowder. Most of the green tea is shipped to Morocco, Tunisia, and Afghanistan, but it can sometimes be found here. It is generally of good quality but not as fine as the better greens of Japan. Pouchong tea is oolong scented before the final firing with gardenia, jasmine, or yulan blossoms. Jasmine, a pouchong which enjoys some popularity here, is available in relatively small quantities. Most of the pouchongs are shipped to the Far Eastern markets.

It is for the Formosa Oolongs that tea lovers are ever and deeply grateful. With their intense pungency and penetrating bouquet, these teas have been characterized variously as "the champagnes of teas," as "liquid sunshine," and as "the philosopher's drink." The liquor, a sparkling brownish-amber in color, possesses an attractive, naturally fruity flavor.

Fifty years ago American tea drinkers were well acquainted with this wonderful tea. Large-scale production of oolong was undertaken to satisfy demand in the U.S. In those days, black tea accounted for only 40 percent of the tea consumed here. Green tea accounted for an equal amount, while oolongs made up fully 20 percent of our tea diet. Today 98 percent of our tea is black. Fully 36 percent of the tea Americans drink is made from instants or instant "tea" mixes. If you would but once savor the ambrosia that is a first rate Formosa Oolong, you could only share our horror at what constitutes tea in America today.

Formosa Oolong tea was first produced in imitation of Chinese oolong. Oolong gets its name from the Chinese words *wu* (black) and *lung* (dragon). Chinese oolong originated in the Province of Fukien halfway between Foochow and Amoy. The cultivation of oolong in Formosa was not undertaken in response to demand from abroad, as was the case with the cultivation of Keemun and Lapsang teas. Many Fukienese who migrated to Formosa missed the tea of their native province and the attempts at duplication were made to satisfy these immigrants. We don't know if the Fukienese were entirely satisfied with the result, but the rest of the world has been delighted to this day. It turned out that the oolong produced on Formosa differed from its Chinese model, and was in fact in all ways a finer, more delicious tea. Where later attempts at duplications would result only in fairly good approximations (*e.g.*, Keemun), oolong found its true home in Formosa.

How is it that the oolong from Formosa is so extraordinary? The plant is the same plant used for all tea. The manufacture of this semi-fermented tea is surely carried out with great care, but not with more or less care than its Chinese prototype. If the plant is the same and the manufacture is the same, only a difference in soil and climate can account for the superiority

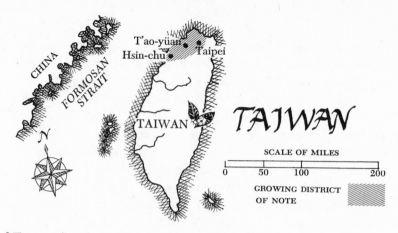

of Formosa's oolong. This is not surprising, for we are accustomed to getting excellent oranges, apples, pineapples, and even coffees from particular regions with special growing conditions. What is somewhat peculiar is the fact that Formosa's green and black teas are not equally great. For although it is true that any region's growth may be manufactured into green, oolong, or black tea, the growing conditions of a particular area may make a tea better suited to one type of manufacture than another. The tea lands of Formosa produce tea which when semi-fermented is perfect. Such tea is not produced anywhere else in the world. Years ago, impressed by the flavor of Formosa's oolong, the tea planters of India and Ceylon commissioned a group of scientists to visit the island and investigate the manufacture of semi-fermented tea. The planters wanted to know if they could borrow from Formosa what Formosa had borrowed from China. The commission reported back that while the manufacturing process could be duplicated, the special conditions of soil and climate could not. Their employers abandoned the hope of competing in the production of oolong tea. The Chinese experience in Keemun provides another example of the relationship between cultivation and manufacture. The renowned black tea is actually the successor to a poor quality green.

Cultivation of Formosa Oolong is practically confined to the northern part of the island, in the counties of Taipei, T'ao-yüan and Hsin-chu. Neither district names nor garden marks are used to identify the teas of Taiwan but an incredibly extensive grading system is rigorously applied by the Government Tea Inspection Office. These grades, which denote actual quality, include: Standard, On Good, Good, Fully Good, Good Up, Good to Superior, On Superior, Superior, Fully Superior, Superior Up, Superior to Fine, On Fine, Fine, Fine Up, Fine to Finest, Finest, Finest to Choice, and Choice.

Most oolong cultivation is done in a small way by families on portions of their land. Tea is grown on hilly land at altitudes of up to 1,000 ft., but in Taiwan high-grown tea is not the best. Most tea is grown on tablelands, also at elevations of up to 1,000 ft., but the island's best tea is not grown there either. The localities famous for quality leaf are on the "teela" or broken lands, many of which are at sea level and none of which are above 300 ft. The reason for this unusual turnabout is that the soil of the teela derives from decomposed rock, and this yellow clay soil is ideal for tea. Good tea is produced in the hilly regions and on the tablelands where the soil is rich reddish loam, but great tea comes from the teela. Even though the teela is actually the lowest region, it is known as the high country because it produces such fine tea. The vintner says, "The poorer the vine, the better wine." The grower of Formosa Oolong says, "Yellow soil, small bush, good tea." The scrawny, scraggly bushes of the teela produce quality, not quantity. To insure against hybridization, seeds are rarely used. On Taiwan the preferred method of propagation is layering.

Oolongs are produced from April to early December. There are five crops, showing much variation in quality. Spring tea (early April to mid-May) has a rough, dry leaf without much tip. The liquor is light in both color and character, with grades usually ranging only from Good to Fine. First summer tea (late May to late June) shows fair body, excellent flavor, and handsome leaf. Late summer tea (early July to mid-August) is very handsome, tippiest of all the crops, and possesses the fullest, richest flavor. From the summer teas come the highest grades. Autumn tea (late August to mid-October) has good leaf and full body, but flavor is not so good. Rarely is this tea graded higher than Good. Winter tea (late October to early December) is, because of unreliable weather conditions, impossible to categorize. They sometimes, but rarely, resemble the teas picked in the spring.

The leaf of Formosa Oolong shows a crisp dry, greenish brown, sometimes tippy. Its color derives from its characteristic manufacture to a state between green and black. The liquor is a sparkling amber. The color of the infused leaf should not be entirely green, for such a tea would not have good flavor or body; it should show fermentation around the edges. The process of making an excellent oolong is difficult; fermentation must be carefully controlled, for if it is allowed to proceed unchecked, the result will be under- or over-fermented tea. The manufacture of black and green tea certainly requires great care, but these processes are less tricky than making oolong, as the products are more clearly defined. When plucked, oolongs are sun-withered for from twenty minutes to an hour. (Taiwan, fortunately, has a sunny period almost every day.) Next the tea is briefly fermented, until the leaf becomes slightly darker and softer, and the characteristic fragrance develops. The tea is then pan-fired to stop fermentation. Only then is the tea rolled. Juices are liberated, fermentation again occurs, only to be almost immediately checked by firing. The result, known as crude tea, will be refired before being packaged. Refiring right before packaging is common with all teas, but in the case of oolong this procedure is crucial to the preservation of its unique character. Appreciate the character of a fine Formosa Oolong straight, or try it blended with Darjeeling. Add lemon or sugar if you must, but not milk.

Lapsang Souchong, originally grown in the Fukien province of China, is known for its smoky flavor. The Chinese version, known also as Tarry Souchong, was made in very small quantities and owed its peculiar character to the locality in which it was grown. Today's Lapsang teas, which come from Taiwan, owe their smoky aroma and taste to the curing process rather than to the soil. Its black leaf has a bold, raggedy appearance. This exceptional tea liquors rich and syrupy, usually producing a clear, bright orange infusion. A pretty clear line can be drawn between Lapsang lovers and everyone else. Like a good Scotch whiskey—to which it bears some resemblance—it will be loved only on its own not uncertain terms. Its devotees drink it straight, but if you're at all uncertain, try blending it with three-quarters Keemun.

JAPAN Japan ranks as the world's third largest tea producer after India and Sri Lanka. Her output has recently increased steadily, and her annual yield is now about 200,000,000 lbs. Virtually all of Japan's tea is green. However, because Japan is a nation of many tea drinkers (annual per capita consumption 2.3 lbs.), only 2 percent, or about 4,000,000 lbs., is available for export. Japan actually imports ten times that amount of tea and so on balance this country is actually a tea importer; in fact, Japan is the U.K.'s biggest tea customer. In 1972, Japan actually exported less tea than such countries as Argentina, Mozambique, and Tanzania. In that same year Kenya, which produced barely half the amount of tea grown in Japan, exported twenty times more than Japan. The United States takes more than 80 percent of Japan's tiny export crop, or well over 3,000,000 lbs. Japan provides the U.S. with more than half of our green tea and this contribution must be considered important, even though only one in forty pounds of the tea drunk in America is green tea.

It is ultimately not as a major producer of tea nor as a major supplier of our small portion of green tea that Japan is primarily important. Japan

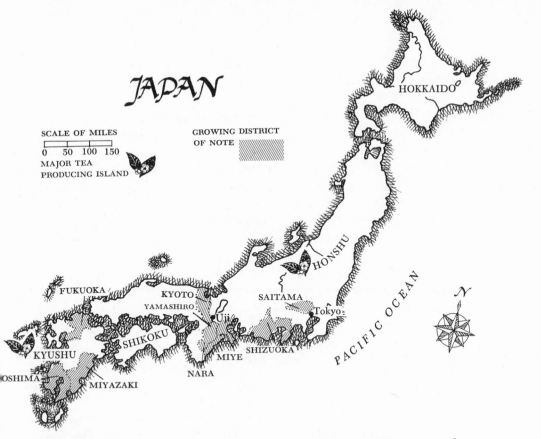

means tea and would mean tea whether it produced ten pounds or ten million. In art, in philosophy, in the history and life of Japan, tea prevails. Whatever tea is made in Japan represents age-old methods of cultivation, manufacture, and appreciation.

The varieties of Japanese teas, known collectively as the white wines of tea, arise primarily from the ways in which they are manufactured and from the districts in which they are grown. Quality depends on the timing and the method of plucking. Japan's teas are size-graded after manufacture, as are most of the world's teas, but they differ in that particular teas from a specific region or of a specific leaf size are specially selected for certain kinds of manufacture. This special relationship between the type of leaf and the treatment it receives reflects the philosophy that certain methods of manufacture are best suited for certain growths, pluckings, and leaf styles. In addition to being classified according to manufacturing methods and leaf style Japanese tea has the following quality gradings: Extra Choicest, Choicest, Choice, Finest, Fine, Good Medium, Good Common, Nibs, Fannings and Dust.

Tea is grown throughout Japan, preferably on land where rice and other crops cannot be grown. More than half the country's tea comes from the prefecture of Shizuoka, with relatively large quantities coming also from Kagoshima, Miye, Kyoto, Nara, Saitama, Miyazaki, and Fukuoka. Tea is grown from May to October and is divided into three crops. The first crop, which furnishes the best tea and accounts for about half the total crop, is plucked from the beginning of May to the middle of June. The second crop is plucked from the end of June through the beginning of July. The third crop is plucked from the end of August till the beginning of September. If a fourth plucking is made, it is a short one in early October. Pickers must pluck the whole leaf, cutting it at the stem. Care must be taken to avoid bruising the picked leaf, for bruised leaf will ferment. Even were the tea destined for manufacture into black tea, this fermentation would be undesirable, as it would be going on uncontrolled, but for green tea any fermentation of leaf must be avoided.

The finest teas of Japan are grown in the district of Yamashiro, near Kyoto. Nearly all Yamashiro tea consists of special grades reserved for domestic use. From the area around Uji in Yamashiro comes Gyokuro tea or "Pearl Dew," the most highly prized tea in Japan. In the Gyokuro garden, just before the picking season, the tea is completely hidden under specially constructed sun shelters. In April, as the buds begin to flush, a trellis is built over the garden. As the buds open into leaves, screens are spread out on the trellis and ten days later are thatched with rice straw. The shading process, carefully carried out, imparts a delicate sweetness to this special tea. The leaves need shade, but young leaves cannot be deprived of the sunlight they need by too much shade too soon. Only the nippings of the tender top buds of the first flush are made into Gyokuro. This tea is carefully handmade into a rolled leaf. When this same leaf is dried in the open natural state, the product is Tencha (also called Hikicha), the leaf from which Mattcha, the ceremonial tea, is made. Tencha is never used as such but is always powdered to make Mattcha. To make Mattcha, the Tencha leaf, thoroughly and painstakingly dried, is broken into small pieces and sorted into Koicha (dark-colored tea) and Usucha (light-colored tea). The small pieces are ground to powder in a mortar.

Practically no Gyokuro, Tencha, or Mattcha is exported, and indeed they account for less than 1 percent of Japan's output. More than 70 percent of Japanese tea and nearly all this country's exported tea is Sencha or "ordinary" tea. As it accounts for such a tremendous quantity of tea, one can readily understand that Sencha is a designation applied to teas from all regions manufactured by a variety of methods. The different methods of manufacture applied to Sencha do produce distinct types known as Pan-Fired Tea, Guri, Basket-Fired Tea, and Natural Leaf Tea. The method of manufacture does not create quality. However, finer teas are often given special treatment by a particular form of manufacture.

All Japan's green teas are steamed, rolled and fired, but all must be refired before export to insure that the tea will be stable, that it will contain no residual moisture. Pan-fired tea is tea refired in a metal pan or its machine equivalent. Tea selected for this type of manufacture is on the small side, well twisted and curly. The curliest of pan-fired teas, which are sorted out during the refiring and fired separately, are known as Guri. The pan-fired Guri is similar to the Young Hyson of China. It has mostly been exported to North Africa and Afghanistan. The dry leaf of these teas will be light in color. Basket-fired teas are refired in baskets, and the finest of this type is known as Spider-Leg or Needle-Leaf tea; used are the young, supple, and succulent leaves which are easily twisted in lengths of up to two and a half inches. This very fine tea was named Tenkachi or "Number One Under The Sky" by a Tokyo tea dealer long ago, but the name no longer holds. There are, also, low-grade basket-fired teas made from older and therefore less pliant leaves. Basket-fired teas are distinguishable from pan-fired not only by the length of the leaf but by color. The curing process imparts a dark olive green hue to the basket-fired teas. The drinking qualities of both depend not on the refiring method but on the quality of leaf used. Natural Leaf teas may be either pan-fired or basket-fired, but they contain a high proportion of coarse leaf. This is a somewhat irregular tea, as the refiring process unevenly affects the not very well sorted leaf. It is this style of tea which was once known as "porcelain-fired" tea, but why it received this name is a mystery. Porcelain pans are not known to have ever been used. Perhaps the white paper pans once used in Japan's tea manufacture were thought to look like porcelain. Little of this type of tea is exported because its quality is unreliable.

The only other major style of tea besides Gyokuro, Tencha, and Sencha is Bancha. Bancha is sometimes characterized as the poorest grade of tea; alternatively, it may be considered a by-product of the manufacture of Sencha. Teas used for this grade are the coarse leaves pruned off the tea plants at the end of the season when the bushes are shaped. Coarse leaf sorted out of earlier plucking as unsuitable for inclusion in the Sencha grade may also be used. Bancha was formerly reserved by the Japanese for home consumption but is now available in the United States as a health food product. Bancha does contain less caffeine than other teas and so its attraction to those who enjoy a less stimulating brew is not incomprehensible. In Japan it has traditionally been regarded as suitable for the elderly and children. It is also popular there for use in institutions because it is very inexpensive. Hojicha is a kind of tea produced by strongly toasting a combination of Bancha leaves and tea stems. A brew made from this tea is brown in color and pungent to the taste. That these teas should have found a certain following is understandable, but that they seem also to have been surrounded with a certain mystique is confusing. They are of low quality and remarkably undelicious. That Bancha is sought after at all is mildly perplexing, but we must admit to being dismayed at the thought that Bancha might be regarded as representative of Japan's green teas. For those who seek the glorious flavor of the subtle and astringent greens, a fine pan-fired Japan is in order. Those who prefer to avoid or reduce their intake of caffeine can do better than Bancha. They can select a delightful mint, a flowery camomile, or a flavory lemon verbena and get something for their trouble.

CHINA   Before World War II China produced nearly 1,000,000,000 lbs. a year, or nearly half the world's tea. By the 1930s, however, this giant was already being dwarfed by India and Ceylon in the field of exports. A century ago China exported close to 300,000,000 lbs. of tea. It is estimated that modern China's total production is little more than that amount. China has recently been exporting about 65,000,000 lbs. annually, or only 6 percent of the world's total exports. It is thought that China wants to regain her position of importance in the world of tea. Some believe that she is having more success in re-establishing quantity than quality, but we have tasted with our own lips the evidence that China still knows how to make great tea. If greater quantities of fine China tea are forthcoming, so much the better. If the days of laboriously handmade teas are gone, so are the long hours of very poorly rewarded work. The introduction of mechanization into China tea manufacture need not result in a reduction in quality, and it will make this country competitive with other producers.

In the old days, Chinese tea merchants recognized fully 8,000 different grades of tea. This incredible number arose from the fact that each tea was classified by how it was manufactured (five ways), the quality of the leaf (four grades), the quality of the manufacture (two grades), and the number of places of origin (200 grades). Tea grown in one locale was sometimes manufactured in various other locales, and the results differed depending on where it was manufactured. When a tea bore the name of a particular place, one could not always be sure whether the name was of the growing region or the place of manufacture. Certain teas were named for districts other than their own simply because they resembled the teas of the other districts. To keep from going completely mad, the non-native tea traders in China developed a much abbreviated system of classification. China is huge, and since tea is grown in sixteen provinces, even the shortened classification system produced a lengthy list. We'll describe the best known teas of China, whose market names will designate where they're from and how they're made.

Black, green, oolong and brick teas are made in China. In China much of the land is good for tea: crumbly, loamy, iron-rich, moist, and well drained. Yet tea is grown mostly, though not exclusively, on hilly ground considered unsuitable for other, more important crops. The high quality of some China teas is indeed remarkable considering how little emphasis is placed on cultivation. The tea-producing season in China is a particularly

short one. There are regularly three pickings; if a fourth is done it is an end-of-season clean-up called *tsew-loo*, or "autumn dew." This gleaning yields only old, coarse leaf. The first plucking, called *show-chun* or "first spring," begins in late April when the delicate leaf buds appear. The quantity secured is necessarily small, but the quality is superior. The second plucking, known as *urh-chan* or "second spring," occurs in early June when the bushes are full. Most tea of medium to good quality comes from this plucking. The "third spring" plucking, also called *san-chun*, is done in July and produces teas of a common sort.

The black teas fall into two great divisions: North China (black leaf) Congous and South China (red leaf) Congous. North China Congous were long ago collectively known as English Breakfast teas, but later that name came to be reserved for Keemun alone. They come from the provinces of Hupeh, Hunan, Kiangsi and Anhwei. The better grades of North China Congous are aromatic, full-bodied, and sweet liquoring. These are the burgundies of China teas. The poorer grades, called Monings, are price teas, producing thin undistinguished liquors.

The three leading varieties of North China Congous are the Keemuns, Ningchows, and Ichangs. Keemun, a district in Anwhei Province whose praises we have already sung, produced until a century ago only an unremarkable green tea. When the district switched to the manufacture of black tea, one of the world's greatest teas was born. Keemun, whose flinty leaf is not particularly attractive, liquors thick and full; its penetrating bouquet is unsurpassed. A lesser known North China Congou called Kintuck, also from Anwhei, resembles Keemun, but is somewhat more delicately flavored. Ningchows, from Kiangsi Province, possess an attractive, small, grayish-black leaf. They produce a bright, light-bodied infusion and are valued blenders. Ichangs are generally attractive small-leaf teas, rich and full-bodied in the cup, with the slightest of smoky overtones. Ichangs are also called Oopacks, a market name for teas from Hupeh province. North China Congous from certain districts of Hunan, generally known as Oonams, are similar to the Ichangs.

The distinguished South China Congous, grown in Fukien province, are the Paklums, Panyongs, Paklings, Padraes, and Ching Wos. China's Lapsang Souchongs also come from the south. The south China blacks, by virtue of differences in soil and climate, have a character and flavor distinct from the northern black teas. They are known as the clarets of China teas. Paklums are very stylish, small-leaf tippy teas. They are bright and flavory but, lacking body, they haven't the character to be good self drinkers. Panyongs are bold leaf teas, brisk, fragrant, and pungent in the cup. Paklings show well made, small black leaf and are heavy-bodied, with a pleasant toasty flavor. Padraes are highly-fired teas with a bold, black, crepe-like leaf. They possess great strength, their flavor reminiscent of black currants. Ching Wos are considered top-notch. The dry leaf is even, tightly-rolled and black. Its bright red infusion has a most delicate aroma and wonderful flavor.

During the war, the tea industry was developed in the southwestern provinces of Szechwan, Kweichow, and Yunnan. We have recently imported some tea from Yunnan. It shows a long, tippy leaf. The liquor resembles that of a smooth high-grown Ceylon, but is somewhat lighter and more fragrant.

China green teas are broadly classified as Country Greens, Hoochows, and Pingsueys. Country Greens comprise all green teas except those coming from the districts adjoining the towns of Hoochow and Pingsuey in Chekiang province. Hoochows, the first of the China greens to appear in the spring, are light-liquoring, sweet-flavored teas of handsome appearance. Pingsueys are handsome teas, but generally not so good in the cup.

The finest of the Country Greens, and of all China Greens, are the Moyunes, made in Anhwei province. Their soft, tender, sappy leaf results in a cup unsurpassed in richness and clarity. The best of the best possess also a wonderful toasty body. Almost equal to the Moyunes are the Tienkais, also from Anhwei province. These have the flavor of the Moyunes but not the body.

Green tea manufacture results in numerous divisions and countless subdivisions which refer to the various makes. The two major styles are Gunpowder, which is good tea rolled into balls, and Young Hyson, which is good tea made into long bold twisted leaf. Another style is Imperial, which refers to older leaf made like Gunpowder but more loosely rolled. Another style called Hyson is made like Young Hyson, but from older, poorer leaf.

China oolongs tend towards roughness, and are no match for the Formosa oolongs from Taiwan. Scented oolongs such as Jasmine also suffer by comparison to the Jasmine of Taiwan, but not so much as do the oolongs themselves. For a full discussion of semi-fermented teas see the section on tea from Taiwan.

You may have heard about brick tea, but we hope you weren't tempted to try it, as we were. It is made in the Szechwan district of China, chiefly from waste left over from the manufacture of black tea, including siftings, tea dust, and stalks. About six pounds are placed in a mold and heavy hydraulic pressure is applied. Although it is not generally imported here, we had some and found it thoroughly unpleasant. In Tibet, where it is used exclusively, it is boiled with salt, butter and other ingredients to form a kind of soup.

OTHER TEA AREAS

u.s.s.r. A little more than 130,000,000 lbs. of tea are grown in the U.S.S.R., much of it for home consumption. This country, even with increased production in recent years, is still very definitely a net importer of tea. Her small amount of exports go mainly to Mongolia, Morocco, Poland, Germany, and Belgium. The United States does not import tea from the U.S.S.R. Tea is grown almost exclusively in the Republic of Georgia, but to some extent also in Azerbaidzhan, and the Caucasus. Most plantations are on the southern slopes of the Adjar Hills, near the eastern shore of the Black Sea. The largest and best known plantation is the Chakve, in the Republic of Georgia. This is the farthest north that tea is cultivated anywhere in the world.

africa Tea is grown in and exported from Tanzania, Kenya, Uganda, and Malawi. Commercial tea production is relatively new to this part of the world but is expanding at a rapid rate. Soil and climate are good for tea and the yields of these countries are popular with large-scale blenders. Other tea-growing countries in Africa include Mozambique, Mauritius, Burundi, Zaire, Cameroon, Rwanda, South Africa, and Rhodesia.

Tea is also produced in Bangladesh, Thailand, Viet-Nam, Iran, Turkey, Argentina, Brazil, Ecuador, and Peru.

TEA BLENDS

Almost all mass-market teas are blends. A blender serving only a particular region may produce a blend containing as few as four or five teas. By limiting the scope of his market, he will have to provide only a certain amount of tea and can be fairly certain that teas suitable for inclusion in his blend will be constantly available. He seeks to maintain the character—that is the flavor, strength, body, leaf style and cost—of his product. The blender with a much wider market also aims for such consistency, but because he must provide a great quantity of tea, to achieve consistency he must include in his blend as many as twenty teas. If he used only a few teas, his demand for any one of them would be great, and should it become unavailable to him in the quantity he required, a substitute would have to be found. He could not make a substitution for one-quarter or one-fifth of his blend and still maintain the character of that blend. So he covers his bets. The wider the market to be reached, the greater the amount of tea required, the less distinctive is the blend. The pressures of cost and the requirement that the teas used be readily replaceable work against the creation of a great tea.

There are, however, blends created only for the excellent, interesting, distinctive cup they produce. Some you will find already packaged, some will be the creations of your tea merchant, some will be creations of your very own. A few thousand distinct types of tea are produced, and the number of blends obtainable by varying the types and proportions is huge. Add to this huge number of theoretical possibilities the blends resulting from the use of various floral scents and herbals, and the new range of possibilities is nearly infinite. Since tea rather than mathematics is our concern, let us describe some of the widely available blends and suggest some guidelines for creating your own.

English Breakfast: traditionally not a blend at all but straight Chinese Keemun. Some packers are faithful to the tradition; others create a blend of teas strong enough to get you started in the morning. Well, we suppose there are many people in England who don't drink Keemun for breakfast.

Irish Breakfast: a blend of high-grown Ceylon with a hearty Assam. The Irish like strong, full-liquoring tea, so small leaf teas are usually used. This is a good blend to put milk in.

Russian Style Tea: The days of the caravans are long gone, as are the days when Russian tea meant tea imported into Russia from China. Tea blended to the Russian taste is marketed today under such names as Russian Caravan, Russian Blossom, and Russian Style. We feel a blend of Keemun, Assam, and China green is a combination well suited to anyone's samovar. Some offerings include only black teas. Tea is now grown in but not imported from Russia.

Earl Grey: This blend, scented in the English manner, is a lovely afternoon tea. Its pungent, flowery aroma derives from the oil of bergamot which is sprayed on variously blended teas. Some offerings are more highly scented than others. The tea base may be all Ceylon, but we prefer a blend of Black China and India teas.

Spiced Blends: To black tea, usually a smooth-drinking Ceylon, is added natural cut clove and bits of either dried orange peel or dried lemon. "Constant Comment" is the famous orange spice tea, but many tea merchants offer their own versions. Other spiced blends include tea with cinnamon, tea with anise, and tea with cardamom. The latter, heavily sugared, is a pleasant accompaniment to Middle Eastern cuisine.

Lu Yu characterized spiced teas as "no more than the swill of gutters and ditches." We are not such purists, but must admit to being somewhat dismayed at the proliferation of flavored teas. Good tea has its own exquisite flavor and does not have to be made to taste like a soft drink.

Mint Tea Blends: An herbal tea may be made from fresh or dried mint, but for a cup not so minty, tea/mint combinations are offered. Peppermint is what most Americans mean by mint, and it may be blended with Ceylon or, as we prefer, Assam. Minted green tea, a great variation, is cool and sharp. Add spearmint to the green, and you have tea as the Moroccans like it. All minted teas make wonderfully refreshing iced tea.

Chinese Restaurant Style: varies from restaurant to restaurant and so do the offerings of various packers. Some may provide, as indeed some restaurants do, only an undistinguished Formosa black. The addition of a little Jasmine helps, but not much. We like a blend of half oolong, one-quarter green, and one-quarter Jasmine. Many cups of this light, flowery blend may be drunk unsweetened with a good Chinese meal.

BLENDING YOUR OWN

Creating your own tea blends can be almost as much fun as tasting the results. Familiarize yourself with the available unblended and blended varieties. Start your day with a hearty Darjeeling. In the afternoon, rendezvous with Earl Grey. Sit back in the evening with a piquant oolong. When blending, use as a base a full rich tea such as Ceylon, Assam, Keemun, or Darjeeling. The latter with one-quarter oolong is delightful. Three-quarters Ceylon may be spiked with one-quarter smoky Lapsang or flowered with one-quarter delicate Jasmine. Mix Keemun, Assam, and green for a Russian-style tea, or Ceylon and Assam for tea as the Irish like it.

5. The Art of Tea and Tea Drinking

FROM *The Book of Tea* by Kakuzo Okakura we learn that there were three schools of tea in China's history, corresponding to the T'ang, Sung, and Ming dynasties. They were cake tea which was boiled, powdered tea which was whipped, and leaf tea which was steeped. The tea ideal of the Sung conformed to their notion of life; that of the T'ang had coincided with their philosophy. It took nothing less than an invasion by the dreaded Mongol hordes to put an end to Sung culture. The Ming dynasty, which marked an attempt at renationalization in the fourteenth century, survived only until the Manchus took control of China in the seventeenth century. It was only at the close of the Ming dynasty that tea drinking became known to Europe, and it was steeped tea that the Europeans took as their model. All older methods had given way to philosophical and political upheaval, and remained unknown in the west.

It was in 1904 that an accident revolutionized the tea-drinking habits of Americans. According to the records, Thomas Sullivan, an enterprising tea and coffee merchant in New York, sent a few samples of his tea to his customers. Such samples usually were sent in small tins. Sullivan decided it would be simpler and less expensive to put the tea in little bags instead. So he ordered several hundred little silk, hand-sewn bags, filled them with tea and sent them to his customers and waited for orders.

Soon the orders began to pour in, but to Sullivan's great surprise, they were for tea packaged in the little bags. His customers had discovered that by pouring boiling water over the bags they could make tea with less effort.

It didn't take a Mongol invasion, nor was the change based on a shift in the religious, moral, and aesthetic outlook of the people. Or was it? Perhaps acceptance of the tea bag found its basis in the religion of convenience, the morality of rugged individualism, the aesthetic of cleanliness. Perhaps only in a country where tea was regarded as coffee's poor relation could such a contraption have captured the consuming public's imagination. In the United Kingdom, where tea reigns, the tea bag is making some inroads but fully 75 percent of the tea made there is from bulk tea.

The school of tea in the twentieth-century United States is the tea bag which is dunked. Tea bags are used to prepare 54 percent of the tea made in American homes. As we have said, delicious tea can be obtained from a tea bag, but bad brewing habits conspire with a generally mediocre product to make delicious tea the exception rather than the rule. To our taste, steeped tea has advantages over even the best of tea bags. We are permitted to see the leaves (and flowers in the case of a tea like Jasmine) as they unfold and swirl in the freshly boiled water. We can enjoy the differences in shape, color, and texture—the tippy shafts of a hearty black Darjeeling, the tightly curled grayish greens of a delicate Gunpowder, the sinewy flats of the broad brown oolongs. Tea bag teas, no matter what they are, must be finely chopped to provide maximum surface area within the confines of the filter paper. The tea in a tea bag is, in a sense, mutilated beyond recognition and further hidden by the filter paper itself. It seems to us that the aroma of steeped tea is fuller and more communicative than that of the tea bag.

Looming on the horizon and fast gaining acceptance is the school of instant tea. Tea in this form represents a total capitulation to convenience and bears as much resemblance to tea as cherry Kool-Aid does to Beaujolais. Americans make 36 percent of their "tea" from instants, the Britons only 1 percent. Its thin, bitter taste is sometimes poorly masked by additives such as artificial sweeteners and lemon flavoring. You just add hot water (some manufacturers say you can use tap water), but the tea has been murdered beyond resurrection. The time you may save in making it is nothing compared to the time you'll waste drinking it.

The Japanese succeeded in repelling two Mongol invasions following the downfall of the Sung, and so preserved the tea ideal of the Sung dynasty (including powdered tea) although it was lost to the Chinese themselves. The tea ideal in Japan, as embodied in the beautiful tea ceremony, is the result of a profound concept of Zen: There is greatness in the smallest incidents of life. You are invited to partake not only of the pleasures of tea but of its wisdom.

Lu Yu, the oldest interpreter of tea, said this about the proper use of tea:

> In the ten thousand objects which Heaven nourishes,
> there is supreme perfection. It is only for ease

and comfort that man works at things . . .

Thus with tea. There are nine ways by which man must tax himself when he has to do with tea:

He must manufacture it.

He must develop a sense of selectivity and discrimination about it.

He must provide the proper implements.

He must prepare the right kind of fire.

He must select a suitable water.

He must roast the tea to a turn.

He must grind it well.

He must brew it to its ultimate perfection.

He must finally drink it.

BREWING TEA

A good tea will yield up its wonderful qualities if treated with only a modicum of care. Experiment with different kinds of tea to discover which ones suit your taste. We strongly recommend that you buy the highest grade of the tea you like, for even the highest quality tea can be had for three cents per cup. You may choose a fragrant Keemun, a lusty Assam, or a delicate, astringent pan-fired Japan. Perhaps your cup of tea is a high-grown Ceylon or a blend of Darjeeling and Formosa Oolong. Be sure the tea you buy is fresh and untainted. Tea is not nearly as finicky as coffee, but will become stale upon prolonged exposure to the air. It should be protected from contamination by anything that has its own strong smell. Store the tea you buy in an airtight caddy or tin. It should be kept in a cool dry place and out of the light. If it is fresh when you buy it, tea stored this way will keep very well for six months.

You brew tea by permitting an appropriate amount of boiling water to draw the valued constituents from a particular quantity of dry leaf for a specified amount of time. If the temperature of the water is correct throughout the brewing process, if the proper amounts of tea and water are used, and if the timing is carefully controlled, the resulting infusions will have flavor, body, stimulation, pungency, and color in balanced proportions. The rules of making good tea stem from the nature of the dry leaf. Understanding the constituents of tea as the dry leaf, and knowing what we desire from tea as a beverage, will make it easier to understand the precepts of sound brewing practice.

The stimulation of tea is provided by caffeine. A pound of tea contains a little over 200 grains of caffeine, this accounting for a little less than 4 percent of the weight of the dry leaf. Since a five-minute infusion extracts only three-quarters of the caffeine, and since we get 200 cups from a pound, a cup of properly brewed tea will contain less than a grain of caffeine. A pound of coffee contains less caffeine than a pound of tea, but a cup of coffee is much richer in caffeine than a cup of tea (1½–1¾ grains). For one thing, the total amount of caffeine in a pound of coffee is distributed among only 40, or one-fifth the number of cups. For another, the extraction of caffeine is more nearly complete in the brewing of coffee. For a discussion of caffeine please see pages 88–89 and page 110.

The color, pungency, and body of fermented teas derive from the water-soluble tannins and tannin oxidation products in the dry leaf. Color is obviously a visual sensation; pungency is, perhaps not so obviously, more a tactile than a taste sensation. Body is a fullness felt in the mouth, the effect of the balance among taste, smell, and touch components.

During fermentation, some of the tannin present in the fresh leaf is oxidized, some combines with protein, and the rest remains unchanged. The tannin oxidation products, sometimes called tannin reds and tannin browns, are responsible for tea's color, and contribute to the strength of the liquor. The pungency or astringency of tea, its pleasantly sour-harsh quality, is due to those tannins unchanged by fermentation. Those tannins that combine with protein during manufacture are rendered insoluble, even in boiling water, and so do not appear in the brewed tea. The more tannins that are rendered insoluble, the less tannins in the final brew, and so the less pungent the brew. The tannin unchanged by fermentation in a black tea usually accounts for about 12 percent of the dry leaf, or half the tannins present in the fresh leaf. It can be seen that, generally, the shorter the fermentation, the greater the amount of unchanged tannin and therefore the more pungent the liquor; the longer the fermentation, the smaller the amount of unchanged tannin, the softer and more deeply colored the liquor. The black teas of China, which even before manufacture have less tannin than other black teas, are very fully fermented. They are known for their fragrance and flavor, not their pungency. High-grown teas like Darjeeling and the High-Grown Ceylons are lower in tannin than their lower-grown counterparts. These teas too are valued for their fragrance and flavor.

One might think that since green teas are unfermented—which means no tannins are used up during manufacture—the amount of tannin available to be infused would be very great. This would be true if the amount of tannin present in the natural leaf of green tea were as high as that in the natural leaf of black tea. However, whereas the tannin content of black tea is about 24 percent, that of green is only 15 percent. Manufactured green tea contains only 12 percent tannin—which is the same as the tannin content of manufactured black tea. The reason that green tea may seem more pungent or astringent than black tea is that green tea's flavor is more delicate; the pungency of green tea is not so mitigated by flavor as is the pungency of black tea, so green tea seems more puckery. Oolong teas, as they are semifermented, exemplify a fascinating marriage of delicacy, pungency, and flavor.

The flavor of green tea comes from the unfermented oils of the tea plant. The flavor, both taste and aroma, of fermented tea is due to the presence in the dry leaf of a water-soluble essential oil developed during fermentation. Present in the dry leaf as only one part in 10,000, this bittersweet complex makes the brew more than stimulating, more than bracing. It gives tea its delicious appeal, and when tea has that appeal nothing else seems to matter.

Only by much skillful manipulation in the fields and factories of tea-growing countries are the virtues of tea created. The flavor of tea is wonderfully subtle but tea itself is simple, direct, immediate. To brew tea you need boiling water, a container of some sort, a minimum of skill, and a modicum of care. Don't hurry. When making tea, you have only time. Let tea be a refuge, a genuine change of pace. Brewing your tea is part of drinking it and drinking it part of your life. Let the tea gently stimulate you to reflect on how the smallest part touches and is touched by the infinite. You can make tea by putting the leaves directly into your cup and adding the freshly boiling water. You may watch the leaves unfold as the tea develops color and puts forth its enticing aroma. If you will be bothered by leaves in your cup of tea, use a tea bag or infuser. An infuser should be large enough to permit the leaves to swell and the water to circulate freely through them. It's advisable to keep the tea hot during brewing by covering the cup with a saucer or lid.

When making tea for a few people, you'll probably want to use a teapot, one whose construction will help rather than hinder the simple process of tea brewing. A teapot doesn't brew tea in the way that a coffee-maker *makes* coffee. A coffeemaker actually participates in and regulates the brewing process, but a teapot is simply a container in which brewing takes place. A poorly designed teapot will not force you to make bad tea—as a poorly designed coffeepot will force you to make bad coffee—but it can mar the pleasures of your personal tea ceremony. Your teapot should be well-balanced; it should not be easily knocked over when at rest, nor should it fall forward when you pick it up to serve. The lid of the pot should remain firmly in place when you pour—it will if the flange of the lid is deep. The lid should have a knob so that you can remove the lid without burning your hand. The handle should be of such a shape that will enable you to grip it firmly without burning your knuckles. The top of the spout must be at least as high as the top of the pot or you won't be able to fill it. The base of the spout should be above the level of the leaves, so that the grid holes don't get blocked up. The pot should be easy to clean. A removable leaf basket is desirable, because it makes it easy to remove the spent leaves from the finished brew. While many teapots are attractive, few measure up to even most of our criteria of good design. It is fortunate that metal pots, injurious to tea flavor, are rarely used for brewing tea. Most are ceramic or glass, both of which have a salutary effect on the brewing process. A beautiful ceramic pot is its own justification, while the modern glass pots have the advantage of showing off the brew.

Here then are the rules of making tea, how they work for your enjoyment, and why deviation from them will yield less than satisfactory results:

1. *Use the highest grade of the type of tea that suits you—one teaspoonful (or one tea bag) for each 5½-ounce cup.*

   In tea drinking, the whole is greater than the sum of its parts. The brew should be a delightful symphony—but can be only if all the notes of flavor, body, color, stimulation and pungency are present in the tea. Using quality tea will insure that goodness is available; using enough tea will insure that you'll get that goodness in satisfying amounts.

2. *Bring freshly drawn, cold tap water to a bubbling boil. Use it when it has just reached the stage of bubbling fiercely.*

   Water that's been sitting around in a hot water tank or a kettle, is flat and insipid. So is water that's been previously boiled, or water that's allowed to continue boiling for some time before it's used. All suffer from de-aeration; tea made from such water will lack liveliness. The point of using freshly boiling water is that only water at the boiling point will both agitate the leaves and open them up sufficiently for proper infusion to take place. The liquor of the tea will be thin, lacking in flavor and character unless a thorough mixing of water and leaf is insured. Underboiled water (*i.e.*, 185°–195°F.) does not have this desired effect on the tea leaves. The harder the water you use, the more aggravated the ill effects of stale or underboiled water. At high altitudes where water boils well below 212°F., good tea is hard to prepare.

3. *Preheat your teapot.*
   This may be accomplished by rinsing the pot with scalding hot tap water
   or boiled water. A hot teapot maintains the high temperature of the
   freshly boiling water as it hits the leaves. A cold teapot would reduce the
   temperature of the water and the result would be the same as if underboiled water were used.
4. *Take the teapot to the kettle; when pouring the boiling water, hold the
   spout of the kettle near the mouth of the teapot.*
   Both these operations insure that the water is not permitted to cool down
   before it hits the tea leaves.
5. *Brew tea for three to five minutes, depending on the tea and your taste.*
   When it comes to tea, time really is of the essence and the essence a
   result of good timing. The tea must be given time to fully infuse. Since
   different rates of infusion result from various leaf styles, a single time
   cannot be recommended for all teas. Flat leaf infuses more quickly than
   well twisted leaf; small leaf more quickly than coarse leaf. Varying the
   brewing time within the three- to five-minute limits is a way of adjust-
   ing the brewing process to suit leaf style and personal taste. Flavor and caffeine are dissolved earliest (after color) in the infusion process. From then
   on, as more tannin or tannin compounds are dissolved, the brew develops
   more pungency and body. Most tea drinkers favor tea made from a five-
   minute infusion, as the shorter infusion times usually produce a "skinny"
   brew. Tea should be brewed, not stewed—infusing tea for longer than
   five minutes will throw the balance the other way. The brew will become
   heavy and increasingly bitter. This bitterness will overshadow the more
   delicate flavor and aroma of the tea.

   Time the brew. Probably the single greatest cause of improperly
   brewed tea here is the tendency of Americans to judge the strength of
   tea by the color of the infusion. As George Mitchell, former United States
   Supervising Tea Examiner, said, we drink tea with our eyes. It seems to
   us that this reliance on color is responsible for the widespread mistreatment of black teas as well as our out-of-hand rejection of semi- and
   unfermented teas. The coloring matter of fermented tea infuses very
   quickly, before the brew has had an opportunity to develop much flavor
   or body or stimulation. The infusion of high quality unfermented green
   tea never develops any but the palest golden green color. In fact, if any
   darkness of color were to show in such an infusion, we would take it as
   a sign of damaged or low quality tea. The widespread use of tea bags
   has probably aggravated this bad habit. People can and do stop the

brewing process when a little color shows, simply by lifting the tea bag out of their cups. If you are enrolled in the school of the dunked tea bag, we recommend that you dematriculate immediately.

6. *Keep the brewing tea hot while infusion takes place.*

A fuller draw is obtained when the temperature of the brewing tea is kept high; but perhaps more important is the fact that you'll want the beverage to be hot when you serve. Use a tea cozy for this; any application of direct heat involves the danger of driving off the delicate aroma in the steam such heat might produce.

7. *Separate the spent, infused leaf from the brewed tea. Stir the infusion and serve.*

This is necessary of course to prevent infusion from continuing beyond the desired amount of time. It's made easier if your teapot is equipped with a removable leaf basket or if you use some sort of perforated tea ball or spoon. If you've used tea bags, just lift them out. If you have not employed either of these devices, and you will not be using all the tea at once, pour the remainder off into a second preheated pot. Before serving tea made in a teapot it is advisable to stir the brew so that you get a liquor of even strength throughout.

tea caddy

bamboo strainer

infuser

teapot

tea strai

8. *Pour the tea.*

Drink just as it is or add sugar or milk (in that order if both), or lemon. Honey is great with tea, or for a change try some raspberry jam. Or drink it just as it is; good tea, well made, offers you a whole symphony of delights and truly needs no accompaniment. To appreciate the full range of flavor, color, pungency, and body, don't just gulp it. Sniff it. Appreciate its color. Sip it. Savor it. Roll it around in your mouth.

9. *If you want more tea, brew more tea—but use fresh leaves or a fresh tea bag.*

Lu Yu recommended that "for exquisite freshness and vibrant fragrance, limit the number of cups [that you drink] to three." Spent leaves have nothing more to offer you than a little color and a little bitterness. If you're having a second cup because you liked the first, don't disappoint yourself by making it with less care.

TEA AS A WAY OF LIFE: CUSTOMS AND CEREMONIES

There is a story told about Rikyu, the great Japanese tea master, who was questioned regarding the supposed secrets of *Cha-no-yu*, the tea ceremony. He replied:

Well, there is no particular secret in the ceremony save in making tea agreeable to the palate, in piling charcoal on the brazier so as to make a good fire for boiling the water, in arranging flowers in a natural way, and in making things cool in the summer and warm in the winter.

The questioner, disappointed with such an apparently bland prescription, exclaimed, "Who on earth does not know how to do that?" Rikyu, unruffled by the inquirer's dissatisfaction, replied, "Well, if you know it, do it."

A true ritual or ceremony expresses an inherent need, makes explicit the implicit nature of things, bridges the gap between inner and outer world. Customs and ceremonies are intuited or felt, not simply "executed." In this sense they must be known to the inner self before they can be successfully performed. Rikyu's questioner, we suspect, never quite attained the inner peace of *Cha-no-yu*.

Ceremonies, customs, and rituals that have grown up around the practice of tea drinking are an integral part of the life and culture of many societies. The great tea traditions have evolved slowly over the centuries, and are uniquely suited to the cultures that fostered them. One of the great traditions of Western culture has been the exploration, exploitation and, occasionally, appropriation of foreign cultures. Of course cultural borrowing has its limits and inevitable misunderstandings, even within single nations. In the mid-nineteenth century *Harper's* magazine reported the following:

> A country lady received a pound of tea from a fashionable friend in the city, and supposing it to be a newly-introduced vegetable, boiled the whole parcel, and had it served up for dinner, throwing away the liquor of course. Another supposed that the leaves were to be eaten as dried fruit; but after giving them a fair trial in this form, acknowledged reluctantly that she could not bring herself to like them.

Curiously enough, some Asian peoples swear by pickled teas and chewing teas that are probably not so distant from the ill-conceived stew of this country lady. Probably you won't want to borrow their cultural habits; some new ideas are simply not as adaptable as others.

The panorama of tea habits that follows is not meant, then, for your uncritical imitation. The ceremony which is your own you know somewhere inside you. Here are some that are known by the various cultures of the world.

IRAN Tea has been the national beverage of Persia for centuries. It is served around the clock: The day starts with a breakfast of tea, bread and cheese; then it's tea at ten and again at four in the afternoon, and tea is served to visitors in the evening. It is not uncommon for Iranians to make perfumed tea by adding heavily scented blossoms or herbs to tea leaves in a cannister, where they remain for several days. Water for tea is brought to a boil in a samovar-like urn, with coconut shell charcoal for fuel, and poured through the tea in a cloth strainer.

MOROCCO Moroccans put green tea into a brass or silver tea pot, add fresh spearmint leaves, and serve the brew with plenty of sugar. In Morocco etiquette requires a guest to have three glasses of tea—not a hardship, for the brew is delicious, and so are the goodies. Typical are *tmarh* (stuffed walnuts) and *kehbousal* (almond crescents), a favorite for centuries. The eldest woman in the house has the honor of pouring tea for guests, usually served with sugar and lemon. She sits on a rug specially reserved for this ceremony.

TIBET To Tibet goes the honor of holding the world's largest tea party.

In 1852 4,000 lamas consumed cauldrons of tea in holy silence at a party given for them by a wealthy pilgrim.

TURKEY For formal occasions a samovar is used, but for daily use, tea is made in two pots: one to hold a tea essence, which is kept warm over the the second pot holding the boiling water. The tea is served in small glasses with sugar and lemon; a special afternoon treat is a cheddar-like cheese on a type of soft pretzel called *simits*.

U.S.S.R. Years ago, the term "Russian tea" meant China brick tea, carried through Manchuria and Mongolia into Russia by caravan. Now, the Soviets consume China, Japan, Ceylon, and Indian teas as well as those from the Georgian Republic. Russia is the home of the samovar, a large vessel for boiling water, usually copper, heated by charcoal in a metal pipe extending vertically through its center. Tea leaves are brewed in a small teapot resting on top of the pipe, where it is then kept hot. The tea is served in glasses with metal holders, about one-fourth strong tea and three-fourths steaming water from the samovar. Russian tea, not as strong as English tea, is usually served with lemon but never with milk. Often a sugar cube is held between the teeth and the tea is sipped hot through the cube. Sometimes a spoonful of jam takes the place of sugar.

Russians drink tea with all meals, and throughout their waking hours. The Frenchman has his café; the Russian his *chainaya* or tea room.

GREAT BRITAIN The stereotype of the tea-drinking Britisher is someone who never has the cup away from his lips. He starts with tea as an eye opener and goes on with tea for breakfast and for the morning break. He has tea for lunch and tea at four, then tea with dinner and tea for a late night snack. The Briton, to be happy, must have his tea, good tea, whenever he wants it —at the railway stations, the tea trolley; on the trains, the tea basket; at the cinema, the tea room.

Great Britain is the world's greatest consumer of tea, although consumption is on a slight decline, probably due to a growing interest in coffee. The British, who once consumed about ten pounds of tea per capita annually, now consume only about eight—which is still nearly three times the per capita consumption of tea in Japan and Taiwan, and ten times the per capita consumption in the U.S.

The use of tea bags is growing in the U.K., but it is still very small. Most Britons seem to know how to make a delicious and satisfying pot of tea.

Blends of India, Ceylon, and China black are favored. Milk is generally added, but sugar is a matter of personal taste. Better hotels and restaurants offer a choice of green or oolong or India tea on the menu. Perhaps the most noticeable difference between American and British attitudes toward tea is the place reserved for it in public life. In London there are hundreds of popular tea rooms, run by Lyons, Lipton, Ridgways, A B C Shops, Slaters. The big department stores like Selfridge's, Harrods, and Barkers have attractive tea rooms. In the summer throughout England it is possible to enjoy afternoon tea in the open. Tea Gardens are operated in the public parks of London, mainly in Hyde Park, Kensington Gardens, and Kew Gardens. In the suburbs, any number of private houses turn their parlors and back yards into tea rooms and gardens, signalled by a modest sign: TEAS.

NEW ZEALAND AND AUSTRALIA   New Zealand, Australia, and Canada present interesting variations on English tea-drinking habits. In New Zealand, those living in the rural areas called "back Blocks" are prone to boil the leaves. In Australia, the bush man on the great sheep farms has a smoke-blackened tin called a "billy can" in which he boils water as soon as he crawls from his bunk in the morning. He throws in a handful of tea and lets it go on boiling until his bacon is cooked. By this time the tea is well stewed and ready for breakfast. Plenty of sugar is used, and often a gum tree leaf is added for flavoring. The meal over, the billy is left simmering; when he returns to his cabin at dusk, he rekindles the fire, warms up the black concoction which has steeped all day, and drinks it with the utmost enjoyment. In urban areas of Australia, British habits seem to prevail.

CANADA   Although Canada is the foremost tea-drinking country in the Western Hemisphere, per capita consumption is only about half the U.K.'s, that is, four pounds per capita annually. Some green tea is favored in the lumber regions.

SRI LANKA (CEYLON)   Tea drinking in Sri Lanka is a comparatively recent habit imported from England. Except for breakfast, it is seldom served with meals. Tea is offered when guests drop in, and the English silver service, if available, has also been adopted. A deviation is the native custom of sitting leisurely among pillows on the floor. Tea customs in the small villages are less British. A cluster of bananas in front of a native shop identifies it as a Tea Boutique. The villager stops off for a cup of tea on his way home from work in one of the lush tea gardens which blanket the country's slopes and terraces. The "cocktail" hour is spent chatting with friends, sipping tea and chewing a bit of betel leaf; the fatigue and tensions of the day are dispelled.

INDIA One of the largest tea producers, India has only recently turned to the use of tea as a beverage on the Western model. Generally the tea is boiled in an open pot together with a few green (unbleached) cardamom seeds, a pinch of fennel, and sugar. Milk is added to the boiling liquid—about one part milk to four parts water. This sweet, fragrant brew is served all over India, in cups and glasses in the cities and towns, and sometimes in crude earthenware "glasses"—which look like miniature flower pots—in remoter vilages. Every station of the Indian railway has at least one tea stand, and at any hour of the day or night, as a train lumbers in, the air is filled with the cries of the tea vendors—"chay-ya! chay-ya!"

SCANDINAVIA Trips to England have taught the Norwegians, Swedes, and Danes the rewarding comforts of tea to escape the cold dreariness of the dark months. Afternoon tea is especially popular. But here there are no scones, as in Britain; instead, it's open-faced smoked fish sandwiches, little sweet cakes and milk, and sugar in the tea.

JAPAN Introduced from China over 1,000 years ago, green tea is favored here, and served throughout each meal, cup after small cup.

The tea ceremony, or *Cha-no-yu*, is essentially an aesthetic experience, evoking relaxation of mind and a worship of purity, beauty and serenity. The special tea room is nine feet square, the number of guests four. Here are some of the rules for the ceremony, written about 600 years ago, that still represent the highest ideals of the ceremony as it is practiced today.

1. It is important on entering this ceremony to have not only a clean face and hands, but chiefly a clean heart.
2. The host must meet his guests and conduct them in. If he is too poor to give them the tea and necessaries for the ceremony, or if the eatables are tasteless, the guest can leave at once.
3. As soon as the water makes a sound like the wind in the fir trees, the bell rings and guests enter from the waiting room.
4. It is forbidden, since long ago, to speak in or out of the house of anything worldly—including politics, and especially scandal.
5. No guest or host may, in any true, pure meeting, flatter either by word or deed.

The performance of the tea ceremony can be separated into approximately three phases. In the first, called *zenseki,* the room is darkened by bamboo screens, the scroll is arranged in the alcove, or in the case of dusk or dawn ceremonies, only flowers are used. The next part, or *nakadachi,* consists of the serving of a simple meal and sweet cakes. After this the guests relax in the garden, or *roji,* for a few minutes. In the final phase of the ceremony, called *nochiseki,* a floral arangement is substituted for the scroll, the tea utensils are brought in, and *temae,* the actual making and serving of the tea, is performed. This is the most important part of the ceremony.

Shuko, who invented *temae* in the fifteenth century and who is known as the father of the tea ceremony, taught that concentrating on the gestures of *temae* could bring about the same sense of deep spiritual meaning experienced during Zen meditation. First the tea utensils, including the tea caddy, the tea scoop, the tea bowl (in which the tea is made), and the tea whisk are arranged and wiped clean. The bowl and whisk are warmed. Three heaping tea scoops per person are placed in the tea bowl, boiling water is added, and the tea is whisked smoothly and slowly until it thickens. This is the highlight of the ceremony. The tea is then sipped in a polite, ritual manner. After the utensils have been washed and wiped the chief guest asks to examine the lacquered tea caddy, or *natsume,* and the tea scoop and he shows them to the other guests. The host leaves the room. When they have finished looking at the utensils the host returns and conversation begins, inspired by a comment on one of the utensils. When this formal talk has ended the fire is smothered and the kettle allowed to die down. Then thin or weak tea is served to signify that the ceremony is over.

The tea ceremony reaches this high ideal in Japan today only in the monasteries and among a small minority of elite tea masters and their acolytes. The ceremony is practiced widely by the middle classes, but it is sometimes difficult to discover the original spiritual principles in those modern versions. Expertise in ritual has been emphasized at the expense of a deeper aesthetic experience. This trend is encouraged by the tea schools who profit by teaching a rigid, complicated set of tea rules. In the past fifty years, 90 percent of the students at these schools have been women anxious to acquire these dubious skills to enhance their chances of marriage. They rarely show any interest in tea after getting their diplomas or marrying.

Tea entertainments of 2,000–3,000 people are common in Japan. Intimacy and spiritualism are all but impossible at these events. Businessmen take up tea for the prestige of owning a tea house and impressive utensils, but leave the actual preparation to a hired tea master. The complex industrial system in Japan has harmed rather than nurtured the tea ceremony—but then, the simple, natural, and pure life has suffered to some extent wherever technology and industrialism have appeared. Perhaps it should be taken as a hopeful sign that the Japanese tea ceremony exists in any form after all these centuries.

6. Tea Recipes and Tea Fortunes

WHEN GRANDPA made tea he put his leaves in a glass measuring cup and poured just a little boiling water on them. After five minutes of steeping he'd have an essence which he'd pour off into tea cups and dilute with more boiling water. He loved his tea and believed in it. He didn't just recommend tea; he prescribed it. A good cup of hot tea was his recipe for a long, full life.

We feel, as Schap did, that a nice cup of hot tea can't be beat. Its charming subtle flavor and gentle stimulation make it delightful in any season at any time of day. The recipes which follow don't improve on the basic brew, but offer some further adventures in the world of tea. You can ice it, spice it, mint it, or make a tea punch. Tea ice cream is refreshing two times over. In the recipes, unless green tea is specified, use black—a good Ceylon, Assam, or Darjeeling.

Fruit Tea

A variation from the usual additions to tea is to make a fruit tea. Brew a cup (5½ oz.) of tea in a mug. Sweeten with sugar or honey and add a finely diced apple or pear, or strawberries. Let the fruit sit in the tea for a few minutes, then eat the fruit and drink the tea.

Cinnamon Tea

Brew the tea in the regular way, but include a stick of cinnamon in the brewing.

Spicy Tea

Brew your tea according to the instructions for regular tea. In each cup place 1½ teaspoons sugar, 1 thick slice of lemon studded with 3 whole cloves, and a stick of cinnamon to use as a stirrer. Stir and strain the tea and pour it over the other ingredients in each glass. If you have them, serve this tea in Russian tea glasses with handles.

Hot Tea for a Crowd

The easiest way to make tea for a large crowd is to make a tea concentrate ahead of time. To make tea for 25, bring one quart of fresh cold water to a full boil and pour over ⅔ measuring cup of tea. Cover and let the tea steep for five minutes—no longer. Stir and strain the tea into a pitcher or teapot. To make tea for 50, just double the amount of water and tea. Keep the tea concentrate covered at room temperature; it should be used within 4 hours. To serve, pour about 2 tablespoons of tea concentrate into each cup and fill the cup with freshly boiled water. By varying the amount of concentrate you can vary the strength of the tea.

Iced Tea

Good iced tea is easy to make. Follow the rules for making hot tea, but use 50 percent more tea, to compensate for the melting ice. For example, you'd use 4 tea bags or 4 teaspoons of loose tea to make 4 cups of hot tea, but to make 4 glasses of iced tea, you need 6 tea bags or teaspoons. Cloudiness doesn't affect the taste of the tea, but to clear it up, you can add a little boiling water. The brewed tea should be poured over the ice in the glasses or pitcher.

Iced Tea for a Party   *30-35 servings*

Bring 1½ quarts of freshly drawn cold water to a rolling boil in a saucepan. Remove from the heat and immediately add ¼ pound of loose tea. It's important to add all the tea at one time, while the water is still bubbling. Stir to immerse the leaves. Brew for 5 minutes. Strain into 5 quarts of cold water (not iced). Serve in ice-filled glasses with sugar and lemon, if desired. To make twice as much, just double the amounts of tea and water.

Sun Tea

This is the way our friend Nancy remembers her family making iced tea. On a hot, sunny midsummer's day, place 8 tea bags or 8 teaspoons of loose tea in 1 quart of room temperature water. Cover loosely to keep out dust and set the container out in the sun for the entire day. The tea will brew in the sun. At the end of the day, serve the tea over ice cubes, with sugar and lemon if desired.

Hot Spiced Party Punch   8 6-oz. servings

5 measuring cups water
10 teaspoons loose tea or 10 tea bags
½ cup boiling water
¾ cup sugar
¼ cup lemon juice
½ cup orange juice
6 whole cloves
1 stick cinnamon

Bring the 5 measuring cups of water to a boil and pour them over the tea. Allow the tea to brew for 5 minutes. While the tea is brewing, pour ½ cup of boiling water over the sugar in a large pitcher or punch bowl. Stir to dissolve the sugar and add the lemon juice, both at room temperature. Add the cloves and cinnamon. When the tea has brewed for 5 minutes, strain it or remove the tea bags and pour the brewed tea over the spices and juice. This punch should be served at once.

Chilled Tea Punch   50 punch-cup servings

2 quarts water
5 level tablespoons tea or 15 tea
  bags
2 cups lemon juice, strained
4 cups orange juice, strained
1½ quarts grape juice
2 cups sugar
2 quarts water
1 quart ginger ale

Brew the tea in 2 quarts of freshly boiled water for 5 minutes. Stir and strain the brew or remove the tea bags, and add the brewed tea to a pitcher containing all of the other ingredients except the ginger ale. Just before serving, pour the mixture into a punch bowl over ice. Stir in the ginger ale.

Tea Lemonade   12 6-oz. servings

2 quarts water
5 level tablespoons tea or 15 tea
  bags
¾ cup cold water
¾ cup sugar
¾ cup fresh lemon juice

Brew the tea as above. To make the syrup, combine and simmer the cold water and the sugar for ten minutes. Add the syrup and fresh lemon juice to the tea. To serve, pour the mix over ice in tall glasses. You can make this punch even more festive by adding a package of frozen strawberries to it.

Minted Teas

For minty refreshment blend a robust black tea like Ceylon or Darjeeling with peppermint or spearmint. The proportion of mint to regular tea in the blend can be adjusted to your taste. To brew, use 1 teaspoon of your blend to each 5½ ounces of water.

If you want something lighter try tea the Moroccan way—a blend of green tea and spearmint.

Minted teas are delightful hot or iced.

Tea Ice Cream

A ceremonial tea ice cream is served in Japan, using Mattcha, the green, powdered, ceremonial tea. (If you can't find Mattcha, grind green tea to a powder.)

1 quart heavy cream	1½ cup sugar
1 pint milk	1 heaping teaspoon Mattcha

Mix the cream, milk, and sugar in a large bowl until the sugar is dissolved. Place the Mattcha in a measuring cup and add enough tepid water to measure ¾ cup. Mix the tea and water into a thin paste. Add this to the cream, milk, and sugar mixture. Place in the freezer until the mixture is frozen about an inch from the sides all around and slushy in the center. Remove and scoop into a blender. Blend for *about* two minutes or until smooth; this breaks up any ice crystals. Return to the freezer until completely frozen. Tea ice cream can be made in a home ice cream machine.

FORTUNES IN A TEACUP

The ancients believed that ringing bells would drive away evil. From this belief the practice of studying the inside of bells for omens developed. The ancient Chinese carried this practice a step further. To them the tea cup was like an inverted bell, and the leaves remaining in the cup after the tea had been drunk formed a mystic pattern to be studied and interpreted. Over the centuries tea-leaf reading spread throughout the world and became one of the most popular methods of fortune telling. Local variations developed. In the Scottish highlands the tea-leaf reader was known as the "spae-wife." She read her own tea leaves every morning from her breakfast cup of tea, and those of her friends who came to visit during the day. She looked not into the far future, but only into the twenty-four hours to come. She would predict such things as the weather, if a letter would come and from whom, whether it was a good day to take the stock to market, whether a sick person would recover. An anonymous Highland seer, author of *Tea-Cup Reading and the Art of Fortune-Telling by Tea Leaves,* claimed that "many of the minor happenings of life could be foreseen with considerable accuracy" but that those who charged for the service and claimed to be able to predict the future were simply exploiting their gullible clients.

Over the centuries the symbols of tea-leaf reading have become generally agreed upon. How much can be read depends on the imagination and experience of the reader or seer. The pictures formed by the leaves are often only stylized silhouettes; they are symbols which must be interpreted in the light of the relationships they form with each other and in the light of their relevance to the questioner. The seer recognizes the symbols, interprets their effects upon each other in the pattern of the leaves, and weaves the interpretation into the life of the inquirer.

The tea should be prepared without an infuser in a regular teacup—one that is fairly shallow and narrow at the bottom, with a wide opening and a handle. The cup should be unfluted and plain white on the inside. A large leaf tea will make for easy reading. The questioner drinks the tea. While drinking he should make a wish or formulate a question and keep it in mind while he drinks. The questioner should leave about a teaspoonful of tea covering the leaves in the cup. The questioner then takes the cup by the handle in his *left* hand and swirls the liquid and leaves three times *to the left*. Gently he turns the cup upside down in the saucer, letting the water and excess leaves fall out. He waits a moment for the cup to drain. The reader picks up the cup and turns it right side up. The first pattern or impression received when the cup is turned over is the response to the tea-drinker's question or wish. The reader must concentrate on the questioner. The cup is turned to various positions as the reader studies the leaves. He lets his imagination take over, and slowly discerns the emerging images and patterns.

The handle of the cup represents the questioner and home. The reading begins at the left of the handle and proceeds around the cup. Symbols farther from the handle are more distant from the person. Symbols close to the rim represent the immediate future; farther from the rim, they pre-dict events farther in the future. At the bottom of the cup the symbols represent the distant future.

The interpretation of symbols depends on the context provided by all the leaf-patterns taken together and by the life of the questioner. Even the most precisely defined symbols may be mitigated by those around them. For example, a bouquet (symbol of good luck) with a small cross (bad luck and suffering) next to it, might indicate a delay in the good fortune. Or, a line around the cup from the handle and back indicates a speedy journey and return home. Breaks or interruptions in the line indicate obstacles or stops; an unfinished line, that the questioner will not return home. The journey could be physical or spiritual. In some cases, the leaves may appear muddled and cloudy. This is said to reflect the state of mind of the ques-tioner. A state of indecision or vagueness may so cloud the mind of the questioner that the reader will be able to distinguish no images or patterns.

Anything from a dinosaur to a rocket ship may be seen in the leaves and interpreted. Following are just some of the more traditional symbols. Their general meanings are given, but no symbol is absolute. These symbols generally indicate good luck: triangles, stars, clover, leaves, anchors, trees, garlands, flowers, bridges, crowns. And these are generally bad luck: coffins, crosses, serpents, rats, hourglasses, church steeples, swords and guns, ravens, owls, monkeys.

anchor—voyage
cat—treachery
cow—prosperity
dog—faithful friends
book—revelation
clouds—doubts, problems
cross—suffering
egg—increase, luck

flowers—love, honors, esteem
heart—love
ladder—gradual rise, advancement
letters of alphabet—initials of
   significant people
tree—good luck, fruitfulness,
   success, happiness
ring—marriage

History tells us that it's perfectly legitimate to read your own tea leaves as well as those of others. The procedure is the same. Reading tea leaves is rather like looking for pictures in clouds or in the flames of a fire. At first you see nothing, but if you stare at them for a while you begin to see things. With a little practice you'll recognize symbols and get better at putting together an interpretation.

HERBAL TEAS

Like plants, most men have hidden properties
that chance alone reveals.
                    La Rochefoucauld, *Maxims*

1. Definitions, History, Cultivation, and Uses

DEFINITIONS

AN HERB has been defined as an aromatic plant and a spice as an aromatic and pungent vegetable substance. American settlers called any plant they ate an herb. This usage reflected the wider meaning of the word—a plant with a fleshy rather than woody stem. What they called herbs we now mostly call vegetables.

In the dictionary definitions of herb and spice the difference seems to hang on the word "pungent"; herbs are aromatic, spices are aromatic and pungent. The sense of taste, like smell (intimately connected with taste) and touch, is considered a primitive animal sense in the West. It is through sight and hearing that we have built an intellectual and technological empire, and these are the senses that have been most thoroughly studied scientifically in our laboratories. Colors and sounds are described accurately in terms of spectrum, wavelengths, and amplitude, if not in words. But descriptions of taste—the word "pungent" for instance—have no such exactitude and drift into shades of personal subjectivity.

Dropping semantics in favor of locale at least gives us a way to distinguish between herbs and spices. In general if the aromatic or fragrant plant originates in the tropics it is called a spice; if it comes from a temperate region it is called an herb. This rule is not all-encompassing, since a tropical product like cinnamon appears both in herbals and spice books and so does the temperate plant sweet basil. Both of these make excellent herbal tea. Classification according to parts of the plant used is also ambiguous. Cloves and camomile are dried flower buds; black pepper and elder are fruits; cinnamon and birch are bark. The first mentioned in each of these pairs is a tropical product and considered a spice; the second is a temperate plant and known as an herb. All but pepper make fine herbal tea.

The line between spices and herbs is indistinct, but it is an uncertainty of little importance. What is important are the tastes and flavors themselves. In the ancient Orient herbs and spices were an organic part of life, used not only as flavorings for food and drink but in incense, embalming, ointments, perfumes, cosmetics, medicines, and magic. Coffee, tea, spices, and herbs all originated in the East and were revered by the people there. Perhaps exaltation of the sense of taste is a reflection of the more mystical sensuous way of life that Westerners must embrace to round out their world of mechanical abstractions. Taste is immediate and individual, experienced more with the body than the brain. It is the perfect sensation to symbolize a philosophy that emphasizes a personal, non-intellectual elevation of the mundane into a state of cosmic awareness. Taste is an adventure—some might say a spiritual adventure—and whether the drink is called herbal tea or spice tea is of no matter; it is the adventure that counts.

Our concern is with herbal tea. Pepper, onion, and garlic would seem to be spices by any criteria of taste or usage, and they appear as such in the spice literature. Yet they also show up in all the herbals, and one manual even suggests as a cure for epilepsy an infusion of bruised garlic bulbs— garlic tea! Only the brave would try such a beverage. Our purpose here is not to recommend it, but to illustrate that the blurring of the lines between spice and herb should not be an impediment to the enjoyment of herbal tea.

THE HISTORY OF HERBS AND SPICES

The history of herbs and spices is more ancient than that of tea and coffee. Primitive man roaming the new earth was attracted to the leaves, fruits, seeds, and roots of fragrant, sweet-tasting herbs like anise, marjoram, and cinnamon, and chose them for food over other plants. He combined them with water to make the first soothing herbal teas. He made unguents for his wounds out of them, on the assumption that their aromatic quality would be beneficial to his ills.

Around 3000 B.C. Marduk, an Assyrian god, was elected to lead the fight against Tiamat and her brood of oceanic monsters. Marduk and his army of lesser gods drank spiced wine in a pre-battle revel; then Marduk split Tiamat in half with his spear and made heaven from one half and earth from the other. This is one of the earliest written references to spices. The Assyrians and Babylonians planted large gardens of spices and herbs for use by their doctors and magicians, and by 700 B.C. hundreds of herbs including cumin, dill, fennel, thyme, saffron, myrrh, and garlic were known. Priests burnt aromatic plants in the temple as an offering to the gods. Fragrance was connected with purity, stink with evil. The streets were fumigated with sweet-smelling spices. At times luxury deteriorated into decadence. Sardanapalus, an Assyrian monarch fond of perfume, cosmetics, and transvestism, was warned of a rapidly approaching foe. He ordered a fire made from a pile of fragrant shrubs, mounted it with his concubines and favorite art objects, and was suffocated by the aromatic fumes. Assyrian sorcerers offered burnt sesame, mint, and garlic to the fire god to help the sick or bewitched. The Babylonians worshiped the moon god, Sin, and so they gathered and prepared medicinal herbs only by moonlight.

Osiris, the Egyptian god of the dead, was also the god of vegetation who knew the uses of all plants. The Egyptians believed that the spirit re-entered the body after death, and so to placate Osiris corpses were preserved from decay by an embalming process using cumin, anise, cinnamon, and marjoram. Doctors used coriander, caraway, saffron, and sesame in medicine. The Egyptians, like the Babylonians and Assyrians, used herbs and spices like myrrh and cassia in perfumes, oils, and unguents. The countless Egyptians who labored twenty years to build the Great Pyramid of Cheops subsisted largely on a diet of onions and garlic.

Joseph, visionary of the Old Testament, was sold into slavery by his older brothers to Ishmaelite spice merchants carrying "spicery and balm and myrrh" into Egypt. The Lord instructed Moses to build a tabernacle in the desert to be anointed with an oil made of cinnamon, cassia, myrrh, and calamus. Sheba visited Solomon in Jerusalem, bringing camel trains of spices as gifts. And in the Song of Solomon, the famous biblical celebration of connubial ecstasy, images of beauty and happiness are set in an ambience of aromatic herbs.

The Assyrians, Babylonians, Egyptians, and early Hebrews all made extensive use of a variety of spices to enrich their lives. Several of the important spices and herbs, including cinnamon and cassia, are not indigenous to the Middle East, but grow in Sri Lanka (Ceylon) and China. Ancient Chinese herbal records are not clear, but cassia is mentioned in the *Elegies of Ch'u* and ginger by Confucius around the fifth century B.C. Pepper, cinnamon, turmeric, cardamom, ginger, mustard seed, and sesame were included in sacred texts written before 1000 B.C. in India. These herbs and spices were used to ward off evil spirits, as sickroom fumigators, in poultices for wounds, to cure obesity, as digestive aids, and to sweeten the breath.

It was the adventurous Arab spice traders, dealers for centuries in aromatics, resins, and gums like frankincense and myrrh, who brought cassia and cinnamon to the Middle East and founded a spice and herb empire that was to last unbroken into the sixteenth century. The Arabs, sagacious traders and experienced, daring sailors, were the first to venture along unknown coasts to bring Oriental spices to the courts of Egypt and the Middle East in 1500 B.C. Sailing out of the Red Sea and the Persian Gulf, they travelled eastward, skirting what are now the nations of Iran, Pakistan and India at the edge of the Arabian Sea. They reached Ceylon, home of cinnamon, and crossed the Bay of Bengal to Burma and Malaysia, source of pepper, cloves, cardamom, cassia, and nutmeg. Here they could also pick up products of China like star anise, cumin, dill, fennel, ginger, sesame, turmeric, and mustard.

South Arabia became the spice and herb center of the ancient world, and the Arabs used all their wisdom and cunning to protect this tremendously lucrative trade. Taking advantage of an age when witchcraft, omens, and magic were commonplace, they spread fantastic stories about the spices they dealt with, obscuring their country of origin, hiding the sea routes they used, and raising the value of the products. The Arabs deceived historians from Herodotus in the fifth century B.C. to Pliny the Elder in the first century A.D. into believing that cinnamon and cassia grew in Arabia when in fact they were imported from the Orient. One fanciful tale, once accepted as truth, concerns the collection of cassia. Men who waded into the marshes surrounding a lake to gather the spice were attacked by hordes of shrieking bat-like monsters who flew straight for their eyes. Luckily they were protected by a covering of ox-hides. Perhaps even more imaginative was the supposed cinnamon collecting process. Giant birds made their nests out of cinnamon sticks amid inaccessible rocks. When the Arabs discovered one of these eyries, they would scatter carcasses of slaughtered oxen and asses on the ground below and hide. The enormous birds would then swoop down and pick up the huge joints of meat and carry them to their nests—which promptly broke under the strain of the additional weight. The Arabs, emerging from their hiding places, would pick up the pieces of fallen cinnamon.

Tales like these protected the Arab monopoly, until increased use of herbs and spices in the emerging Greek and Roman civilizations and new geographical discoveries precipitated a lively challenge to Arab domination. In 331 B.C. Alexander began a series of campaigns which would spread the Greek emblem from the Mediterranean to India. He founded the city of

Alexandria, which was to be renowned under both Greeks and Romans as the greatest herb and spice port in the eastern Mediterranean. Cargo from India and Indonesia was shipped to Greece and Italy from Alexandria to play an ever larger role in the life style of the people of the western Mediterranean. Greek soldiers slept on beds of spices and decorated their weapons with laurel leaves. Athletes were rubbed down with spice-scented oil and, when victorious, wore crowns of laurel. Anise, caraway, coriander, cumin, ginger, and mint were used as seasonings for sauces and relishes. Anise seed, basil, garlic, and fennel were mixed with wine or food as aphrodisiacs. Cardamom, cinnamon, cassia, and marjoram were blended for perfumes. Parsley was scattered over graves.

Since magical properties were associated with certain herbs and spices, they could be avoided, used to advantage, or employed to bewitch an enemy or gain favors from a loved one. Anise dispelled nightmares. Basil provoked hatred. Cumin was the symbol of avarice. Fennel was good for the eyes. Laurel made one prophetic. Parsley prevented drunkeness. Marjoram insured a happy marriage.

Hippocrates, the famous Greek physician who practiced around the fourth century B.C., is celebrated for directing medicine toward science and away from magic, and for formulating a code of ethics that still bears his name today. Among other herbal remedies he prescribed anise to prevent sneezing, coriander to stop heartburn, and mint to put an end to vomiting. Theophrastus, of the third century B.C., a contemporary of Plato and Aristotle, wrote two books: *On Odors* and *An Enquiry Into Plants*, which contained all that was then known about herbs and spices.

The Roman scholar Pliny the Elder worked on his 37 books of *Natural History* in the first century A.D. To save time servants read to him during meals and he dictated notes from his bath. In his remedies herbs were mixed with everything from asses' milk to axle grease and used to cure a range of ills from madness (raw garlic) to hiccups (mint). His insatiable scientific curiosity led to his death in 79 A.D., when he ventured too close while inspecting an eruption of Vesuvius. Dioscorides, a contemporary of Pliny, was a Roman army surgeon who mentioned aniseed, caraway, cinnamon, ginger, peppermint, and thyme as cures in his massive *De Materia Medica*, a standard medical authority for the next 1,500 years.

The Romans were among the world's most prolific users of spices and herbs at the dawn of the Christian era. Most people, soldiers included, were heavily perfumed. Great quantities of spices were used at funerals, and spiced wine, oil, and lamp oil were in constant demand. Romans slept on saffron-stuffed pillows to protect themselves against getting a hangover. Physicians prescribed spices and herbs lavishly.

As the trade in herbs and spices increased, gold and silver drained from the Roman treasuries and into the hands of the Arabs. Prices rose, the unfavorable balance of trade worsened, and a solution was sought. First the Romans tried military conquest, but their attempt to invade southern Arabia was a dismal failure. Where force of arms failed, commerce succeeded. Other spice traders were skeptical about the cassia bats and cinnamon birds. The merchants of Alexandria knew of the long Arab voyages and were increasingly suspicious about the cargoes. Greek and Roman sailors who began venturing out of the Red Sea into the Indian Ocean slowly built up a knowledge of the distant oceans: where the safe harbors were, the paths of the most perilous storms, where various spices and herbs could be obtained. Early in the first century A.D. the great breakthrough came: Greek and Roman navigators unlocked the secret of the monsoon winds. These seasonal winds, which the Arabs had been using to advantage for centuries, cut the trip to India and back by more than half—it now took less than a year. The southwest monsoon blew toward India from April to October, and the northeast shifted from October to April, blowing fair winds for the voyage home. This discovery prompted the Romans to increase the size of their fleet, and for the next three centuries both Roman and Arab vessels plied the Indian Ocean to the Orient.

In 476 the Roman Empire began to crumble. The rout was completed by the Arab takeover of Alexandria in the mid-seventh century. For the next four centuries the seat of culture and learning shifted to Mecca, where the Arab golden age flowered under the teachings of Mohammed. Islam eventually spread from Spain to the borders of China and to Ceylon, Java, and India. The spice and herb trade remained a secure Arab monopoly until Western encroachment during the Crusades and the Turkish conquests in the eleventh, twelfth, and thirteenth centuries. Still, the Muslim hold on the spice trade was not to be broken by the West until the voyages of discovery and the Renaissance in the fourteenth, fifteenth and sixteenth centuries.

Mohammed was a shrewd spice merchant who married a wealthy older woman, a widow, to secure a position as leader of her camel caravan. He dealt in myrrh, frankincense, and other spices from a shop in Mecca. One night in a dream Gabriel named him the Apostle of God and took him on a journey through hell that Dante would later depict in his *Divine Comedy*. Mohammed chose at the start of the voyage to drink from a vessel of milk and leave a vessel of wine untouched. By this choice wine became forbidden to his followers, and coffee became the Muslim drink.

Mohammed's worshippers created a flourishing commercial network across their empire. Islamic scientists developed ways of extracting scents from flowers and herbs and methods of distilling the essential oils from aromatic plants. These oils were then combined with sugar to form syrups, elixirs, and extracts. Muslim scientists synthesized a number of chemical compounds and excelled in mathematical optics and astronomy. Avicenna and Rhazes were Arab physicians whose medical and therapeutic writings influenced the universities of Europe until the seventeenth century. At the court Arab aristocrats and warriors developed a life style based on individual prowess, a taste for poetry, enjoyment of the senses, and a decorous code of behavior that was contrapuntal to the devout, unalterable precepts of the Koran. At the same time Arab merchants and scholars spread trade and learning throughout the land. This mixture created a civilization of vast depth and variety, richer than any known in Europe at the time. Undoubtedly it is to this great age, based largely on the riches of the spice and herb trade, that the Arabs of today look in their bid to recapture glory —a glory to be based this time on oil instead of spices.

Although spices were in great demand in medieval Europe to flavor and preserve the dull food of the time, and to hide the numerous unpleasant odors caused by poor sanitary conditions, they were in short supply. Hostility between the Christian and Islamic worlds, pirates, thieves, poor roads, and exorbitant taxes accounted for the diminished spice and herb trade. Charlemagne encouraged the cultivation of temperate herbs like fennel, anise and fenugreek throughout his realm. The Christian church, often credited with preserving whatever learning and culture could be found in these times, also grew sage, thyme, parsley and coriander in monastery gardens. The few costly Oriental spices like cinnamon, cumin, pepper, and cloves that reached Europe usually wound up with the clergy, as church records of gifts received and shopping lists show.

Partly responsible for keeping trade lines open between East and West in the ninth and tenth centuries were traveling Jewish merchants, who were accepted by Christian and Muslim alike. They brought wool, furs, swords, eunuchs, and European female slaves to the Orient, and returned to Europe with perfume, jewels, and spices. During the Crusades of the eleventh, twelfth, and thirteenth centuries, the West obtained a foothold on the edge of the Holy Land, which it used to supply the soldiers with food and metal and to ship fruit, precious stones, and spices back home. In time the increased flow of Oriental goods could hardly keep up with the demands of the prospering nobility and Church. Italy received valuable trading privileges for aid given in the Crusades and this enabled Venice, because of her unique geographical location, to pour Arabian spices into the expanding European market. The merchants of Venice became incredibly wealthy as sacks of cloves, nutmeg, and mace from Java, and pepper, cassia, and ginger from China piled up in their warehouses alongside the pearls, precious stones, and rugs. The gold and silver of Europe filled Venetian banks and made Arabs and Venetians alike fantastically rich.

By the end of the fourteenth century the use of spices and herbs had permeated all classes of medieval life. The extraordinary changes in the normally insipid diet included such Oriental products as dates, figs, citrus fruits, almonds, rice, and sugar. Cloves and cinnamon for garnish, anise and mint for gravies, caraway and cumin for soup and cheese, nutmeg and mace oil for butter, and sweet marjoram and thyme for puddings and cake were samples of culinary art in the Middle Ages. Medieval doctors and sorcerers prescribed dill for itch, fennel for coughs, marjoram for burns, mint for cuts, garlic for dog bites, laurel for cramps, parsley for black eyes, and onion to make hair grow. Spices and herbs appeared in the works of Boccaccio, Chaucer, and Shakespeare.

While Venice prospered and the Arabs grew affluent, the rest of Europe became slowly more powerful. They built larger, stronger ships, avidly pored over geographers' maps, perfected navigational instruments, and made tentative forays south along the coast of Africa in an effort to break the Venetian-Islamic stranglehold on spices. Marco Polo's tales of the interior of an Orient teeming with jewels, marble palaces, burning fountains of petroleum, polar bears, cannibals, sea beds of pearls, and untold quantities of every variety of spice and herb made the Western seamen even more eager to discover a sea route to the Orient. In 1453 the Ottoman Turks conquered Constantinople, and Venice entered into a long series of crippling wars with the Turks. Bartholomeu Dias discovered the Cape of Good Hope in 1488, and in 1498 Vasco da Gama became the first European to reach India by sea. This was a staggeringly long voyage with many hardships, but it enabled traders to avoid Islamic and Venetian control and taxes. It meant the end for Venice and the Arabs. No longer would the West be dependent on Venetians for their spices, and no longer would the Arabs be able to charge exorbitant tariffs of up to one-third the value of the spices they delivered.

The lure of spices drew Columbus and John Cabot west just before the end of the fifteenth century. They never found the spice lands, but they discovered the New World. In the meantime the Portuguese exploited Vasco da Gama's route to the fullest. They sent fleet after fleet to India, the Malabar Coast, Ceylon, Java, Sumatra, and the other spice islands. They captured ports and fortified them, built spice factories, and ruthlessly put down the natives who opposed them. Portugal replaced Venice as the herb and spice capital of the world. As riches flowed into Lisbon at the start of the sixteenth century, Spain, England, and Holland made plans to end Portugal's monopoly. Magellan's fleet sailed under the Spanish flag in 1519, found a Western route to the Orient through the straits that bear the great explorer's name, and were the first to successfully circumnavigate the globe, returning in 1522. Sailing for Queen Elizabeth in the *Golden Hind* in 1577–78, Sir Francis Drake steered around the southern tip of South America and returned to England around the world from the Orient laden with cloves and other spices. And before the end of the sixteenth century Van Houtman, sailing for the Dutch, followed Da Gama's route around the Cape of Good Hope to Sumatra and the spice islands.

These voyages of discovery set the stage for a great struggle for supremacy in the spice trade between Portugal, Holland, and England. The Dutch, envious of Portugal's accumulated wealth, were determined to drive her from the Orient at any cost. Holland had developed a large, powerful fleet of her own since she carried spices north from Lisbon to Amsterdam. Her profits from this and other ventures in grain, salt, and fish enabled her to build superior fighting ships manned with well-trained soldiers. The Dutch launched upon a merciless policy of massacre, torture, and slavery which crushed the Portuguese and brought the natives of the Malay Archipelago, Ceylon and Java completely under their control by the end of the seventeenth century. To maintain high spice prices they uprooted acres of clove trees and burned huge quantities of cinnamon and nutmeg.

In the meantime France and England stole closely guarded spice seedlings from the Dutch-controlled spice islands and cultivated clove, nutmeg, cinnamon and other spice plants in the West Indies, South America, Africa, and the Seychelles and Réunion in the Indian Ocean in an effort to break the Dutch monopoly. Spices from English-controlled India competed with spices from Holland. Piracy, smuggling and a war with England in 1780 finally resulted in the bankruptcy of the Dutch East India Company and the fall of Holland at the end of the eighteenth century. Britain controlled the spice trade for about three-quarters of the nineteenth century, but her interests gradually turned to India and tea and the Dutch regained their former spice eminence in the late nineteenth and early twentieth centuries. The United States enjoyed a brief monopoly in the Sumatra pepper trade from about 1800–1850. Fast clipper ships from New England carried fish, tobacco, flour, candles, beef, soap, and butter to the Orient and battled storms, Malay pirates and French privateers to return with pepper, tea, coffee, cassia, ginger, cinnamon, and cloves. Cargoes like the 1,000,000 lbs. of pepper carried by the *Eliza* in 1806 from Sumatra to Salem helped make America's first millionaires.

The spread of spice plants from the East Indies to Indochina, the West Indies, Africa, Japan, and Central South America, coupled with the decline of the great monopolies and the rise of free maritime commerce, has created a modern, decentralized spice and herb industry that includes countless independent importers, exporters, manufacturers, wholesalers and retailers throughout the world. But still locked in the shriveled leaf, dried bark, and twisted root is the essence of the past. The spicy aroma of brewed herbal tea once floated across the Arabian desert, wafted through the streets of ancient Rome, and graced the gardens of medieval monasteries. Spice flavors were so valued that a horse was worth a pound of saffron, a pound of ginger could buy a sheep, and a serf in medieval France could buy his freedom for a pound of pepper. Men no longer battle vast, unknown oceans in search of spices, or murder for cinnamon and nutmeg, but while the shifts of fortune and imperatives of history surrounding the storied spice trade have faded, the tastes remain to add a refined and elegant savor to our lives.

HERBALS: BOUGHT, GROWN OR GATHERED

There are three ways of obtaining the ingredients for herbal tea: buying them, growing them, or gathering them in the wild. These choices set herbal tea apart from *Camellia sinensis* since, unless you live in a tea-growing region like India or China, the only way you can obtain tea is to purchase it. Growing or gathering herbs for herbal tea offers the adventure of firsthand participation in some of nature's most basic processes.

Buying herbal tea is probably the easiest way to enjoy the beverage. It is less time-consuming than gardening or foraging and permits you to choose from a wider variety of teas. Herbal teas can be purchased at specialty tea shops, health or natural food stores, herb and spice emporiums, and herb farms. You can use dried herbs that you have around the house for cooking to make herbal tea, as well as fresh herbs. Herbal teas can be combined in an almost infinite variety. Colonial tea—peppermint, cloves, lime peel, and nutmeg—was used by American settlers during the embargo of British tea and is known as a good digestive. Trapper's tea—catnip, anise seed, and sage—is warming on winter or rainy days. Squaw tea—spearmint, rose hips, and sage—was popular with the American Indians and is rich in vitamin C. Feel free to adapt, alter, or ignore these blends, or create your own, according to taste. You may also want to consider adding herbals to regular tea.

Growing herbs is more difficult that purchasing them, but it is also extremely rewarding. Herb gardening, like any other type of gardening, requires first of all a plot of ground (or a decent-sized planter) and sun. It also requires planning, planting, cultivating, watering, weeding—in other words, time, patience, and a certain amount of strength and energy, all depending on how extensive a garden you want to keep. Herbs have this advantage: They do not need much space and, having been around for thousands of years, they are generally hardier than many flowers and vegetables. Some herbs, like parsley, will survive all winter outdoors. Lavender and chives last several years, and rosemary is a perennial which will keep coming up year after year. Tea made from fresh herbs is tastier and healthier than that made from their dried counterparts. If you live in the city or have only limited space you can easily cultivate a small herb garden in your window, balcony, or on your roof. This is quite common nowadays and five or so different herbs can be grown in a couple of square feet. The time and effort spent working on a garden will be considered a disadvantage only if you overextend yourself. No matter how big a garden you have, the variety of herbs will be limited by climatic factors. Probably the best choice is to grow what is practical to grow and buy either what cannot be grown or what you are not familiar with. In any case do not underestimate the intangible satisfactions of gathering herbs from your own garden and drinking tea made from them.

Going into the woods and fields after wild herbs may be at once the most difficult and satisfying way to enjoy herbal teas. This is the way the ancient Chinese first experienced tea; American Indians gathered teas this way for centuries and taught the settlers the secrets of native herbs, which were followed until less than a century ago. *Camellia sinensis* is undoubtedly the queen of tea, and its superb flavor and bouquet was the reason, thousands of years ago, that it was chosen as the tea of commerce out of all the plants that were available. But what of the other, forgotten, tea-giving plants—the strange, the rare, or the difficult to cultivate? These plants are still in the forests, meadows, and swamps, in the same primeval state as tea was at the dawn of time. They are the wild relatives of cultivated herbs and spices like sage and mint, and all herbalists admit they are better than their domestic counterparts; they are flowers like dandelion and wild rose, and wild plants like sassafras, coltsfoot, and alfalfa.

There are disadvantages to wild food gathering. The most obvious is the chance of error; there are plants that kill, and in quite a few cases these deadly growths so closely resemble a desired species that only someone with great experience can tell them apart. Another disadvantage of seeking herbs in the wild is the limitations of climate and geography; only plants near home are usually available, and winter means a scarcity of plants and uncomfortable hiking conditions.

But there are many definite benefits to foraging for herbal teas. You are encouraged to become intimate with nature, you learn to be at ease in the woods and to recognize poisonous as well as desirable plants, you are in tune with the flow of the seasons. We cannot provide you here with a handbook for embarking on this promising path toward self-education. There are, however, quite a number of books available; some of these, including the lively books of Euell Gibbons, are included in the Suggestions for Further Reading. Next time you go backpacking, why not take one along and do some searching for herbs?

STORING, DRYING AND PREPARING HERBAL TEAS

Store dry herbs that you buy in airtight glass containers or jars in a dry, dark, cool place. A general rule for preparing herbal teas is to use ¼–½ teaspoon of the herb per serving of tea, though this may vary according to your taste and the strength of the herb; in the case of milder herbs you may want to use as much as double the amounts above. Herbs which are flowers or leaves are usually prepared by infusion. Pour freshly boiled water over the herb and let steep, covered, about fifteen minutes. Herbs used in the form of root, bark, or seeds are usually prepared by decoction. To make a pint of tea (16 oz.), boil an ounce of the herb in 1½ pints of water for thirty minutes. Some herbal teas are now available in tea bags, but if you use loose tea, strain the beverage before serving.

Pick fresh herbs from the garden or woods on a dry, clear spring or summer day, after the sun has dried the dew but before the day has become hot. This preserves the strength of the plant's aromatic oils. If the leaves are not to be used immediately, hang them in bunches in a shaded, warm, dry, well-ventilated room to dry. Afterwards crumble them up and store them as described above.

HERBS AND MEDICINE

Medicine began in the kitchen. The earliest cooks realized that the sick needed different foods than the well and ministered to them with soothing herbs. This was the start of the ancient connection between herbs and healing. Magicians, who used thyme to see elves, ginger to dispel incubi, celery seeds to fly, and parsley to summon the devil, tried their hands at curing also; herbs and spices were employed by sorcerers, who ground bits of animal and vegetable matter into an incantation-fueled brew. As magic and superstition slowly gave way to the science of medicine, the sorcerers became spicers and pepperers pulverizing healing herbs with their mortars and pestles. These in turn became apothecaries, who were the forerunners of the modern pharmacologist or physician.

Probably partially responsible for the disrepute surrounding herbal remedies is the primitive and ancient doctrine of signatures, championed by Paracelsus in the sixteenth century. Paracelsus renounced his orthodox training as a physician, burned his medical texts and studied with gypsies, thieves, and wizards to perfect his knowledge of this doctrine, which is still subscribed to by many serious herbalists. The theory holds that some peculiarity in the plant—color, shape, odor, taste, or habitat—points to its effectiveness as a curative. Skullcap cures insomnia because it resembles a human skull. Eyebright is good for sight because it looks like an eye. Red plants purify the blood. Stinking arrach helps foul ulcers. Willow aids rheumatism because it grows in damp places. Yellow plants cure jaundice. The spotted leaves of lungwort are used for diseased lungs. Some of these remedies may be effective, but the doctrine of signatures itself seems somewhat far-fetched.

More interesting are recent studies that indicate ancient cures of the herbal art were based on an instinctive or dimly understood knowledge of vitamins and minerals. Fantastic claims to cure poor eyesight, itch, pimples, dandruff, and infection sound unbelievable, yet all these ailments could be the result of a lack of vitamin A and if that were the case, would be immeasurably aided by drinking tea made from dandelion leaves, which contain seven times more vitamin A than lettuce or carrots. Loose teeth, poisoning, scurvy, infections, wounds, and broken bones that do not heal might all be caused by a vitamin C deficiency. If this were true, tea brewed from wild rose hips, which contain four times more vitamin C than oranges, would be an excellent remedy.

Because herbs have been part of medical lore for thousands of years, every herb has a reputation for curing one or more ills. These will be included in the descriptions of the teas, but a warning is in order. In spite of the fact that a growing body of evidence suggests herbal cures are not as far-fetched as they seem, herbal medicine is not nearly so sophisticated as the orthodox medical establishment. Do not hesitate to experiment with some of the herbal remedies, but if you really do not feel well, see a doctor.

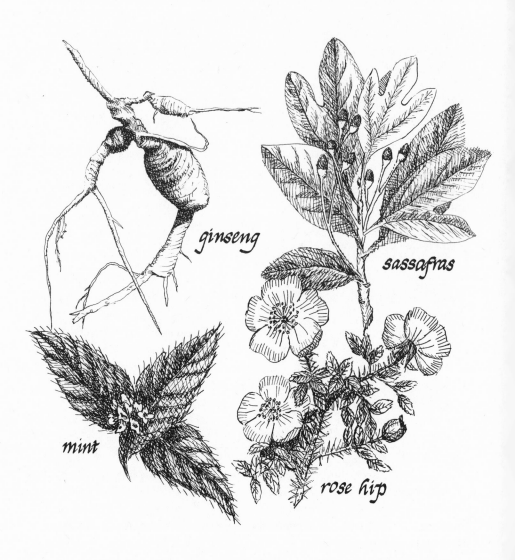

ginseng

sassafras

mint

rose hip

2. A Catalogue of Herbal Teas

Agrimony (*Agrimonia eupatoria*)

This plant, also known as church steeples, sticklewort, and cocklebur, is deep green with a thin, hairy stem and reaches a height of 2–3 ft. The serrated leaves are long, slender, and pointed at the ends, and the golden blossoms are star-shaped. Agrimony grows in Europe, North America, and other north temperate regions and may be gathered along roadsides and field edges or cultivated in the garden. It was considered a magical sleeping potion in medieval England and was thought to heal warts, snake bites, and harquebus wounds. The leaves and flowers make a spicy, aromatic tea resembling apricots in flavor. Agrimony is considered a strengthener of the liver, good for the skin, and a cure for sore throats.

Alfalfa (*Medicago sativa*)

Alfalfa, or Lucerne, is a leguminous herb with trifoliate leaves and blue or violet cloverlike flowers. The plant, which is 1–1½ ft. high, grows wild in Europe, the Orient, and North America and may be found along streams, wet meadows, and roadsides. It is grown extensively in the United States as forage for cattle. First mentioned as a vegetable by a Chinese emperor in 2939 B.C., alfalfa was also praised by Virgil, and Spanish friars planted Mexican alfalfa in the fields surrounding their California missions. A bland and somewhat grassy tea is made from the young leaves and flower heads. Alfalfa contains extraordinarily high quantities of vitamins A, E, D, and K, and eight important digestive enzymes, and is a rich source of minerals, iron, and organic salts. This herb, which contains more protein than wheat and corn, cleanses the kidneys, is good for ulcers, arthritis, and rheumatism, and aids in the building of muscle and flesh.

Angelica (*Angelica archangelica*)

Commonly called archangel or wild parsnip, this large, aromatic plant has a thick six-foot stem, bright green leaves that are three feet long and reddish-purple at the base, and branches bearing clusters of white, pale purple, or yellow flowers. It is native to northern Europe, but other varieties grow in North America and Asia. Angelica may be cultivated in the garden or found wild in swampy areas, along stream banks, and in open fields. Linked with angels in almost every European language, this herb, according to legend, was revealed by an angel in a monk's dream as a cure for the plague. Popular as a remedy for poison, witchcraft, and enchantment, angelica was known as "the Root of the Holy Ghost." It may be eaten as a vegetable, candied for a confection, or used to flavor liqueurs. A musky, aromatic sweet tea similar in taste to juniper is made from the leaves, chopped stems, or ground root. It is supposed to cure diseases of the lungs, indigestion, and gout.

Anise (*Pimpinella anisum*)

Also known as sweet cumin or anise seed, this plant has dainty white flowers and feathery bright green leaflets and stands about 18 inches high. Originally from Egypt and Greece, anise spread to Central Europe in the Middle Ages and can be cultivated in America. Wild anise may be gathered on dry, sunny hillsides. Anise was mentioned in the Bible, used as a spice in Vergil's time, and considered protection against the "evil eye" and nightmares. Widely used as a flavoring for liqueurs, the seeds also make a spicy, sweet tea with a strong flavor reminiscent of licorice. Anise is thought to help coughs, flatulence, and digestion.

Balm (*Melissa officinalis*)

This herb, commonly called lemon balm or bee balm, has cream-white flowers surrounded by dark green, wrinkled leaves and grows 1–2 ft. high. A native to southern Europe, this fragrant plant also grows in the Orient, Northern Africa, and the United States. It can grow in the garden and is found wild in the woods. Paracelsus called balm the elixir of life. It had a great reputation for restoring youth, driving away melancholy, and closing up wounds. Highly attractive to bees, it was rubbed on beehives to keep them from straying. One of the most popular herbal teas, pungent and lemon-flavored, is made from the leaves and flowering tops. Balm is good for reducing fever, aiding nervous disorders and prolonging life.

Basil (*Ocimum basilicum*)

Basil, the herb of hatred, grows 2 ft. high with white flowers that grow in whorls and oval leaves that are glossy above and grayish-green beneath. Originally from India, basil now grows an all warm and temperate countries and may be cultivated or gathered wild on sunny banks. Sacred to the Hindu religion, a basil leaf is buried with Indians as a passport to paradise. One possible origin of the word is thought to be from the Greek word for king (*basileios*); another is from lizard or *basilisk*, the dragon that kills with a look. Scorpions were thought to breed from basil and Salome put the head of John the Baptist in a pot of basil. Basil leaves produce a tea with a taste somewhere between cloves and anise. Basil relieves nausea.

Bay (*Laurus nobilis*)

The bay, or laurel, whose motto is "I change but in death," is also the herb of prophecy. A tall tree whose height can reach 60 ft., it is usually grown as a bush throughout the Mediterranean. The bay, with its thick, shiny, dark, evergreen leaves was sacred to the Greek god Apollo, was worn by victors in war or athletic games, or as protection from lightning and a good luck charm. The tea is fragrant and slightly bitter. Bay is said to ease childbirth, stop stomach cramps, cure coughs, and clear the brain.

Bergamot (*Monarda didyma*)

This herb, also called bee balm, horse mint, or Oswego tea grows up to 4 ft. in height, has narrow, gray-green leaves and clusters of white, purple, or scarlet flowers. The bergamots, including the lemon and wild varieties, are North American aromatic herbs of the mint family that can be grown in the garden or discovered in upland woods, thickets, and prairies. Used by the Winnebago Indians as a cure for acne, it was also preferred by the settlers around Oswego, New York during the American Revolution. Bergamot is highly fragrant and has a slightly bitter, citric taste. Tea made from the leaves and flowers helps bronchial problems, stomach disorders, and headaches.

Birch (*Betula alba*)

Commonly known as white birch or sweet birch, this familiar tree may grow quite tall and can be found in Europe from Sicily to Iceland as well as in North America and northern Asia. The young branches are a rich red or orange-brown and the trunk is white. Birch is an ancient tree; its name probably stems from the Sanskrit *bhurga* (bark for writing on). Coleridge named it "Lady of the Woods." Powdered inner bark has been eaten with fish eggs by the Russians, baked in bread by Swedes, and smoked by Alaskan Indians. Wine and beer is made from the sap and canoes are made from the bark. A delicious tea with a wintergreen taste is made from the bark, leaves, or young twigs. Good for skin diseases, intestinal complaints, and kidney stones.

Borage (*Borago officinalis*)

Known also as cool tankard, miner's candle, and talewort, and as a symbol for courage, this plant is from 1¾–2 ft. with hairy rough dark green leaves shaped like ox tongues, a stem covered with white bristles, and beautiful, brilliant blue star-shaped flowers. It grows in Europe, north Africa, Asia Minor, and North America. This herb may be cultivated or found as a weed in waste places, woods, and pastures. Introduced to Europe by the Crusaders, borage had a great reputation as an exhilarating herb that would dispel sorrow and make people glad and merry. A cooling, refreshing tea is made from the leaves and flowers, with a taste and aroma suggestive of cucumber. Borage aids lung complaints, increases the flow of mother's milk, and increases the action of the kidneys.

Burnet (*Sanguisorba officinalis*)

Sometimes called garden burnet, this herb, its smaller cousin salad burnet and wild varieties grow 10–20 in. high and have small, sharply serrated leaves and tiny deep red or purple flowers. The burnets grow in Europe, North America, and Asia and are discovered in the wild in sheltered, moist valleys, particularly in chalky soil. Chaba, a medieval Hungarian king, was said to cure the wounds of 15,000 soldiers with the juice of burnet. Like borage, the tea is cooling and reminiscent of cucumber. Highly regarded for stanching bleeding and as an aid to dysentery.

Camomile (*Anthemis noblis*)

Known as manzanilla or sweet camomile, this trailing herb seldom grows more than a foot high. With feathery, light-green leaves and a yellow center surrounded by 18 white rays, camomile resembles the daisy. It grows in North America, Europe, and temperate zones of Asia both in gardens—where its curative powers with respect to other growths earned it the name of "plant's physician"—and in wild, sunny waste places as a weed. The Egyptians dedicated camomile to their gods for its power to cure ague. In the Middle Ages it was planted in paths, for when walked on it gives off a strong, aromatic apple-like scent. Camomile tea is slightly bitter, a soothing sedative, and will end an attack of *delirium tremens*.

Caraway (*Carum carvi*)

Also called Kummel this popular herb is between 1½ and 2 ft. high, with finely cut feathery leaves and umbrels of tiny cream-white flowers. It is found in Europe, northern Asia, and North America, either cultivated or in the wild, in fields and waste places. One of Europe's oldest condiments, caraway seeds were found in a 5,000-year-old archeological dig in Switzerland, were used by the Romans, and were mentioned by Shakespeare in *Henry IV*. It was thought that any container holding the seeds could not be stolen, and that lovers who ate caraway would remain always faithful. Tea made from the small horned fruit, or seeds, has a warm, sweet, biting taste. That made from the leaves, which can be eaten as a salad, has a milder taste, somewhere between dill and parsley. Caraway is useful as a digestive, to ease the pain of toothache, and as a sweetener of the breath.

Catnip (*Nepeta cataria*)

Commonly called catmint or field balm, this herb of the mint family has a downy 2–3 foot stem bearing greyish heart-shaped leaves and a spike of white or pink flowers dotted with scarlet spots. Catnip grows in Europe, temperate zones of Asia, and North America. It can be cultivated or gathered wild along fence rows, stream banks, and roadsides. Beloved of cats, catnip was a popular tea in Roman times and in the Middle Ages was used as a flavoring for meat and in salads. It was a tea in England long before the first Oriental tea came to Europe and was popular with American Colonists. The tea is made from the leaves and flowering tops and has a bitter, aromatic, minty taste. Because it produces perspiration the tea is good for fevers. It relieves pain in the abdominal area and brings on delayed menstruation.

Cinnamon (*Cinnamomum zeylanicum*)

Cinnamon comes from an evergreen tree of the laurel family that sometimes reaches 20–30 ft. but normally is trimmed back to bush size under cultivation in the East Indies, China, and Malaysia. The leaves are glossy and leathery, the flowers white, and the fruit purple. The young shoots are green speckled with orange. Their dried inner bark becomes cinnamon. In ancient Chinese mythology this tree, growing in paradise at the headwaters of the Yellow River, yielded immortality to whoever ate its fruit. One of the world's oldest spices, cinnamon is mentioned in the Bible. Nero burned a year's supply of cinnamon in grief at his wife's funeral. Cinnamon was among the strongest spurs to the voyages of discovery. Tea made from the bark has a warm, sweet taste and a fragrant aroma. It is said to be useful for stomach ailments and as a stimulant.

Clover (*Trifolium pratense*)

Also known as trefoil or red clover, this familiar flower has as its motto "think of me." Growing 6–16 in. high, the downy stems support leaves with darker green markings and round purple or red blossoms. Mainly cultivated as a fodder plant, clover grows wild in fields and mountains in Europe, northern Asia, and North America. One of the earliest of cultivated herbs, the plant was highly valued by the Druids, Celts, Greeks, and Romans. The four-leafed variety is considered lucky. Clover is high in protein, calcium, and phosphorus. American Indians enjoyed the leaves and flowers raw and boiled. The flower heads make a strong, soothing tea said to help ulcers, skin ailments, and cancer.

Cloves (*Eugenia aromatica*)

The clove tree, native to the islands of Southeast Asia, is a beautiful evergreen from 20–30 ft. high with grey bark, large, bright green leaves, and flower buds that gradually turn from a rosy peach color to yellow and red. At this point the undeveloped flowers are harvested and the dried seeds inside them become cloves. The trees which may bear for a century were popular in 300 B.C. with the Chinese, who called cloves the "chicken-tongue spice" because of their shape. Cloves were known in Greece and Rome, smoked in Java, and today are chewed in India along with betel. As cloves are extremely strong and pungent, the tea should be made with care or used in combination with other teas. It is highly stimulating and antiseptic.

Coltsfoot (*Tussilago farfara*)

This wild plant, sometimes called coughwort or ass's foot, is one of the first flowers to appear in the spring in Europe and North America in damp woods and alongside stream banks and roadside ditches. The asparagus-like stem, which grows 4–18 in. high, is topped by a bright yellow dandelion-like blossom and surrounded by large sea-green leaves resembling the outline of a horse's hoofprint. Coltsfoot was praised by Pliny and Dioscorides as the best herbal remedy for coughs and lung ailments. It was taken as tea and also smoked. Apothecaries in medieval France painted a picture of the leaf on their doors as the most powerful symbol of herbal medicine. Today coltsfoot is the main ingredient in British Herb Tobacco. It makes a sweet, strong tea.

Comfrey (*Symphytum officinale*)

A wild weed which may be cultivated in a herb garden, comfrey, also known as knitbone, bruisewort, and boneset, has a thick stem 2–3 ft. in height that supports large, hairy, rough, pointed leaves and clusters of white, cream-yellow, pale pink, or blue flowers. Called "the healing herb," comfrey grows in Europe, temperate Asia, and North America in shady, wet places. Famous since the Middle Ages as a cure for battle wounds and broken bones, it was found in 1912 to contain allantoin, a cell proliferant that causes injured cells to heal rapidly. A pleasant tea, made from the leaves and ground root, is recommended for ulcers and dysentery.

Dandelion (*Taraxacum officinale*)

Another wild herb, called priest's crown and swine's snout, it has a purple stem topped by the familiar bright yellow crown and shiny, jagged leaves resembling lion's teeth, which give the plant its name (*dent de lion*).

The dandelion grows practically everywhere in the temperate zones. First mentioned by Arabian physicians of the tenth and eleventh centuries, the dandelion has been cultivated in India for liver diseases; the flowers are made into wine, the leaves eaten as a nourishing salad, and the root ground as a coffee substitute. Children tell time by counting the number of puffs required to blow all the dried seeds away; and to dream of dandelion is bad luck. Extremely high in vitamin A and rich in potassium and calcium, the slightly bitter tea made from the leaves or ground root is supposed to aid kidney and liver disorders.

Elder (*Sambucus nigra*)

Sometimes called elderberry or pipe tree, this is a large wild bush or tree reaching 10 or more ft. with green or gray-brown bark. The leaves are elliptical and sharply serrated, the blossoms arranged in creamy flat clusters, and the berries are purplish black. Elder, which can be domestically cultivated, grows wild in Europe, west Asia, and North America along fences, walls, ditches, banks and streams. The elder is rich in legend and mystery; it is said to be the wood of Pan's Pipes, the Cross of Calvary, and the tree from which Judas hanged himself. While medieval Europeans would not burn it and carried twigs of elder to drive away evil spirits, Danish mothers feared to place their children in elder cradles for fear the Elder Tree Mother would strangle them. The berries make a famous wine; the leaves and flowers make a honey-like, slightly bitter tea which is said to be the best cure for chills and influenza.

Fennel (*Foeniculum vulgare*)

A large herb often reaching 6 ft. in height, this member of the parsley family has bright green feathery leaves and golden flowers. Native to southern Europe and Asia, fennel also grows wild in most parts of Europe and North America. The ancient Chinese used fennel for snake bite, Romans cultivated it for salads, and medieval farmers rubbed fennel ointment on their cows' udders to prevent the milk from becoming bewitched. The seeds make a delightful tea which has the flavor properties of anise, peppermint, and licorice. Fennel is reputed to improve memory, cure obesity, and stop chronic coughs.

Fenugreek (*Trigonella foenumgraecum*)

Also called bird's foot, Greek hayseed, and goat's horn, fenugreek is a herb that grows up to 2 ft. tall, has light green leaves, small white flowers, and crescent-shaped pods 6 in. long, each containing around 20 yellow seeds. This plant, indigenous to the eastern Mediterranean, is also cultivated in India, Africa, Egypt, and temperate zones of North America. The ancient Egyptians used fenugreek as a food and as one of the ingredients of their "holy smoke." Sprouting seeds were used in salads; powdered seeds were said to cure baldness. Boiled seeds were eaten with honey in Greece, and Arab bread was made with fenugreek. A tea made from the seeds or leaves has a strange taste somewhere between celery and burnt sugar. This herb is said to be effective in preventing fevers, soothing to the stomach, and useful for diabetes.

Flax (*Linum usitatissimum*)

Flax, or linseed, is a plant reaching 2 ft. in height with many narrow, pointed leaves, turquoise blossoms, and round seed pods. One of the world's most widespread herbs, it has been cultivated in all temperate and tropical countries since earliest times and can be found in a wild state all over the globe. Flax made the linen Egyptian mummies were wrapped in, the curtain of the Tabernacle in Exodus, and the white sails in Homer's *Odyssey*. Greeks and Romans used the seeds to make bread; Bohemians believed seven-year-old children who danced in fields of flax would become beautiful adults. A soothing tea made from the seeds is said to be a remedy for colds and coughs.

Ginger (*Zingiber officinale*)

This spice grows to about 3 ft. in height in the form of a green stalk with narrow leaves and white or yellow purple-edged flowers. It is found cultivated in Africa, Asia, and India, and grows wild in North America in shaded, wooded areas. Ginger was mentioned in the *Analects* of Confucius. It was eaten by Egyptians in the form of the famous gingerbread confection in the time of Cheops, while the recipe itself was first written down 500 years later, by a Greek baker on the island of Rhodes in 2400 B.C. Queen Elizabeth I started the fashion of molding the cake in likenesses of her guests. Pieces of the odd-shaped root, which sometimes resembles a hand, add piquancy to meat and fish dishes, and the ground root makes a hot, spicy-sweet tea. It is stimulating and warming and is said to be effective for gastritis.

Ginseng (*Panax quinquefolium*)

Known as "wonder of the world," ginseng is a wild root that is also called man's health, five fingers, sang, red berry, and man-root. The erect stem supports whorls of three palmate leaves, small flowers, and red fruit. The root is fleshy and forked, often assuming the shape of a human form. It takes 5–7 years to mature; in 1952 the Russian Journal of Botany reported a 400-year-old root. Ginseng grows in cool, fertile woods in the eastern and central United States, Japan, Korea, and southeastern Manchuria. Mentioned by the Chinese Emperor Shèn Nung 5,000 years ago, ginseng was thought to be a fabulous cure-all which contained the essence of the earth in a condensed form. Among the extraordinary powers attributed to ginseng in the Orient were: aphrodisiac, stimulant, tonic, and prolonger of life. The more the ginseng root resembled a human body the stronger it was supposed to be. Mentioned in Ezekiel as pannag, ginseng was known to the American Indians as garantoqueen and discovered by Canadian missionaries in the early eighteenth century. To replenish exhausted Oriental sources, Daniel Boone and other mountain men hunted and sold ginseng root for export to China—more valuable than lynx, beaver, and mink, ginseng was worth its weight in gold. In 1966, 100 tons of ginseng worth $4,000,000 were exported from the United States to China. Today Russian astronauts take ginseng to prevent infection in space, and California mystics put ginseng chips under their tongues. The tea, made from the ground root, has a pleasant licorice-like taste and reportedly stimulates the cardiovascular system, raises hormonal levels in the blood, aids digestion, cures dysentery, and acts as a pain-killer.

Goldenrod (*Solidago canadensis*)

Also called blue mountain tea and sweet goldenrod, this plant is from 1–3 ft. tall and has smooth, clear green leaves and clusters of small daisy-like flowers whose rays and disk are both yellow. Goldenrod is a wild native of eastern North America that grows in open, sunny places where there is sandy soil. It can be cultivated in the garden; and there are numerous varieties in Europe. Given the name blue mountain tea by German settlers in Pennsylvania, goldenrod was so highly regarded as a tea that it was exported to China, where only the aristocracy could afford it. The leaves and flowers make a fragrant, golden tea with a warm, anise-like flavor. Goldenrod is recommended to reduce high fever, as an aid to digestion, nausea, and jaundice, and to dissolve kidney stones.

Hawthorn (*Crataegus coccinea*)

Sometimes called Mayblossom, quick, whitethorn, and haw, this relative of the apple tree may grow 3–30 ft. tall and sometimes lives to a great age. Crooked, irregular branches support crimson, pink, or white five-petaled flowers and fierce 5-in. thorns. Hundreds of varieties of hawthorn grow in Europe, temperate zones of Asia, north Africa, and North America. It can be cultivated in the garden as a shrub or discovered wild in thickets and woods. Considered a sacred tree because it was believed to have formed Christ's Crown of Thorns, it was thought in medieval times that bringing a hawthorn branch into the home foretold death. It was the device of Henry VII, was used in hedges by early Germans to divide their land, and makes the hottest wood fire known to man. The leaves and berries make a sweet, astringent tea said to aid cardiac diseases, sore throats, and kidney ailments.

Hollyhock (*Althaea rosea*)

Hollyhock, or purple malva, is a flower that has been cultivated for centuries for its beauty. Tall, stately branches grow deep red, purple, or pale yellow blossoms. Originally from China, the flower can be cultivated or found wild in Europe and North America. The leaves were used in Egyptian cookery. The flowers were brought to Europe at the time of the Crusades and cultivated in the Royal Gardens of the Duke of Orleans in France and by Lord Burlington in his London garden. A tea made from the blossoms is said to be effective for chest complaints and as an aid to digestion.

Hops (*Humulus lupulus*)

Known as northern vine and bine, this twining climber sometimes reaches 20 ft. or more and has an extremely tough, flexible stem. The leaves are dark green, heart-shaped and have finely toothed edges. The male flowers are in loose bunches and the female flowers are small yellow-green cones.

Hops grows in Europe and North America, can be cultivated in the garden or foraged for along streams, roadsides, and in open fields. Romans ate young hops shoots like asparagus. The female cones have been used throughout Europe since ancient times for brewing beer, the pulp can be used to make paper, and in Sweden the fibers were made into linen. Hops tea can be made from the flowers and leaves. It has a bitter taste and induces sleep, improves the appetite, and aids in combating alcoholism.

Horehound (*Marrubium vulgare*)

Called seed of Horus, bull's blood, or eye of the star by Egyptian priests, horehound grows a foot high, has wrinkled hairy leaves that are oval and tooth-edged, and small cream-white flowers. A member of the Mint family, horehound can be cultivated in Europe, North Africa, Asia, and North America or found wild in pastures, by roadsides, and in waste places. Believed in ancient times to be an antidote to magical poisons, horehound is one of the five bitter herbs eaten by the Jews at Passover. The leaves and flowers make a bittersweet, musky tea. Through the ages this herb has been one of the most popular remedies for coughs, asthma, consumption, and all pulmonary complaints.

Hyssop (*Hyssopus officinalis*)

Hyssop, called the sacred herb, means "sold in herb shops." It is a pretty everygreen shrub growing up to 2 ft. in height with dark green, dull linear leaves and tiny white, deep blue, or pink flowers. This member of the Mint family is native to Europe, temperate zones of Asia, and North America. A popular garden herb, hyssop also grows wild in shady spots with sandy soil. Used by the ancient Hebrews to cleanse lepers, hyssop dipped in lamb's blood marked their doorposts on Passover eve. A prayer of King David was "Purge me with Hyssop, and I shall be clean." Hyssop was offered to Jesus at the time of the Crucifixion. The whole plant is used for tea that tastes bitter, resinous and minty, with traces of camphor and rue. Hyssop is supposed to cleanse the body, calm the nerves, regulate blood pressure, and cure nose, lung and throat infections.

Iceland Moss (*Cetraria islandica*)

This is a lichen composed of a fungus and an alga growing together.

Growing from 2–4 in. high, this mossy plant has no leaves but consists of branching stems which form tangled masses of gray, brown or red. The fruits are thin, stalk-like sprouts piercing through the mat in numerous places. Iceland moss is a wild herb found in northern Europe, Canada, Alaska, and the northern United States. A survival food of the North, Icelanders regard it as the bread of God from the rocks. It forms the diet of moose, grouse, deer, caribou, elk and reindeer. A highly nutritious, bitter tea is made from powdered Iceland moss that has been treated to remove its bitter acids. It is recommended for bronchitis and tuberculosis.

Labrador Tea (*Ledum groenlandicum*)

Also called Hudson's Bay tea, this member of the Heath family is a small evergreen shrub ranging from 1–4 ft. tall whose narrow, leathery leaves curl under at the edges and have a dense red felt underneath. Tiny white five-petaled flowers form thick umbrella-like clusters. The plant grows in Newfoundland, Alaska, Canada, and the northern United States in bogs, woods, swamps and damp mountain meadows. Brought back to England two centuries ago for its beauty, Labrador tea was highly popular with miners. mountain men, and American colonists during the Revolution. The young leaves make a spicy, refreshing beverage reminiscent of Oriental tea.

Lavender (*Lavandula spica*)

A familiar shrub with clusters of small light purple flowers borne upon woody branches and surrounded by long narrow leaves, lavender grows in gardens and in the wild in all sunny, temperate regions. Originally from India, this fragrant plant was cultivated by the Romans for use in perfumed bath water, and gradually spread throughout the Mediterranean. Grown for centuries in European gardens for its beauty and aroma lavender is a popular ingredient in sachets and potpourri and is important in perfume production. The blossoms make a highly aromatic, mild tea said to be good for nervousness, heart palpitations, and halitosis.

Lemon Verbena (*Lippia citriodora*)

The lemon verbena tree grows from 5–15 ft. tall with grooved, downy, red-marked stems and small white flowers. Its crisp, oblong leaves 2–3 in. long, are yellow-green with interesting veining. One of the few herbs originating in the New World, lemon verbena is native to Central and South America. It was imported to England in 1784 from Chile and quickly spread throughout Europe. It also grows in India, Martinique, Réunion, and North America. The tea has a characteristic lemon flavor and aroma. Reportedly it is effective in reducing fever, as a sedative, and for indigestion.

Linden (*Tilia vulgaris*)

Sometimes called basswood or lime, this tree can grow to 100 ft. in height. The branches, which spread out at the bottom, bear bright green, finely toothed oval leaves of from 2–6 in. and bright red buds which open up into creamy white, fragrant, five-petaled flowers arranged in flat clusters. Several varieties of linden grow in Europe, where it has been popular as a shade tree, and North America. In ancient times the inner bark was used as an antiseptic. One of the world's best honeys is made from the blossoms, and the white, fine-grained soft wood has always been in demand by wood-carvers. One of the most popular herbal teas is made from linden flowers; its taste is sweet and fragrant, and it is said to calm the nerves, promote restful sleep, and relieve cramps.

Licorice (*Glycyrrhiza glabra*)

Also known as sweet root, black sugar, and Spanish juice, this favorite confection is a shrublike plant growing 1–3 ft. tall with purple-blue or green-white flowers. Originally from southern Europe, northern Africa, and Persia, licorice can be cultivated in all temperate regions and found wild in waste places with clay soil or wet mountain draws. Licorice was a panacea in China and Egypt for untold centuries; a great quantity of it was found in the tomb of the pharaoh Tutankhamen. Chewed as candy since the time of Christ, this herb is sweet and thirst-quenching. A bittersweet tea is made from the root and is supposed to be good for throat and chest ailments and ulcers, and helpful to people who want to stop smoking.

Mallow (*Malva sylvestris*)

Sometimes called marshmallow, this plant ranges from 2–6 ft. in height and has thick, downy, coarsely toothed leaves and large, pink, five-petaled flowers. It is native to Europe and Asia, but there are now varieties of mallow all over the temperate zones. It can be cultivated or discovered wild in swamps, marshes and near coastal areas. One of the oldest food herbs, mallow was raised at Apollo's temple at Delos as a symbol of man's first nourishment. It is mentioned in the Old Testament as a meat substitute. But it is most famous as an ingredient of the puffy confection roasted over campfires. The roots, flowers, and young leaves are used to make a mild, sweet tea. Mallow's high mucilage content makes it soothing for colds and sore throats.

Marigold (*Calendula officinalis*)

This flower, the symbol of despair, is also known as Marybud, gold, summer's bride, and solsequia. A dark green, rigid stem supports long, pale green leaves and a brilliant orange spherical flower formed of a myriad of tiny petals. The marigold comes from Asia and southern Europe, but can be found in all temperate zones; it is one of the easiest blossoms to grow in a garden. This plant is sacred in India, where it decorates shrines in Hindu temples. In Brittany a girl who walks barefoot over a marigold will forever know the secret language of the birds. According to the Gypsies, it is one of the ingredients necessary to see the fairies. In Mexico and Germany it is the emblem of death. Marigold flower tea has a slightly bitter, saffron taste. It is said to be good for the complexion and useful in treating ulcers and fevers.

Marjoram (*Majorana hortensis*)

Known as "joy of the mountains" to the Greeks, this aromatic herb grows 1–2 ft. high, has a square purple-brown main stem with wiry red side branches and small, elliptical, downy green-gray leaves. Tiny cream-white flowers bloom from knots along the stem, giving the plant its other name: knotted marjoram. A Mediterranean native, marjoram spread to Asia, Europe, and North Africa. Wild marjoram, or oregano, is found in cooler temperate zones. Sacred to Shiva and Vishnu in India, dedicated to Osiris in Egypt marjoram was planted on graves by the Greeks and Romans to insure peaceful rest for the dead. Newlyweds were crowned with this fragrant herb. When Venus first cultivated marjoram, it was odorless—it was the constant touch of the goddess that gave the plant its magic aroma. A favorite of the "Strewer of Herbs" in the twelfth-century court of King

Stephen of England, marjoram was called "the herb of grace" by Shake-speare. It remains one of the most important herbs in European cuisine. Marjoram tea, made from the leaves, has a warm, sweet, slightly oily taste which is related to thyme. It is supposed to strengthen the brain, relieve nervous headaches, induce sleep, and aid indigestion.

Meadowsweet (*Filipendula ulmaria*)

Meadowsweet, bridewort, lady of the Meadow, or queen of the Meadow is a common flower that reaches 2–3 ft. in height and has dense, fragrant clusters of tiny cream-white flowers. Widespread in all temperate zones, meadowsweet can be cultivated as a garden herb or gathered along the banks of streams and in wet meadows. This was a favorite flower of Queen Elizabeth I, who had it scattered over the floors of her apartments. A tea of meadowsweet flowers is sweet and delicate. It is recommended for upset stomach, rheumatism, and kidney complaints.

Mint (*Mentha spicata*)

Perhaps the most famous and well-liked herb for tea, mint, the plant of virtue, has many varieties. Spearmint (*Mentha spicata*) is the mint of com-merce and the oldest in the family. Peppermint (*Mentha piperita*) is a sec-ond common favorite for flavoring. Lemon mint, applemint, and water mint are three of the hundreds of mint hybrids, which have folk names like heart-mint, garden mint, lamb mint, and mackerel mint. Ranging from 12–20 in. in height, the square purplish stem bears veined and wrinkled, highly aro-matic, toothed leaves and clusters of white, lavender, or deep purple trum-pet-shaped flowers. Mint is cultivated all over the temperate zones and may be found growing wild in wet, shady places. When the nymph Minthe was discovered in the arms of Pluto by his wife Persephone she crushed her sav-agely underfoot. Out of pity, Pluto metamorphosed Minthe into a sweet-smelling plant. Zeus and Hermes, disguised as traveling strangers, were entertained in the humble cottage of Philemon and Baucis, who rubbed their table with mint leaves as a sign of hospitality. In gratitude the hut was transformed into a temple. Ancient Hebrews covered their synagogue floor with mint leaves. The Greeks and Romans used them as a bath scent and ate them to strengthen the nerves, while athletes used them to perfume their bodies and considered mint leaves a source of power. Arabs took them to increase virility. Spearmint tea, made from the leaves, is fragrant, flavorful, aromatic, sharp and with a trace of camphor. Peppermint tea has a more pungent flavor than spearmint, with a characteristic cool aftertaste due to the large menthol content. Mint tea aids in the cure of upset stomach, rheumatism, chills, poor circulation, influenza, lack of appetite, nausea, and colic.

Mint Tea Punch and Mint Syrup

A *mint tea punch* can be made, using 2 cups orange juice, ½ cup sugar, 12 sprigs mint, ¼ cup lime juice, and club soda or seltzer. Bring 1 cup of orange juice, sugar, and mint to a boil. Remove from the heat and strain out the mint leaves. Add the rest of the orange juice and the lime juice. Fill tall glasses two-thirds full of the syrup and one-third full of club soda. A jigger of gin may be added if desired.

For *mint syrup* you will need 20–30 fresh mint leaves, 1 cup sugar, and 1 cup boiling water. The mint leaves should first be bruised in the sugar. Add the boiling water and stir over heat until the sugar dissolves. Simmer for 3–5 minutes to thicken the syrup and then strain out the mint leaves. Use the syrup as a flavoring in drinks, punch, or even homemade ice cream.

Mugwort (*Artemisia vulgaris*)

Mugwort, the symbol of forgetfulness, is sometimes called fellon-herb. Growing 4 ft. tall, this plant has a firm brown stem, green leaves with white undersides, and flowers of a yellow-brown color. Mugwort can be cultivated in the garden or discovered in waste places, near water or along roadsides in north temperate regions. The centaur Chiron taught Diana the uses of Mugwort; the goddess so esteemed it that she gave the plant her name, Artemis. It was believed that whoever slept on a pillow stuffed with mugwort would dream prophetic dreams, that it was protection against lightning and the devil, and that a traveler who put mugwort in his shoes in the morning could walk 40 miles before noon without tiring. Used instead of hops to make beer, mugwort was a highly regarded tea in England before Oriental tea. A strong drink made from the flowers and top leaves is reputed to dissolve gallstones, cure sciatica, aid bronchitis and regulate the menstrual cycle.

Mullein (*Verbascum thapsus*)

Known as velvet dock, beggar's blanket, clown's lungwort, witch's candle, and Aaron's rod—among other common names—mullein is an imposing herb that sometimes reaches 8 ft. in height. The stalk bears large leaves, 10–16 in. long near the base, that diminish toward the top, which is crowned with a steeple of five-petaled, sulphur yellow flowers. Mullein grows wild throughout the temperate zones of Europe, Asia, and North America in dry, sunny pastures and along roadsides. It is cultivated in herb gardens in Europe but considered an obnoxious weed in this country. Called "herb of love" in medieval times, mullein was the *moly* that Hermes gave Odysseus to use as a charm against Circe's enchantments. Devil worshipers burned torches of dried mullein and so did invading Roman armies entering England. In India this herb was thought to be protection against black magic, and in seventh-century Europe it was considered so important that mullein was named *herbe de St. Fiacre* after the Irish saint who became the patron saint of all gardeners. Tea made from the flowers is sweet, that made from the leaves slightly bitter. This tea must be strained to catch the fine hairs with which the plant is covered. Mullein is recommended as a cure for coughs, asthma, bronchitis, and hay fever, and as a sedative.

Nettle (*Urtica dioica*)

Nettle, the plant of spite, is also called stinging nettle and seven-minute-itch. Ranging 1–8 ft. tall, this herb has green, finely toothed, heart-shaped leaves and clusters of small green flowers. The entire plant is covered with stinging hairs containing a venom of formic acid. Common to northern temperate regions in waste grounds, the nettle is one of the most despised of weeds because of its painful properties and at the same time highly prized by herbalists for its rich iron, protein, Vitamin A, and Vitamin C content. Carefully imported into Britain as a medicinal herb by Roman soldiers, nettles have been used for centuries as a potherb and soup. Scottish nettle-linen was thought to be finer than linen made from flax. When boiled the young shoots and leaves lose their stinging quality and make a tea that is said to cure consumption, asthma, diabetes, bronchitis, and help those trying to lose weight.

New Jersey Tea (*Ceanothus americanus*)

Perhaps the most famous of American beverage plants is New Jersey tea, or wild snowball and red root, a small shrub growing up to 3 ft. in height with oval, pointed leaves that are gray-green in color and have finely toothed edges. The tiny white flowers are borne in dense oval clusters. This herb may be found growing in dry, open areas, woods and rocky ledges from New England to Florida. American colonists and soldiers brewed New Jersey tea from the leaves of this plant during their boycott of English tea, and the resulting drink tastes much like Oriental tea.

Nutmeg (*Myristica fragrans*)

This popular spice comes from a large evergreen tree that grows from 40–60 ft. tall, has dark gray bark, glossy, oblong dark green leaves and tiny, bell-shaped, light yellow blossoms. The bright yellow or tan fruit, about the size of an apricot, conceals a shiny, dark brown, oily seed—the nutmeg of commerce. Indigenous to the East Indies, nutmeg grows in tropical Indonesia and Grenada in the West Indies and prefers to be near the sea. First mentioned by the Persian philosopher Avicenna in 1000 A.D., nutmeg was scattered over Roman streets during festivals, described by Chaucer as "nutemuge put in ale," and considered an aphrodisiac by the Arabs. Centuries ago sterling silver nutmeg graters were carried by ladies for making nutmeg tea. The flavor of this drink is warm, sweet and spicy. Nutmeg is reported to cure headaches, intestinal malfunctions, fevers, kidney ailments, and bad breath.

Pennyroyal (*Mentha pulegium*)

Sometimes called squaw mint in America, this aromatic herb has a creeping, spreading maroon stem that often reaches 18 in. in height, oval leaves with round-toothed edges, and lavender or purple flowers growing in dense whorls. Native to Europe and North America, pennyroyal is an ornamental garden herb that can also be discovered wild in dry fields and meadows. Pennyroyal was used as a flea repellent by the Romans and is still used today by woodsmen to drive insects away. This plant was a favorite among American settlers and makes one of the most flavorful wild teas. The leaves are used to make a strong, minty beverage said to cure asthma, indigestion, headaches, and whooping cough.

Purslane (*Portulaca oleracea*)

Purslane, or pussley and pigweed, is a trailing, sprawling herb rarely reaching more than several inches into the air. The fleshy stems, which are red, green, or purple in color, support narrow, fat leaves that are reddish-green and small, yellow five-petaled flowers. Purslane originated in the sub-tropics but due to its tenacity and the enormous amount of seeds on a single plant—over 50,000—purslane has spread all over the world. Cultivated over 2,000 years ago in India and Persia as a potherb and salad, purslane was strewn around beds in the Middle Ages to protect sleepers from the devil, made into a royal salad by the master cook of Charles II, brewed as a tea by American Indians, and eaten boiled by Thoreau at Walden Pond. A healthy tea with a slightly acidic and sour taste can be made from the leaves. Purslane is recommended for fevers, coughs, and insomnia.

Raspberry (*Rubus strigosus*)

Raspberries are crimson fruits made up of tiny, plump kernels, each containing a hard seed. They are borne from 2–7 ft. on thorned reddish canes with clusters of oval, toothed leaves. Among the hundreds of varieties of raspberries growing in Europe, northern Asia, and North America are blackberries, baked-apple berries, salmonberries, cloudberries, dewberries, and thimbleberries. Mentioned by Pliny, this plant has been cultivated for centuries for its delicious fruit and enjoyed by ages of wild berry pickers in woods, fields, and thickets. A famous tea, soothing and aromatic, is made from the leaves. Raspberry-leaf tea is best known as a curer of problems connected with women: frigidity, menstrual discomfort, labor pains, and difficult menopause.

Rose (*Rosa canina*)

By far the most renowned of blossoms. There are 10,000 varieties of roses, the flower of love. Among the most popular strains are the damask rose, cabbage rose, and Provence rose. Roses exhibit a wide range of colors including crimson, white, amethyst, pink, yellow, purple, and scarlet. These flowers grow several feet high on thorned stems bearing toothed, oval green leaves. Roses have been cultivated since ancient times for their beauty, as an herb, and for food, and now flourish in gardens and roadsides, clearings, waste places and fields all over the temperate zones. Originally from Persia, the rose was extolled by the Persian philosopher Zarathustra, who claimed it was the mother of all nutritious fruits. The Greeks considered the rose an emblem of beauty and love and said its color was from the blood of Aphrodite. Romans covered the floors of festival rooms with imported Egyptian rose petals, slept on rose-filled mattresses and bathed in rose wine. Clothes of Arabic emirs were washed in rose water. Muslims believed it holy, and the rose was a symbol of Christ's sufferings. Glorified for centuries by artists for its beauty, perfume, mystery, and perfection the rose has also been used as a food since its beginning. Consumed in a soup by Scandinavians and eaten whole in a ragout throughout China, the rose is famous in the form of jam, jelly, syrup, conserve, and crystallized rose petals, the world over. Rose water, called "dew of Paradise" by the Arabs, is used by them as a glaze for roasting fowl. A sweet, astringent tea is made from the petals or from the rose hips, the swelling fruit of the rose plant, located at the end of the stem under the wilted flower. Rose hips are noted for their extremely high Vitamin C content—one cup contains as much of this vitamin as 150 oranges—and for concentrations of Vitamins A, B, E, K, and P, and Niacin, iron, calcium and phosphorous. The rose is said to be beneficial to the heart and brain and good for colds, coughs, and kidney complaints.

Rose Hip Soup

To make a *rose hip soup* you need the following: 2 cups (½ lb.) crushed, dried rose hips, 1½ quarts water, ½ cup honey (to taste), and 1½ tablespoons arrowroot. In a saucepan bring the water and rose hips to a boil, reduce the heat, and let the brew simmer, covered, for 45 minutes. Strain and discard the rose hips. Mix the arrowroot with enough water to bring the total liquid back up to 1½ quarts. Add the arrowroot mixture to the rose hip liquid and stir over a low heat until the mixture thickens. The soup should then be covered and chilled. Rose hip soup can be served either as an appetizer or as a dessert garnished with whipped cream.

Rosemary (*Rosmarinus officinalis*)

Rosemary means "sea dew" and is sometimes called old man. It is an evergreen shrub that grows up to 6 ft. high with spiky, glossy, grey-green leaves of a leathery texture. The flowers may be pale blue, bright blue, or lavender-blue. Rosemary is native to Spain, Greece, Italy and North Africa, where it is both cultivated and wild, and it can be raised in the milder temperate zones of Britain and North America. Garlands of rosemary were worn by Greek students before examinations to clear the mind and refresh the memory. It was mentioned as a cure-all by Arabian and Roman physicians and considered, since Roman times, a symbol of fidelity between lovers. Burnt as incense in religious ceremonies and used as a charm against witches, rosemary was exchanged at weddings for luck and distributed at funerals to guard the dead. Its wood was used to make lutes. When Mary was fleeing from Herod with the Christ Child she washed her blue cloak one night and hung it on a rosemary bush, whose flowers were white, to dry. The next morning the rosemary flowers had turned blue, and they have remained that color ever since—the rose of Mary. The rosemary tree—33 years old and 6 ft. tall—was supposed to be a symbol of Christ's life on earth. In *Hamlet*, Ophelia poignantly alludes to the tradition of fidelity surrounding this mystical, legendary herb: "There's rosemary, that's for remembrance." The tea has a fresh, clean taste somewhere between mint and pine with a trace of camphor. Rosemary is reported to be good for the liver and heart and helpful for nervous and digestive disorders.

Sage (*Salvia officinalis*)

The herb of wisdom whose Latin name means "healthy," sage comes in 700 varieties, some of which are pineapple sage, red sage, ash-leaved sage, Cyprus sage, and lavender sage. This aromatic member of the Mint family is a shrub reaching 3 ft. in height with a grey, woody branched stem bearing grey-green, oblong hairy leaves that have a pebbly texture, and whorls of blue or purple flowers. Indigenous to the northern Mediterranean coasts of Yugoslavia and Italy, sage is cultivated in all temperate zones and can be discovered wild in dry, sunny waste places. It was used by the Greeks to strengthen the brain and in Roman baths to ease aching feet. The countless virtues of sage led Italian physicians at Salerno to frame the rhetorical question, "Why should a man die who grows sage in his garden?" Charlemagne ordered sage grown in the imperial gardens. The reputation of this herb to heighten the senses and memory and strengthen the muscles and nervous system gave rise to the couplet, "He that would live for aye/Must eat sage in May." Sage was so highy esteemed by the Chinese as a tea that they gave seventeenth-century Dutch traders 4 lbs. of oriental leaves for 1 lb. of sage. The English employ sage leaves in stuffed goose, the French pickle them, the Germans cook them with eels, and the Italians grind them up with sausage meat. In the Mediterranean area roast thrushes are wrapped in sage leaves and in the Middle East sage shoots are eaten as salad. Sage tea has a powerful, warm flavor that is slightly bitter and peppery with traces of camphor. It is supposed to cure colds, headaches, delirium, and other nervous disorders.

Sarsaparilla (*Smilax officinalis*)

Also known as bindweed, small spikenard, spignet and China root, sarsaparilla is a climbing, tangled evergreen shrub with bristly stems, oval, spined leaves, thick umbrels of white flowers, and globular purple-black berries. This trailing pine is found in Central and South America, China, and Japan. Wild North American varieties grow in dry soil in clearings and open woods. Sarsaparilla was introduced to Europe from Mexico in the sixteenth century. It was thought in the Middle Ages that giving sarsaparilla to an infant would make the child immune to all poisons for life. Pirates drank the tea to cure syphillis, and American Indians used it for rheumatism, gout, and skin diseases. Sarsaparilla tea, made from the ground root, has a bitter, licorice flavor and is said to be effective for relief of pain in the joints or head.

Sassafras (*Sassafras variifolium*)

Sometimes called ague tree, cinnamon wood, saxifras, or smelling stick, this member of the Laurel family may range from a shrub 15 ft. in height to a tree 100 ft. tall. The leaves are long and oval, often with 2 or 3 lobes, the flowers are greenish-gold and bell-shaped, in dense clusters, and the fruits are dark blue berries borne upon red stalks. Sassafras is a wild North American plant that flourishes in thickets, dry woods and along roadsides. Known to the American Indians and noticed by the Spaniards in 1512 when they first touched Florida, sassafras was first mentioned as a medicine and tea by the Spanish doctor Monardes in 1569. Sassafras was one of the first exports from the New World to Europe and considered almost as valuable as gold. It was a favorite tea during Revolutionary times, and is used today to flavor and thicken Creole soups and gravies. An aromatic and spicy tea is made from the ground bark of the root. Sassafras is reputed to cleanse the system, and aid in the treatment of gout, arthritis, rheumatism, and dysentery.

Savory (*Satureia hortensis*)

Summer savory, or the pepper herb, is 1–2 ft. high with slender, erect hairy stems, small linear leaves of a bronze-green color, and tiny pink, white, or lavender flowers. Savory, originally from southern Europe and the Mediterranean, is a hardy garden herb and can be found growing wild in warm temperate areas in sunny places with light soil. Used by the Greeks and Romans in fish and meat sauces before pepper was available, savory was the favorite herb of the satyrs who gave it its reputation as an aphrodisiac. Vergil grew savory for his bees. In the Middle Ages drops of savory and rose oil were thought to cure deafness. Shakespeare mentions it in *The Winter's Tale*. Savory was one of the first herbs brought from England by American colonists. The tea tastes peppery and resinous with a hint of camphor. It is recommended for colds, fevers, and intestinal disorders.

Strawberry (*Fragaria vesca*)

There are hundreds of varieties of this popular fruit, symbol of foresight, including garden strawberry, pine strawberry, green strawberry, alpine strawberry, perpetual strawberry, wood strawberry, scarlet strawberry, and Virginia strawberry. Plants have been cultivated with white, yellow, purple and black fruit, fruit tasting of pineapple, and leaves striped with gold and silver. The common variety has a woolly pink stem 3–12 in. high, sharply toothed, veined shiny leaves arranged in groups of three, five-petaled white flowers and scarlet, conical fruit. Strawberries are cultivated all over the temperate zones and grow wild on open slopes, in clearings and rocky woods and along roadsides where the leaves can be collected even in winter. Vergil called the fruit "child of the soil," and Ovid mentions it as food of the golden age. Shakespeare wrote "I saw good strawberries in your garden there." The berry was so esteemed in Elizabethan England that a few seeds sold for a guinea and strawberry leaves decorated the coronets of British nobility. American Indians ate the fruit and made tea from the leaves. American settlers at Salem in 1630 came ashore and feasted on strawberries. Strawberry shortcake has become a national dessert. A cooling, healthy tea made from the leaves is recommended for diarrhea, fever, and anemia.

Thyme (*Thymus vulgaris*)

Among the 50 species of thyme, symbol of activity, are wild thyme, orange thyme, caraway thyme, and lemon thyme. This widely used little shrub rises 6–8 in. on many-branched, amber stems which bear glistening grey-green tiny leaves shaped like arrowheads and small lavender flowers. Thyme first grew in the Mediterranean and southern Europe, spread to western Asia, Europe, North Africa and the Canary Islands and now grows throughout the world in temperate zones. Wild thyme flourishes on hills, mountains, dry banks, and heaths. It is an important flavoring in European cooking and New England clam chowder, and is also an ingredient of the world-renowned thyme honey from Mount Hymettus in Greece. Thyme was taken by the Romans to make them brave, and it was in the manger of the Virgin Mary and Christ Child as part of the bed of straw. In the Middle Ages a knight going to war would carry a scarf embroidered by his lady with a sprig of thyme. In *A Midsummer Night's Dream*, Shakespeare suggests seeking Titania, Queen of the Fairies, on "a bank where the wild thyme blows." Thyme tea is warm and aromatic and helps hangovers, nervousness, and headaches and is said to be antiseptic.

Vervain (*Verbena officinalis*)

Vervain, the herb of enchantment, is a small perennial plant with a long stem, lance-shaped leaves, and hooded, mauve flowers. It is found in temperate regions and may be cultivated or discovered as a weed. Mentioned by Hippocrates, vervain was used by the ancient Druids to cast spells and as a cure for plague. To Persian sorcerers it was a wish-granting herb. The Romans, to whom it was holy, sprinkled it on the altar of Jupiter. Considered an aphrodisiac, it was an ingredient in Tudor love philters. Magicians wore a crown of vervain as protection when summoning demons from another world. Vervain tea has been taken for the kidneys, liver, asthma, and epilepsy.

Wintergreen (*Gaultheria procumbens*)

Also called checkerberry, partridgeberry, mountain tea, deerberry, teaberry, and woodsman's tea, wintergreen is a trailing shrub that sends out slender, vertical stems 3–6 in. high with glossy, oval leaves that are red or green, white, bell-shaped, waxy flowers, and bright red berries. Wintergreen is a wild plant native to North America. Well known to American Indians and early settlers, wintergreen tea, made from the leaves, has a pleasant, warm flavor. Since the oil contains methyl salicylate, an ingredient of aspirin, the tea can be used whenever that medicine is required—for colds, influenza, aches, and coughs.

Yarrow (*Achillea millefolium*)

Yarrow, also known as bunch of daisies, old man's pepper, soldier's woundwort, field hops, thousand weed, and devil's plaything, is a feathery herb from 1–3 ft. in height, with dark green fern-like leaves and dense clusters of tiny white, magenta, or dark pink flowers resembling miniature daisies. A common weed in Europe, Asia, and America in fields and along roadsides, yarrow can also be cultivated in the garden. Used by Achilles in the Trojan War to stanch his soldiers' wounds, yarrow was garlanded about medieval homes on Midsummer's Eve to drive away witches, and carried to weddings by brides hoping for seven years of married bliss. Taken by American Indians for earache, upset stomachs, and toothache, yarrow was used in Scandinavia and Africa instead of hops to make a potent beer. The leaves make a hot, bitter tea that is reputedly cleansing, stimulating, and healing.

Yerba Maté (*Ilex paraguensis*)

Sometimes called Paraguay tea or Brazilian tea, Yerba Maté is an evergreen shrub with leaves that are from 6–8 in. long and forked clusters of small white flowers. The plant fluorishes in Paraguay and southern Brazil and Yerba Maté is consumed throughout South America. The tea has been used by the Indians for thousands of years; its name is part of the ancient Inca language. The leaves are dried and withered like Oriental tea, ground to a coarse powder, and packed into bags to be marketed. Yerba Maté can be brewed in cups or consumed in the South American fashion: Sugar and a small amount of hot water are placed in a gourd, Yerba Maté is added, and the vessel is filled with hot milk, boiling water, and burnt sugar or lemon juice. This mixture is sucked up through a straw called a *bombilla*. Yerba Maté contains caffeine and is an invigorating beverage.

Shopping Guide

HERE ARE OUR SUGGESTIONS on how to get your hands on some good coffee and tea. Your best bet is the specialty coffee and tea store, and we had hoped to provide so complete a listing of specialty stores that you'd be able to find a good one in your area. Although this type of shop is on the rise, they are still few and far between. In our listing at the end of this section we've described those shops that responded to a questionnaire we sent to all the shops we knew about. (NOTE: The approximate prices supplied by our respondants are those that were in effect prior to the July, 1975 frost in Brazil. Expect coffee prices to be considerably higher.) Listed without comment are the names and addresses of sources we heard about just before we went to press.

A growing number of better food shops and department stores have coffee departments with a variety of coffees to be ground at the time of purchase. Ideally, this type of marketing could be a step in the right direction, but as practiced, it often has shortcomings. What's needed is greater integrity on the part of those who supply these departments and greater know-how on the part of those who run them. You should not have to be confronted with stale beans, overpricing, or improper labeling. In general, the more well run a shop is, the better the coffee department is likely to be. Since the specialty coffee store is likely to be found only in the larger, more cosmopolitan areas, we hope that well stocked, well supervised coffee departments will proliferate. They could become an excellent way for good coffee to become easily accessible to everyone.

The tea department in a specialty food shop or department store may be a good source of tea for you. Packaged teas are widely distributed by such companies as Twining, Bigelow, Wagner, Jackson's, and Celestial Seasonings (herbal teas). Their offerings include a good selection of blended and unblended teas, in bulk and tea bag form. Prices are sometimes a bit high, but quality is generally good. Turnover in a well run tea department is likely to be good, so your chances of getting fresh tea are good. If the tins are dusty, go elsewhere; they've been around too long.

For both coffee and tea, you should definitely consider mail order. Many specialty firms will mail coffee and tea to you. While direct contact in the shop is nicer, you'll still benefit from the specialist's expertise and high standards. Even with the cost of shipping, prices are often lower than some of the alternate shopping methods.

The supermarket is usually a wasteland for someone looking for good coffee or tea. It usually succeeds only in providing a nondescript product (national, regional, or house brand) at a competitively low price. Accommodating a mass market, the supermarket rarely offers high quality, fresh roasts, straight growths, or even a proper choice of grind. Supermarket teas are usually limited to a "wide" range of similarly mediocre tea bag blends. Even if the supermarket does carry a line of specialty teas, be cautious; try to ascertain how good the turnover is. Tea keeps well but not forever; and tea becomes stale more quickly when it's packed in small packets.

Here are some points to keep in mind when visiting a shop:

1. In general, use your good sense as a shopper. Does the shop give you the feeling that it's well managed? Is it orderly and clean? Are you getting the hard sell or are you getting helpful service from a friendly person?

2. Ask questions to determine expertise and integrity. For example, if you're offered a Guatemalan blend, ask "just what does that mean?" Ask how teas are selected.

3. Don't assume that high price means high quality. High prices may mean too many middlemen or high overhead. Price is the result of supply and demand. Supplies can be affected by poor growing conditions over the short term, by cartels, or what have you. Demand can be artificially high as a result of notoriety. You certainly don't want to pay a premium price for an ordinary product. You can get extraordinary coffee and tea at fair prices.

4. Coffee should be freshly roasted. If roasting is done on the premises, when? If roasted by a regional roaster, was it roasted to order? When was it roasted? When delivered?

5. Are teas brought in in packets or chests? Who determines the blends? Are quality teas used for tea bags?

We believe the future of everything we've discussed here—fresh roast, proper grind, fair price, greater availability of unblended teas and coffees, more numerous sources of supply (maybe even supermarkets)—depends on you. Armed with your new-found knowledge, press for quality. You'll force the industry to make it happen. Here's a list of some of the people who are trying to do the job now:

NORTHEAST

Ancramdale Coffee and Tea
P.O. Box 75
Ancramdale, New York 12503
518–329–1344

Joel and Diane Schapira have just set up shop in Ancramdale, New York, a restored town in the Berkshire foothills. We are roasting coffee daily in three old twenty-five pound Royal roasters that had been prematurely retired to various basements in Brooklyn and upstate New York. Bulk teas and tea bags are available. We have facilities to serve restaurants and inns in the area and specialize in setting up coffee departments in specialty stores. (One such department is in the Ancramdale General Store right next door to us.) We also wholesale coffee and tea to food co-ops. If you're taking a drive in the country. stop by, say "hello," and have a cuppa with us. Or drop us a line—we can fill mail orders.

Bell-Bates Company, Inc.
107 West Broadway
New York, New York 10013
CO 7–4300

In addition to tea and coffee, the present owner writes, "We carry a substantial number of other items: a full line of jams and jellies, dried fruits and nuts, fresh ground peanut and cashew butter." Established eighty-five years ago, this shop sells a variety of coffees, received twice weekly from a local roaster, for about $2.00 lb. A good assortment of bulk teas priced at $2.20–$4.50 lb. are supplemented by the teas of the two London firms of Twining and Jackson's. Some wholesaling is done, also mail order.

Caravel Coffee Company
P.O. Box 554
Jackson Heights, L.I., New York 11372
212–HA 6–5691

This firm, established over forty years ago, sells coffee and tea by mail only. Our questionnaire elicited nothing but a 1970 mail order form. A nice variety of teas, but coffee is limited to four blends, no straight growths. Prices shown on the form are obviously out of date.

The Coffee Grinder
348 East 66 Street
New York, New York 10021
212–988–2471

Recently opened, this firm sells a variety of coffees roasted outside at prices from $2.05–$2.90 lb. The list includes "Mocha Style." A number of bulk teas from $2.75–$6.00 per lb. and a line of teas from Jackson's of Piccadilly are offered. Coffee appliances, herbal teas, and freshly ground peanut butter can also be obtained here. Mail orders are accepted.

The Coffee and Tea Market, Inc.
1030 Lexington Avenue
New York, New York 10021
212–744–1196

In midtown Manhattan, this new shop offers a substantial variety of coffees, priced from $1.50–$2.50 lb., roasted outside. Bulk teas, herbal teas, and tea bags are also stocked and can be obtained by mail.

Paprika Weiss Importer
1546 Second Avenue
New York, New York 10028
212–BU 8–6117

Established over fifty years ago, this large and well-known gourmet shop is presently operated by a third generation Weiss, Edward. The specialty here is Middle European foods and cookware. Additional quality items from other countries have been added through the years. A current example—over a dozen fine teas from mainland China.

A good variety of coffees are received a few times a week and are priced at $2.50 per pound. Bulk teas are sold for $2.00 per quarter pound. A full line of Twinings Tea and Tea bags, and an extensive selection of herbal teas are available.

Until you visit Weiss in New York's Yorkville area, a mail order catalog is offered.

M. Rohrs
1692 Second Avenue
New York, New York 10028
212–HA 7–8319

Chris Harris, current operator of this shop, writes, "oldest, continuous family run coffee and tea store in N.Y., established 1896. Original furnishings and equipment still in use. We no longer roast coffee, but have it roasted and delivered four times a week."

Eight coffees, average price about $1.70 lb., and about a dozen bulk teas reasonably priced at $2.00 to $3.60 lb. are sold here. Honey, cocoa, coffee grinders, coffee makers and herb teas complete the list. They do mail order and some wholesale, too. A good, old-fashioned establishment.

Schapira Coffee Company
117 West 10 Street
New York, New York 10011
212–OR 5–3733

Our shop, The Flavor Cup, started by Morris Schapira over seventy years ago, continues to operate as a coffee roaster and tea importer. The Schapira family is still at the helm. A good variety of coffees and teas, with coffee prices about $1.90 and teas averaging $3.50. Many of the bulk teas are also available in tea bags.

Coffee roasting is done on the premises about three times weekly. Over the years this firm has earned a fine reputation and has developed a substantial trade; retail, wholesale, and mail order.

Simpson and Vail, Inc.
53 Park Place
New York, New York 10007
212–344–6377

Current owners of this reputable firm write "a no-nonsense coffee and tea mail-order firm established in 1929. Coffee is custom roasted and delivered for us twice weekly." Coffee list is limited, but some types are reasonably priced. Variety of tea is good, prices are fair. Mail orders and wholesale orders are welcomed. Tea is emphasized and worth trying.

Zabar's
Broadway at 80th Street
New York, New York 10024
212–TR 3–3144

This popular and successful specialty food store contains an impressive appetizer department, bulk cheeses, excellent bread, and an extensive selection of general delicacies. Saul Zabar buys coffee green and has it roasted once a week. Mr. Zabar is proud of his coffee department and carefully supervises the selection and roasting of good coffees. Prices average close to $2.00, with most of the selection in blends rather than straight growths. An exception is Jamaican Blue Mountain at $3.98 per lb.—an exclusive import in the East and not always available.

Amber Waves of Grain
Carmel, New York

Aphrodesia (herbals)
28 Carmine Street
New York, New York

The Coffee Connection, Inc.
36 Boylston Street
Cambridge, Massachusetts 02138

The Country Cheese Store, Inc.
40 Montauk Highway
Hampton Bays, New York 11946

Edgartown Coffee, Tea, and Spice
    Company
North Water Street
Edgartown, Massachusetts 02539

The Elephant Emporium
15 Rock City Road
Woodstock, New York 12498

Food for Thought
Stowe, Vermont

Herb Garden
658 Monroe Avenue
Rochester, New York 14607

McNulty's Tea and Coffee Co.
109 Christopher Street
New York, New York

Noble and Bowman
136 Seventh Avenue South
New York, New York 10014

People's Gourmet
50 Cedar Street
Dobbs Ferry, New York

Porto Rico Importing Co.
201 Bleeker Street
New York, New York

The Rye Country Store
50 Purchase Street
Rye, New York

Summer Meadow Herb Shop
319 Eddy Street
Ithaca, New York 14850

Warren Store
Warren, Vermont 05674

Woodcocks Gourmet
60 East Main Street
Chester, New Jersey 07930

MID-ATLANTIC

Bon Appetit
213 S. 17 Street
Philadelphia, Pennsylvania 19103
215–RI 6–8059

This appears to be a shop worth visiting in the Philadelphia area. Owner Ellen Steiner opened seven years ago with an extensive line of kitchen items, and expanded last year to include a cafe. You will also find a very complete assortment of coffee brewers and coffee grinders.

Roasted bean coffee is received here once a week and the variety is good. Prices per pound are $1.90 to $3.00. No bulk teas are offered but many packaged specialty teas are.

Capitol Hill Wine and Cheese
611 Pennsylvania Avenue S.E.
Washington, D.C. 20003
202–543–0880

Gene Nolan and John Rusnak opened this shop three years ago and are doing well. They get roasted coffee delivered weekly, 16 types, all $1.99 lb. A dozen bulk teas are offered, averaging $4.00 lb. Mail orders and whole-sale trade are solicited.

M. E. Swing Company, Inc.
1013 E Street N.W.
Washington, D.C. 20004
202–628–7601

In answer to our questionnaire the owner writes, "We are in our third generation of coffee selling. Have been in business since 1916. Our coffees are roasted by us on premises."

In addition to a good list of coffees and bulk teas, appliances and package teas are also sold. This well established firm deserves a visit, or write for a brochure. Prices seem fair.

Nicholas Coffee Company
23 Market Place
Pittsburgh, Pennsylvania 15222
412–261–4226

Response to our questionnaire did not indicate what teas or coffees are offered, or prices. They did write that they have been in continuous operation since 1919, that business is mainly wholesale, and roasting is done daily. If you're in the Pittsburgh area, see what they offer.

Old Georgetown Coffee House
1330 Wisconsin Avenue
Washington, D.C. 20007
202–FE 8–2366
This popular and successful firm was started fifteen years ago; it offers many food and appliance items in addition to tea and coffee. Roasted coffee is delivered twice weekly. Prices are a bit lower than average.

THE SOUTH

The Coffee Bean Inc.
217 King Street
Alexandria, Virginia 22314
703–836–9242
   This firm also roasts their own coffee (about fourteen kinds) daily. Prices average about $2.25 lb. There is a large assortment of bulk teas and other food specialties.

The Creative Hand, Ltd.
307 Kempsville Plaza s/c
Virginia Beach, Virginia 23462
804–497–1857
   This new firm sells a substantial number of handcrafted items, such as needlepoint, pottery, etc. In addition an interesting variety of bean coffees (roasted coffees are delivered weekly) and bulk teas are offered. Coffee brewing appliances are in stock.

Anderson & Company
Austin, Texas 78731

Cheese Wedge and Keg
Brevard, North Carolina 28712

Your Favorite Things, Inc.
Eden, North Carolina 27288

La Bonne Femme
516 Simpson Street
Greensboro, North Carolina 27401

The Coffee Grinder
711 Saluda Avenue
Columbia, South Carolina 29205

THE MIDWEST

The Coffee Bean
Burlington Mall
777 Guelph Line
Burlington, Ontario, Canada
416–639–5474

Stan and Frances Kenny opened this shop September 9, 1974. Eight types of coffee beans are sold here for about $1.95 lb. Delivery of roasted beans is once a week. Some canned specialty coffees are also stocked. A small variety of bulk tea, reasonably priced, is available, plus Twining and Constant Comment. Tea and coffee making equipment complete the inventory. Stan and Frances mention the "individual service and advice we offer our clients."

The Coffee Trader
2619 North Downer Avenue
Milwaukee, Wisconsin 53211
414–332–9690

John Gardiner and his wife opened this shop in 1971, and write, "we have grown in size, and product knowledge ever since." In addition to a good list of coffees at about $2.00 lb. and teas at about $5.00 lb., he writes, "we also specialize in imported cheeses, herbs, and many other specialty food items." Mail orders are accepted.

Northwestern Coffee Mills
217 North Broadway
Milwaukee, Wisconsin 53202

Visit this firm if feasible, or write for their price list, which we found interesting and intelligently done. The variety of coffees is good, prices on average are about $2.00, and roasting is done on the premises. Bulk teas— all the types you will want—go for about $3.50–$5.00 lb. You'll find just about all the herbal teas, herbs, spices, and seasonings you'll need.

Nuts and seeds are offered, the nuts freshly roasted. Coffeemakers, coffee grinders, and tea infusers are listed. You may order by mail.

Charleville Coffee Store
10411 Clayton Road
St. Louis, Missouri 63131

ROCKY MOUNTAINS

A. & D. Coffee, Tea and Spice Company
Cinderella City
Englewood, Colorado 80110
303–761–7578

Responding to our questions, A. & D. writes, "A one-man operation, show-ing a nice increase in business going into the third year. . . . No roasting is done. Roasted coffee is delivered as required."

A brochure shows a small variety of coffees with an average price of $2.00. Bulk teas go for $2.00–$5.00 per pound. Also offered are Twining, Wagner, and Bigelow. Fresh ground peanut butter, spices, herbs, and some food specialties complete the picture. Mail orders are accepted.

American Tea, Coffee and Spice Company
1511 Champa Street
Denver, Colorado 80202
303–534–4557

For information on this interesting shop we are using answers to our questionnaire plus a copy of a recent article in the *Denver Post*, all mailed to us by Leland Long, owner since 1970. It was started back in 1900 as a grocery store and stocks spices, raw nuts, roasted nuts, baked goods, home-made candies, and other specialty foods.

An excellent variety of coffees, varying in price with the market, are roasted on the premises every day. The tea list too is extensive, with prices from $2.00–$12.00 per pound. Everything seems to point to a substantial, well managed establishment, and a photo of the interior has the look of a large, well stocked emporium. Mail orders, too.

WEST COAST

Bagozian Coffee Co.
119 W. Church St.
Santa Maria, California 93454
805–922–1255

Response to our questionnaire tells us the dozen coffees offered are deliv-ered every two weeks, the bulk teas number eight, and the year it all started was 1972. No prices are given. Many coffee and tea accessories are in stock.

Barclays Coffee, Tea, & Spice Co., Ltd.
9020 Tampa Avenue, Suite N
Northridge, California 91324
213–885–7744

Steve Kandell and Jay Goldenberg started this charming shop in 1973. There is a very complete list of coffees (19). Beans are received roasted about once a week and go for $2.00 to $5.00 lb. Barclays carries 14 varieties of bulk teas, all $1.75 per quarter pound; also 16 herbal teas. A large variety of spices and coffee and tea accessories is stocked. A mail order form is available. At the shop capuccino, espresso and many teas are served to customers.

Chez Fromage
10250 Santa Monica Blvd.
Los Angeles, California 90067
213–553–5582

This cheese shop and restaurant also has a coffee and tea department. The folder we received listing twenty coffees does not contain prices. Some descriptive material is inaccurate.

The Coffee Barrel
235 State Street
Los Altos, California 94022
415–948–1166
649 Laurel Street
San Carlos, California 94070
415–591–2141

Recently established, The Coffee Barrel carries a good variety of coffees, teas, and herbal teas. Coffee prices are about $2.10 lb.; roasting is done outside about twice weekly. No information about mail order.

The Coffee Bean Company
2465 Hilyard Street and 765 Williamette Street
Eugene, Oregon 97405

These two shops, established since 1972, seem reputable. Roasting is done daily on the premises. The coffee variety is good, with prices about $2.00–$2.40 per lb. There is a good choice of teas costing $2.50–$6.00 per lb.

Write for a mail order form if distance makes a visit difficult.

Graffeo Coffee House
733 Columbus Avenue
San Francisco, California

We gladly include this shop in our list as an example of the small roaster that was once found in every Italian neighborhood and is now a rarity. We remember them well.

Mr. Reppetto writes, "We sell no tea, only Italian coffee, which we roast constantly in small batches. We sell no appliances, no other items, have a little wholesale trade and are since 1935 San Francisco's oldest continuous independent roaster."

How appropriate that he is located on Columbus Avenue!

The Kobos Company
533 S.W. Macadam
Portland, Oregon 97201
503–222–5220

"We roast our own coffee in the front of the shop, currently three times a week." Although this firm only started in 1973, the brochure has an air of knowhow and integrity. The variety of coffees is interesting; prices go from $2.00–$3.25 lb. Their tea list is equally attractive. Coffee and tea appliances, about 100 spices, and an abundance of herbal teas and gourmet cooking utensils are also listed. Worth a visit, or try the mail.

Murchie's Tea and Coffee Ltd.
1008 Robson Street
Vancouver, British Columbia 5, Canada

This well established firm, with three branches in Vancouver, is almost a century old and has been continuously operated by the Murchie family. They do wholesale, retail, and will send you an interesting brochure for mail order. A fair-sized coffee list is marred by quite a few strange descriptions (*e.g.*, Mexican coffee is described as having a smoky flavor!?). They have an *extensive* list of teas and tea bags and prices are very reasonable.

The Pannikin
1296 Prospect Street
La Jolla, California 92037
714–459–7956

At present there are a number of tea and coffee shops on the West Coast, and this seems to be one of the better firms. Established in 1967 by Robert and Eden Sinclair, the shop roasts coffee almost every day. Average price is $2.00 lb. for a very satisfactory variety of coffees, and bulk teas are about $3.00–$6.00 per lb. Unusual cooking equipment, herbal teas, herbs, and spices are also offered.

Specialty shops and local restaurants are supplied and mail orders are solicited. Robert Sinclair, in his response to our questionnaire, adds this postscript, "As roasters and responsible merchants, we are very conscious of a number of people in the coffee business who should not be there. We are hoping your consumer's guide will point out the importance of learning about coffees so that the poor consumer will not be buying a package of Jamaican Blue Mountain that is in fact Nicaraguan—as an instance."

The Perfect Recipe
1120 Burlingame Avenue
Burlingame, California 94010;
1970 Broadway
Oakland, California 94612;
76 Stanford Shopping Center
Palo Alto, California 94304

In answer to our request for some history of the firm, we received this reply: "The basic concept was for retail trade of coffees and teas, with the related accessories. We started the business with doing the retail and a limited restaurant-'coffeehouse.' The restaurant introduces people to the taste of good coffees and teas. As can be seen on our Menu, a person can order any coffee we sell, brewed in an individual filter; or any tea by the pot. Therefore, you can taste it before you buy it."

Coffee is bought green and delivered once a week. Pay them a visit if you can, or send for a brochure.

Starbucks Coffee Company
2000 Western Avenue
Seattle, Washington 98121
University Village Shopping Centre
Seattle, Washington 98105
205 5 Avenue
Edmonds, Washington 98020

We quote Jerry Baldwin in answer to our questionnaire: "We're the only people in Seattle willing to go to the trouble to do the whole thing correctly." They do their own roasting three times weekly, have a special grinder for Melitta, and offer a sufficient variety of coffees and teas at fair prices. They certainly seem worth a visit, or send for the mail order brochure.

Sun Harvest Natural Foods and General Store
404 T Street
Eureka, California 95501
707–442–6957

This three year old business is in an old Victorian house on Highway 101. Louis, the owner, says that his customers can't figure out how he gets all the grains, teas, herbs, juices, wine, beers, coffees, grinders, and pots into the place. He tells us he has "all coffees from House Blend to Tanganika, Antigua to Venezuelan." Coffees, roasted in San Francisco, are delivered twice monthly.

Tony's Coffee, Tea and Cheese
1101 Harris Avenue, Fairhaven District
Bellingham, Washington
206–733–6319

Jill Mosher and Michael Ring now own this shop which was established three years ago by Tony Cambell. They do their own roasting daily, using an old Jabez Burns. A very complete line of coffees go for $1.85 to $2.15 per pound, and the assortments of bulk teas and herbals are good. All manner of coffee and tea appliances are available.

Espresso coffee is served, and there are plans for an outdoor cafe next year. A small wholesale trade is developing and a mail order form is in the works.

The Coffee Mill
1014 C. Coast Village Center
Santa Barbara, California 93108

Suggestions for Further Reading

THIS IS not meant as a definitive bibliography, but merely as a guide to those who want to delve further into the history, science, and lore of coffees and teas. Since the literature on herbals is vast, we have only included a few of the high spots.

Angier, Bradford. *Feasting Free on Wild Edibles.* Harrisburg, Pa.: Stackpole Books, 1972.

Bramah, Edward. *Tea & Coffee:* A Modern View of 300 Years of Tradition, Mystic, Conn.: Laurence Verry, Inc., 1972.

Brautigan, Richard. "Coffee," in *Revenge of the Lawn.* New York: Simon & Schuster, 1971.

Conway, David. *The Magic of Herbs.* New York: E. P. Dutton & Co., Inc., 1973.

Gibbons, Euell. *Stalking the Healthful Herbs.* New York: David McKay Company, Inc., 1966.

Gray, Arthur (ed.). *Over the Black Coffee.* New York: Baker & Taylor Co., 1902.

Harler, Campbell R. *Tea Manufacture.* New York: Oxford University Press, 1963.

Law, Donald. *The Concise Herbal Encyclopedia.* New York: St. Martin's Press, 1974.

Lu Yu. *The Classic of Tea.* Translated with an introduction by Francis Ross Carpenter. Boston: Little, Brown & Co., 1974.

Okakura, Kakuzo. *The Book of Tea.* New York: Dover Publications, Inc., 1964.

Parry, John W. *The Story of Spices.* New York: Chemical Publishing Co., Inc., 1953.

Rosengarten, Frederic, Jr. *The Book of Spices.* New York: Pyramid Books, 1973.

Shalleck, Jamie. *Tea.* New York: The Viking Press, 1972.

Sivetz, Michael. *Coffee.* 1973. Mimeographed, available from 3635 N. W. Elmwood Drive, Corvallis, Oregon, 97330.

Stobart, Tom. *Herbs, Spices and Flavorings.* New York: McGraw-Hill Book Company, 1970.

Stryk, Lucien and Ikemoto, Takashi. *Zen: Poems, Prayers, Sermons, Anecdotes, Interviews.* New York: Doubleday & Company, Inc., 1965.

Tanaka, Sen'ō. *The Tea Ceremony.* Translated by Takashi Nishikawa. New York: Kodansha International Limited. 1974.

Ukers, William H. *All About Coffee.* New York: The Tea & Coffee Trade Journal Company, 1935.

Ukers, William H. *All About Tea.* 2 vols. New York: The Tea & Coffee Trade Journal Company, 1935.

Uribe C. Andres. *Brown Gold.* New York: Random House, 1954.

Index

Note: Page numbers in *italics* refer to illustrations and maps.